Excel 2007 Miracles Made Easy

by

Bill Jelen

Holy Macro! Books

Excel 2007 Miracles Made Easy

© 2007 Bill Jelen

Written by: Bill Jelen

Copy Editor: Linda Delonais

Printing, Design & Layout: Fine Grains (India) Private Limited, New Delhi, India.

Cover Design: Shannon Mattiza, 6'4 Productions

Published by: Holy Macro! Books, PO Box 82, Uniontown OH 44685, USA

Distributed by: Independent Publishers Group

First Printing: January 2007. Printed in India

ISBN: 978-1-932802-25-2

Library of Congress Control Number: 2006931385

About the Author

Bill Jelen is the host of MrExcel.com and the author of sixteen books about Microsoft Excel including Special Edition Using Excel 2007, Pivot Table Data Crunching for Excel 2007, VBA & Macros for Microsoft Excel, Learn Excel 2007 from MrExcel, Excel for Marketing Managers and Guerilla Data Analysis Using Microsoft Excel. He has made over 50 guest appearances on TV's Call for Help with Leo Laporte. You can find him entertaining people with his Power Excel seminar anywhere that a room full of accountants will gather. He has produced over 300 episodes of his daily 2-minute video podcast, available for free for anyone with a computer.

Before founding MrExcel.com in 1998, Jelen spent twelve years "in the trenches", as a financial analyst for the accounting, finance, marketing, and operations departments of a publicly held company. Since then, his company automates Excel reports for hundreds of clients around the world.

Dedication

To David Gainer and the rest of the Excel 2007 team.

Acknowledgements

The author would like to thank David Gainer and everyone on the Excel 2007 team for creating a great new version of Excel. Thanks to Michael Fosmire and everyone in the Microsoft MVP program.

Thanks to Linda Delonais for copyediting and Paramjeet Singh and his team for layout and printing of the book. A color book is a bit initimidating - they made this one easy.

Thanks to Lora White, Tracy Syrstad and Barb Jelen for keeping MrExcel running while I wrote. As always, thanks to the hundreds of people answering 30,000 Excel questions a year at the MrExcel message board.

Thanks to Dan Bricklin and Bob Frankston for inventing the computer spreadsheet. Thanks to Mitch Kapor for Lotus 1-2-3. Thanks to my brother Bob Jelen for being my brother. Thanks to Jerry Kohl for endless cool ideas about Excel.

Podcasting is the wave of the future. Thanks to Leo Laporte for suggesting the MrExcel podcast and thanks to Lora White for actually making sure a podcast gets edited and posted five days a week. Thanks to Dick Debartolo of the Daily Giz Wiz and Mad Magazine. It isn't often that one gets to meet a childhood hero.

Finally, thanks to Josh Jelen, Zeke Jelen, and Mary Ellen Jelen.

Contents

Introduction

Excel 2007 is the best new version of Excel.

This book is a short, quick look at Excel 2007 and is designed to introduce you to its wonderful new features. It was originally conceived to have 25 cool things. In the end, there are 40 chapters. Excel 2007 has so many cool visual features that I decided to publish the book in color.

The first 20 or so chapters are features that are new in Excel 2007. The major new stuff is up front, followed by some minor features. Chapters 20-34 are a mix of features that have been improved, or perhaps old features that I think you might not have discovered. Chapters 35-40 show you some of the things you can do with the new Excel.

I've been using pre-release versions of Excel 2007 since October 2005. I am finishing this book on November 12, 2006 – the day that that RTM version of the product was made available to corporations. I've long since gotten over the trepidation of not being able to find anything on the ribbon and I see that this is a great new release. I hope that my experiences over the last year will help you to enjoy this release of Excel.

Bill Jelen

Introducing the Ribbon

If you are a regular at MrExcel.com, you undoubtedly know and love the File – Edit – View – Insert – Format – Tools – Data – Window – Help menu bar that has been at the top of Excel for two decades.

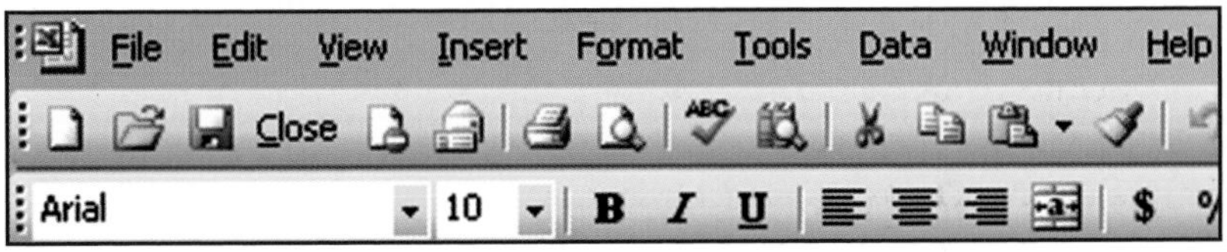

Figure 1.1
If you are an Excel pro, you probably know this menu bar inside and out.

Unfortunately, Microsoft no longer loves the menu bar. In fact, they have completely abandoned the menu bar and the toolbars in favor of something called the Ribbon.

Why would they fix something that was not broken? Well, perhaps the menu system actually was broken. Excel pros knew where to find everything on the menu, but it was pretty hopeless for a person new to Excel to ever navigate to Edit – Fill – Justify to learn that you could have Excel behave a little bit like a word processor. The chances of them finding Data – Import External Data – New Web Query to learn that their dashboards could put data from a table directly on a website were bleak.

In fact, I've heard that the Office team will visit customers and ask what new features the customer would like in Excel. Most of the time, someone asks for something that was added 10 years ago. The conclusion: There is a lot of powerful functionality in Excel that customers have not been able to discover. Instead of adding new features, Microsoft could instead make it easier for everyone to find the features that already exist. (In reality, Excel 2007 offers many fantastic new features, plus a new menu system that will help customers find previously existing features. Excel 2007 is the best new version of Excel since Excel 97.)

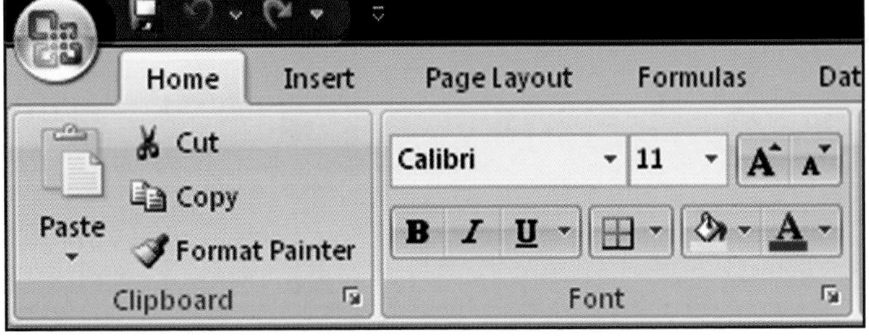

Figure 1.2
Icons are classified in logical groups within each ribbon tab

The ribbon is the new user interface at the top of Excel, PowerPoint, Word, and Access 2007. The ribbon is also present in the Compose Mail portion of Outlook 2007.

The ribbon is comprised of icons and words grouped into several tabs. In Excel, many of the editing icons are on the Home ribbon. Within the Home ribbon, icons are further classified into groups. In Figure 1.2, there are four icons in the Clipboard group of the Home ribbon and 11 icons in the Font group of the Home ribbon.

When I wrote Special Edition Using Excel 2007, the editorial style included the group name in the menu path. For example, the QUE book might say to "Select Home, Clipboard, Format Painter". During the course of writing the book, I started to think it was a bit strange to indicate that someone should select Clipboard. In reality, you would click on Home and then click on the Format Painter within the Clipboard group. In this book, I will say "Select Home – Format Painter".

The Most Important Choices Are Behind the Office Icon!

In the original version of Excel 2007, there was a File choice along the ribbon. For some unknown reason, Microsoft replaced the File choice with a funny looking round Office icon. This is downright confusing, because the most important commands for working with Excel are behind this icon.

Click the Office Icon and you will find most of the settings that used to be on the File menu in Excel 2003 (see Figure 1.3).

Figure 1.3
Why Microsoft would hide the most important commands behind an icon instead of the word "File" is a mystery.

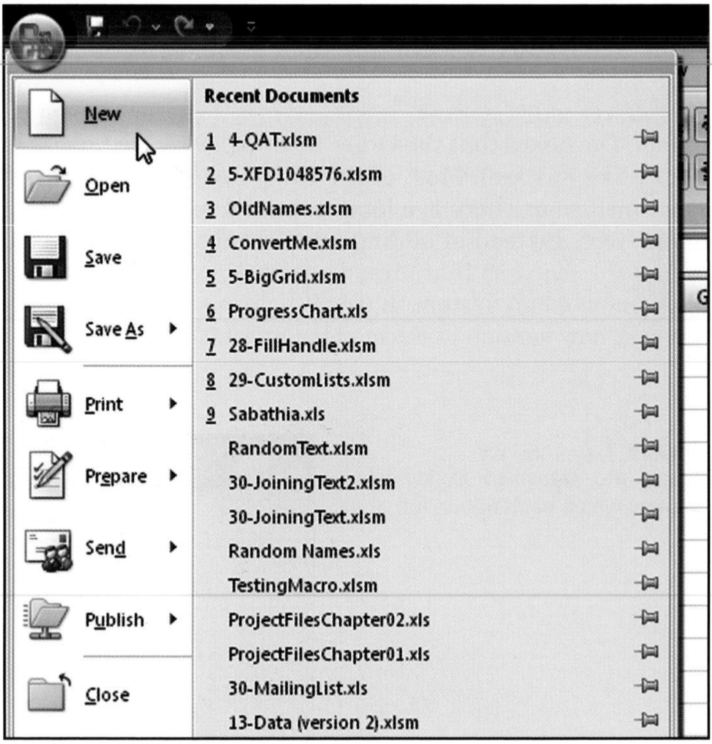

Using Dialog Box Launchers

In the lower right corner of some ribbon groups, you will see a tiny icon showing a diagonal arrow. This icon is a dialog box launcher. Click the icon to open a dialog box similar to the dialogs with which you are familiar from Excel 2003.

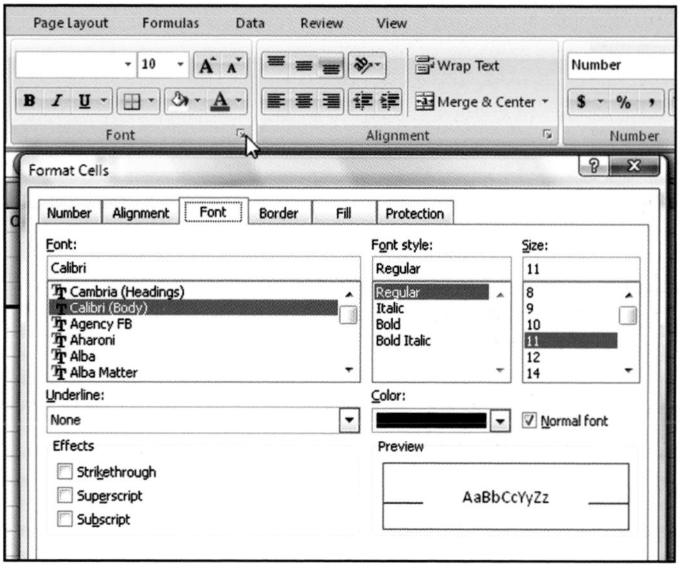

Figure 1.4
The mouse pointer is pointing to the dialog box launcher in the Font group of the Home ribbon. You will find another dialog box launcher in the Alignment tab of the ribbon.

Making the Ribbon a Bit More Like a Menu

While there is nothing you can do to bring back the legacy Excel menu and toolbars, you can make the ribbon behave a bit more like a menu.

Type Ctrl+F1 or right-click the ribbon and choose Minimize the Ribbon. Excel hides the ribbon as shown in Figure 1.5.

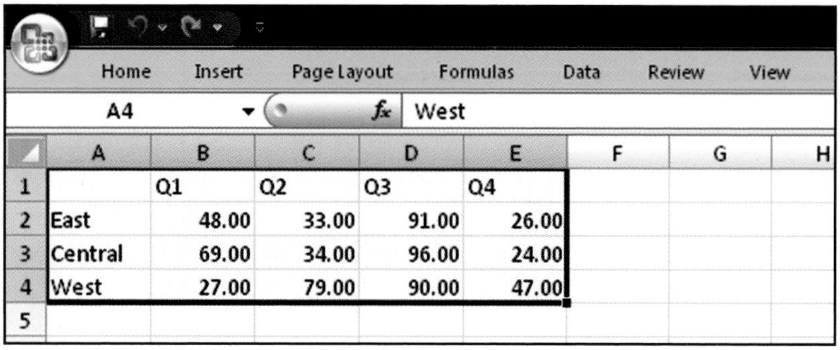

Figure 1.5
Ctrl+F1 hides the ribbon, leaving only the tab names.

After the ribbon is hidden, you have more room to work with your document. You also can click any ribbon tab name at any time to open the ribbon temporarily. In Figure 1.6, I've selected Page Layout – Size – Legal. After clicking Legal, Excel returns the ribbon back to the view in Figure 1.5. (At least this feels more like a typical menu system.)

Figure 1.6
Click a selection and the ribbon expands.

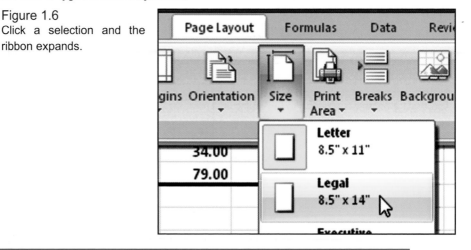

Tip: See Where Can I Find That on the Ribbon? on page 9 for a complete mapping from the old menu to the new ribbons. See Keyboard Shortcuts on page 19 for information on how to add buttons to the Quick Access Toolbar.

Using Context-Sensitive Ribbons

Occasionally, new tabs will appear on the right side of the ribbon. These ribbons will appear when the current selection includes SmartArt graphics, Charts, Drawings, Pictures, Pivot Tables, Pivot Charts, Worksheet headers, Tables, or Ink, or when you are in Print Preview mode.

These new ribbon tabs will stay visible as long as you are working on the selected object. When you select a cell outside of the object, Microsoft Excel 2007 will immediately put away the ribbon tabs.

Figure 1.7
The SmartArt Tools are controlled using two ribbon tabs: Design and Format

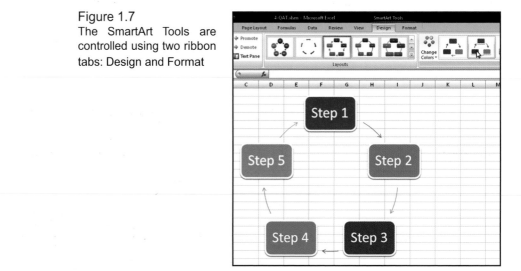

Selecting from a Gallery in the Ribbon

Some ribbon elements are comprised of a gallery of many different options. In Figure 1.8, the Chart Layouts gallery shows three thumbnails at a time.

Figure 1.8
Three buttons at the right side of the gallery allow you to scroll up, down, or to open the entire gallery.

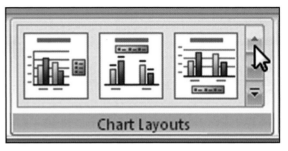

You can use the up and down arrow button to scroll through three thumbnails. Or, click the More button to open the gallery and see all of the options at once (see Figure 1.9).

Figure 1.9
The third button next to the gallery is the More button. Click that button to see all of the choices at once.

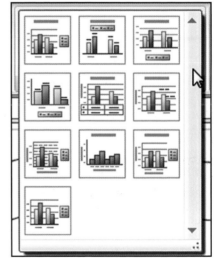

Using Live Preview

Many features of Excel 2007 offer a Live Preview feature. With Live Preview, you can simply hover over a choice and see a preview of that choice in the worksheet. This allows you to quickly browse many settings without actually committing to a change.

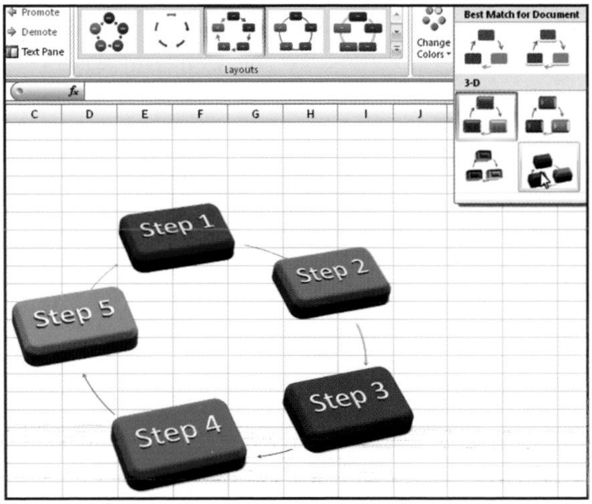

Figure 1.10
This setting is called Bird's Eye Scene. I think this setting is very hard to read, so I appreciate that I can hover, see how awful it is, and then go on to something better.

Unfortunately, it is an odd mix of features that supports Live Preview. You will have to use trial and error to identify these features.

If your computer is slow, you can turn off Live Preview. Use the Office Icon menu – Excel Options. In the Popular category, uncheck the box for Enable Live Preview.

Figure 1.11
Use the Office Icon menu – Excel
Options to disable Live Preview if
it bogs down your computer.

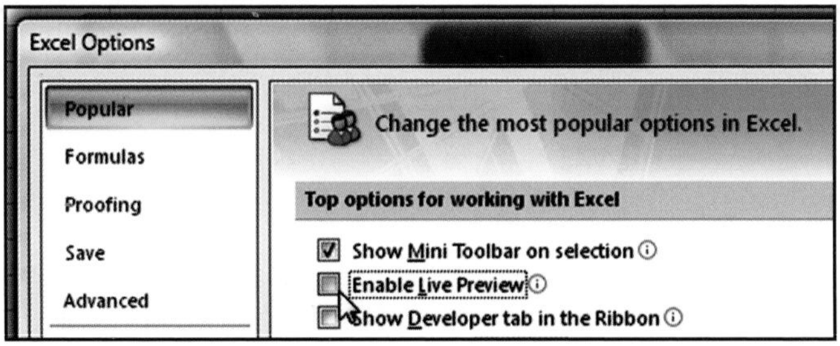

Customizing the Ribbon

While it used to be easy to customize any toolbar, Microsoft has removed this functionality from the Excel user interface. To customize the ribbon, you now need to be able to write XML code.

Patrick Schmid has authored a COM add-in that will let you easily customize the ribbon. Patrick plans to offer a freeware and a premium version at http://pschmid.net.

Learning Where to Find Things

The most difficult part of the new Ribbon is figuring out where to find commands that you knew from Excel 2003. The next chapter, Where Can I Find That on the Ribbon?, provides a mapping to show you how to find the popular commands.

✳ ✳ ✳

Chapter 2

Where Can I Find That on the Ribbon?

The number one problem for someone upgrading to Excel 2007 is figuring out where to find a particular feature in the ribbon.

After upgrading, I found myself wondering, "Where would they have put pivot tables? Are they on the Data ribbon?". (No – they are on the Insert ribbon!)

This chapter is going to map, in color, where to find all of the menu items from Excel 2003. It will cover the regular menu plus the Standard and Formatting toolbars.

For the purpose of this chapter, I've color keyed the Excel 2007 ribbon tabs:

Figure 2.1
The colors used on this graphic correspond to colors used in later figures.

The File Menu

Most of the commands on the legacy File menu are now on the Office Icon button (yellow squares in Figure 2.2). The Workspace functionality is on the View ribbon. Web Page Preview is no longer on the ribbon – you can add it to the Quick Access Toolbar (QAT) if it is a feature that you use. See Taming the QAT & Finding the Mini Bar on page 25 for more information on the QAT.

The Edit Menu

Nearly the entire Edit menu is on the Home ribbon. Undo & Redo are on the QAT. The Links command is now buried deep under Office Icon – Finish. For object editing, watch for context sensitive ribbon tabs to appear when you have selected the object.

View Menu

About half of the old View menu is now located on the View ribbon. The concept of toolbars and the task pane has been removed from the interface. Other commands are spread among the Insert, Review, and Page Layout ribbons.

The Insert Menu

The top selections on the Excel 2003 Insert menu have been promoted to the Home ribbon. Other commands are on the Insert, Page Layout, and Formulas ribbons.

Figure 2.2
Excel 2003 File menu
The pink blocks on the right side corresponds to the Page Layout tab in pink in Figure 2.1.

Figure 2.3
Excel 2003 Edit menu

Figure 2.4
Excel 2003 View menu

Figure 2.5
Excel 2003 Insert menu

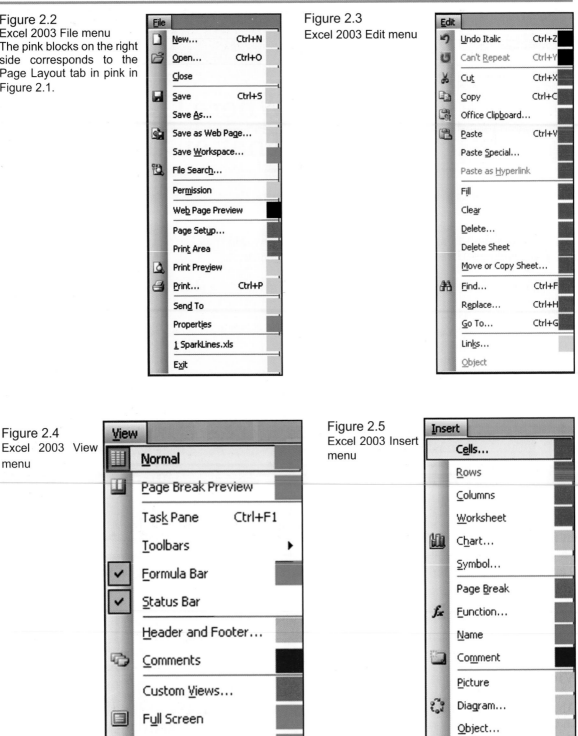

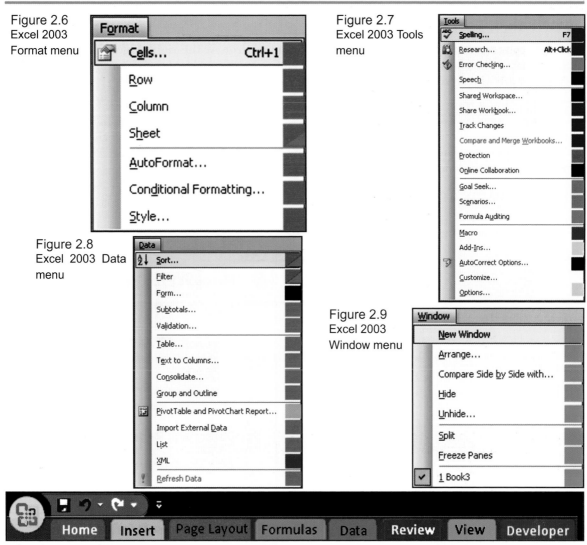

Figure 2.6 Excel 2003 Format menu

Figure 2.7 Excel 2003 Tools menu

Figure 2.8 Excel 2003 Data menu

Figure 2.9 Excel 2003 Window menu

The Format Menu

Nearly all of the commands on the Format menu now appear on the Home ribbon. One command, Format – Sheet – Background, is now on the Page Layout ribbon.

The Tools Menu

The former Tools menu commands have been broken up between several different ribbon tabs. You will find the commands on the Review, Formulas, Home, Data, and Developer tabs. The Add-Ins and Options commands are now in the Excel Options button, located on the Office Icon menu.

The Data Menu

Most of the Excel 2003 data menu is on the Excel 2007 Data ribbon, but several key elements are elsewhere. Filter & Sort appear on both the Home and Data ribbon. Pivot Tables – the most powerful feature in Excel – are, strangely, located on the Insert ribbon. The XML commands have been moved to the Developer ribbon.

The Window Menu

The entire Excel 2003 Window menu is now on the Excel 2007 View Menu.

The Help Menu

The Help command has been moved to a question mark icon at the right edge of the ribbon. The Office Assistant has been completely removed from the program. All of the remaining items on the Help menu are now in the Resources category of Excel Options.

The Standard Toolbar

The former Standard toolbar has been split between the Office icon, the Review ribbon, the Home ribbon, the QAT, and the Insert tab. Read Taming the QAT & Finding the Mini Bar on page 30 to learn how to put these icons on your Quick Access Toolbar.

The Formatting Toolbar

The entire Formatting toolbar is now on the Home ribbon.

Figure 2.10
Excel 2003 Help menu

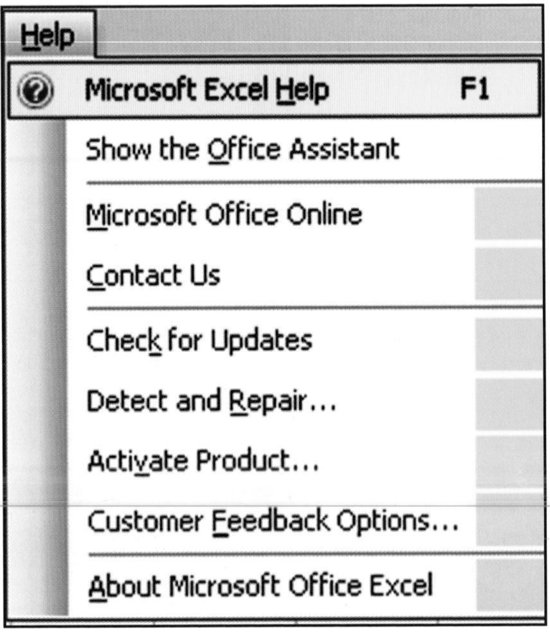
Help
Microsoft Excel Help F1
Show the Office Assistant
Microsoft Office Online
Contact Us
Check for Updates
Detect and Repair...
Activate Product...
Customer Feedback Options...
About Microsoft Office Excel

Figure 2.11
Excel 2003 Standard toolbar – the colors underneath the toolbar correspond to the tab colors in Figure 2.1.

100%

Figure 2.12
Excel 2003 Formatting toolbar

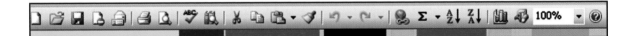

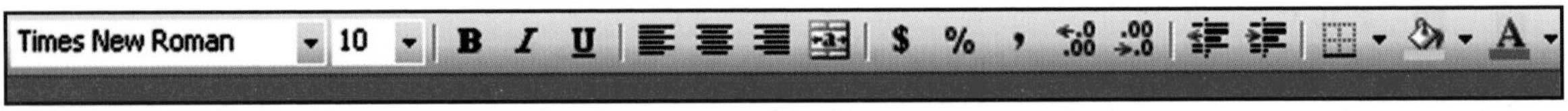
Times New Roman
10

Home
Insert
Page Layout
Formulas
Data
Review
View
Developer

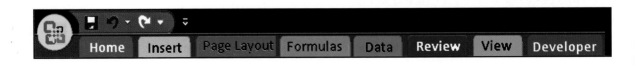

The File Menu	
Excel 2003 Menu	Excel 2007 Ribbon
New...	Office Icon – New
Open...	Office Icon – Open
Close	Office Icon – Close
Save	Office Icon – Save
Save As...	Office Icon - Save As - Save As Web Page from Save As dialog options
Save as Web Page...	Office Icon - Save As
Save Workspace...	View - Window - Save Workspace
File Search...	No equivalent
Permission - Unrestricted Access	Office Icon - Finish - Restrict Permission - Unrestricted Access
Permission - Do Not Distribute...	Office Icon - Finish - Restrict Permission - Do Not Distribute
Permission - Restrict Permission As...	Office Icon - Finish - Restrict Permission - Restrict Permission As
Web Page Preview	Add to QAT using Excel Options
Page Setup...	Page Layout - Page Setup
Print Area - Set Print Area	Page Layout - Page Setup - Print Area - Set Print Area
Print Area - Clear Print Area	Page Layout - Page Setup - Print Area - Clear Print Area
Print Preview	Office Icon - Print - Print Preview
Print...	Office Icon - Print – Print
Send To - Mail Recipient	Add to QAT using Excel Options
Send To - Mail Recipient (for Review)...	Add to QAT using Excel Options
Send To - Mail Recipient (as Attachment)...	Office Icon - Send - E-Mail
Send To - Routing Recipient...	No equivalent
Send To - Exchange Folder...	Add to QAT using Excel Options
Send To - Recipient using Internet Fax Service...	Office Icon - Send - Internet Fax
Properties	View - Show/Hide – Properties
1 c:\Filename.xls	Office Icon – 1
Exit	Office Icon - Exit Excel

The Edit Menu	
Excel 2003 Menu	**Excel 2007 Ribbon**
Undo	QAT - Undo
Repeat	QAT - Repeat
Cut	Home - Clipboard - Cut
Copy	Home - Clipboard - Copy
Office Clipboard...	Home - Clipboard
Paste	Home - Clipboard - Paste
Paste Special...	Clipboard - Paste - Paste Special
Paste as Hyperlink	Home - Clipboard - Paste - Paste as Hyperlink
Fill - Down	Home - Editing - Fill - Down
Fill - Right	Home - Editing - Fill - Right
Fill - Up	Home - Editing - Fill - Up
Fill - Left	Home - Editing - Fill - Left
Fill - Across Worksheets...	Home - Editing - Fill - Across Worksheets
Fill - Series...	Home - Editing - Fill - Series
Fill - Justify	Home - Editing - Fill - Justify
Clear - All	Home - Editing - Clear - Clear All
Clear - Formats	Home - Editing - Clear - Clear Formats
Clear - Contents	Home - Editing - Clear - Clear Contents
Clear - Comments	Home - Editing - Clear - Clear Comments
Delete...	Home - Cells - Delete
Delete Sheet	Home - Cells - Delete - Delete Sheet
Move or Copy Sheet...	Home - Cells - Format - Move or Copy Sheet
Find...	Home - Editing - Find & Select - Find
Replace...	Home - Editing - Find & Select - Replace
Go To...	Editing - Find & Select - Go To
Links...	Office Icon - Finish - Edit Links to Files
Object	Context specific ribbon tabs

The View Menu	
Excel 2003 Menu	**Excel 2007 Ribbon**
Normal	View - Workbook Views - Normal
Page Break Preview	View - Workbook Views - Page Break Preview
Task Pane	No equivalent
Toolbars - Standard	No equivalent
Toolbars - Customize...	Office Icon - Excel Options - Customization

Formula Bar	View - Show/Hide - Formula Bar
Status Bar	No equivalent
Header and Footer...	Insert - Text - Header & Footer
Comments	Review - Comments - Show All Comments
Custom Views...	Page Layout - Sheet Options - Custom Views
Full Screen	View - Workbook Views - Full Screen
Zoom...	View - Zoom - Zoom

The Insert Menu	
Excel 2003 Menu	**Excel 2007 Ribbon**
Cells...	Home - Cells - Insert - Insert Cells
Rows	Home - Cells - Insert - Insert Rows
Columns	Home - Cells - Insert - Insert Columns
Worksheet	Home - Cells - Insert - Insert Sheet
Chart...	Insert - Charts
Symbol...	Insert - Text - Symbol
Page Break	Page Layout - Page Setup - Breaks - Insert Page Break
Function...	Formulas - Function Library - Function Wizard
Name - Define...	Formulas - Named Cells - Name Manager
Name - Paste...	Formulas - Named Cells - Use In Formula - Paste
Name - Create...	Formulas - Named Cells - Create from Selection
Name - Apply...	Formulas - Named Cells - Name a Range - Apply Names
Name - Label...	Formulas - Named Cells - Name a Range
Comment	Review - Comments - New Comment
Picture - Clip Art...	Insert - Illustrations - Clip Art
Picture - From File...	Insert - Illustrations - Picture
Picture - From Scanner or Camera...	Insert - Illustrations - Picture
Picture - AutoShapes	Insert - Shapes - Shapes
Picture - WordArt...	Insert - Text - WordArt
Picture - Organization Chart	Insert - Illustrations - SmartArt
Diagram...	Insert - Illustrations - SmartArt
Object...	Insert - Text - Object
Hyperlink...	Insert - Links - Hyperlink

The Format Menu	
Excel 2003 Menu	Excel 2007 Ribbon
Cells...	Home - Cells - Format - Cells
Row - Height...	Home - Cells - Format - Height
Row - AutoFit	Home - Cells - Format - AutoFit
Row - Hide	Home - Cells - Hide & Unhide - Hide Rows
Row - Unhide	Home - Cells - Hide & Unhide - Unhide Rows
Column - Width...	Home - Cells - Format - Width
Column - AutoFit Selection	Home - Cells - Format - AutoFit Selection
Column - Hide	Home - Cells - Hide & Unhide - Hide Columns
Column - Unhide	Home - Cells - Hide & Unhide - Unhide Columns
Column - Standard Width...	Home - Cells - Format - Standard Width
Sheet - Rename	Home - Cells - Format - Rename Sheet
Sheet - Hide	Home - Cells - Hide & Unhide - Hide Sheet
Sheet - Unhide...	Sheet - Unhide...
Sheet - Background...	Page Layout - Page Setup - Background
Sheet - Tab Color...	Home - Cells - Format - Tab Color
AutoFormat...	Home - Style - Format as Table
Conditional Formatting...	Home - Style - Conditional Formatting
Style...	Home - Style - Cell Styles

The Tools Menu	
Excel 2003 Menu	Excel 2007 Ribbon
Spelling...	Review - Proofing - Spelling
Research...	Review - Proofing - Research
Error Checking...	Formulas - Formula Auditing - Error Checking
Speech - Show Text To Speech Toolbar	No equivalent
Shared Workspace...	Add to QAT using Excel Options
Share Workbook...	Review - Changes - Share Workbook
Track Changes - Highlight Changes...	Review - Changes - Track Changes - Highlight Changes
Track Changes - Accept or Reject Changes...	Review - Changes - Track Changes - Accept or Reject Changes
Protection - Protect Sheet...	Home - Cells - Format - Protect Sheet
Protection - Allow Users to Edit Ranges...	Review - Changes - Allow Users to Edit Ranges
Protection - Protect Workbook...	Review - Changes - Protect Workbook
Protection - Protect and Share Workbook...	Review - Changes - Protect Sharing
Online Collaboration - Meet Now	Add to QAT using Excel Options

Online Collaboration - Schedule Meeting...	Add to QAT using Excel Options
Online Collaboration - Web Discussions	No equivalent
Goal Seek...	Data - Data Tools - What-If Analysis - Goal Seek
Scenarios...	Data - Data Tools - What-If Analysis - Scenario Manager
Formula Auditing - Trace Precedents	Formulas - Formula Auditing - Trace Precedents
Formula Auditing - Trace Dependents	Formulas - Formula Auditing - Trade Dependents
Formula Auditing - Trace Error	Formulas - Formula Auditing - Error Checking - Trace Error
Formula Auditing - Remove All Arrows	Formulas - Formula Auditing - Remove All Arrows
Formula Auditing - Evaluate Formula	Formulas - Formula Auditing - Evaluate Formula
Formula Auditing - Show Watch Window	Formulas - Formula Auditing - Show Watch Window
Formula Auditing - Formula Auditing Mode	Formulas - Formula Auditing - Show Formula
Formula Auditing - Show Formula Auditing Toolbar	No equivalent
Macro - Macros...	Developer - Code - Macros
Macro - Record New Macro...	Developer - Code - Record Macro
Macro - Security...	Developer - Code - Macro Security
Macro - Visual Basic Editor	Developer - Code - Visual Basic
Macro - Microsoft Script Editor	No equivalent
Add-Ins...	Office Icon - Excel Options
AutoCorrect Options...	Add to QAT using Excel Options
Customize...	No equivalent
Options...	Office Icon - Excel Options

The Data Menu	
Excel 2003 Menu	Excel 2007 Ribbon
Sort...	Data - Sort & Filter – Sort
Filter - AutoFilter	Home - Editing - Sort & Filter - Filter
Filter - Show All	Home - Editing - Sort & Filter - Clear
Filter - Advanced Filter...	Home - Editing - Sort & Filter - Advanced
Form...	Add to QAT using Excel Options
Subtotals...	Data - Outline - Subtotal
Validation...	Data - Data Tools - Data Validation
Table...	Data - Data Tools - What-If Analysis - Data Table

Text to Columns...	Data - Data Tools - Convert Text to a Table
Consolidate...	Data - Data Tools - Consolidate
Group and Outline - Hide Detail	Data - Outline - Hide Detail
Group and Outline - Show Detail	Data - Outline - Show Detail
Group and Outline - Group...	Data - Outline - Group
Group and Outline - Ungroup...	Data - Outline - Ungroup
Group and Outline - Auto Outline	Data - Outline - Group - Auto Outline
Group and Outline - Clear Outline	Data - Outline - Group - Clear Outline
Group and Outline - Settings...	Data - Outline - Settings
PivotTable and PivotChart Report...	Insert - Tables - Pivot Table
Import External Import Data...	Add to QAT using Excel Options
Import External New Web Query...	Data - Get External Data - From Web
Import External New Database Query...	Add to QAT using Excel Options
Import External Edit Query...	Add to QAT using Excel Options
Import External Data Range Properties...	Data - Manage Connections - Properties
Import External Parameters...	Add to QAT using Excel Options
List - Create List...	Data - List - Create List
List - Resize List...	Design - Properties - Resize Table
List - Total Row	Design - Table Style Options - Total Row
List - Convert to Range	Design - Tools - Convert to Range
List - Publish List...	Design - External Table Data - Export - Export to List
List - View List on Server	Design - External Table Data - View on Server
List - Unlink List	Design - External Table Data - Unlink List
List - Synchronize List	Add to QAT using Excel Options
List - Discard Changes and Refresh	Add to QAT using Excel Options
List - Hide Border of Inactive Lists	No equivalent
XML - Import...	Developer - XML - Import
XML - Export...	Developer - XML - Export
XML - Refresh XML Data	Developer - XML - Refresh XML Data
XML - XML Source...	Developer - XML - XML Source
XML - XML Map Properties...	Developer - XML - Map Properties
XML - Edit Query...	Developer - XML - Edit Query
XML - XML Expansion Packs...	Developer - XML - Expansion Packs
Refresh Data	Data - Manage Connections - Refresh

The Wndow Menu	
Excel 2003 Menu	**Excel 2007 Ribbon**
New Window	View - Window - New Window
Arrange...	View - Window - Arrange All
Compare Side by Side with Macro to List MenuBars.xls	View - Window - View Side by Side
Hide	View - Window - Hide
Unhide...	View - Window - Unhide
Split	View - Window - Split
Freeze Panes	View - Window - Freeze Panes
1 Book1	View - Window - Switch Window

The Help Menu	
Excel 2003 Menu	**Excel 2007 Ribbon**
Microsoft Excel Help	Question mark at right end of ribbon
Show the Office Assistant	No Equivalent
Microsoft Office Online	Office Icon - Excel Options - Resources - Microsoft Office Online
Contact Us	Office Icon - Excel Options - Resources - Contact Us
Check for Updates	Office Icon - Excel Options - Resources - Check for Updates
Detect and Repair...	Office Icon - Excel Options - Resources - Detect & Repair
Activate Product...	Office Icon - Excel Options - Resources - Activate Product
Customer Feedback Options...	Office Icon - Excel Options - Resources - Customer Feedback Options
About Microsoft Office Excel	Office Icon - Excel Options - Resources - About Microsoft Excel

The Standard Toolbar	
Excel 2003	**Excel 2007 Ribbon**
New	Office Icon - New
Open	Office Icon - Open
Save	Office Icon - Save
Permission	Office Icon - Finish - Restrict Permission - Unrestricted Access
E-Mail	Office Icon - Send - Email
Print	Office Icon - Print - Quick Print
Print Preview	Office Icon - Print - Print Preview
Spelling	Review - Proofing - Spelling
Research	Review - Proofing - Research
Cut	Home - Clipboard - Cut

Copy	Home - Clipboard - Copy
Paste	Home - Clipboard - Paste
Format Painter	Home - Clipboard - Format Painter
Undo	QAT - Undo
Redo	QAT - Repeat
Insert Hyperlink	Insert - Links - Hyperlink
AutoSum	Home - Editing - Sum
Sort Ascending	Home - Editing - Sort & Filter - Sort Ascending
Sort Descending	Home - Editing - Sort & Filter - Sort Descending
Chart Wizard	Insert - Charts
Drawing	No Equivalent
Zoom	View - Zoom - Zoom
Help	Question mark at right end of ribbon

The Formatting Toolbar	
Excel 2003	Excel 2007 Ribbon
Font	Home - Font - Font
Font Size	Home - Font - Font Size
Bold	Home - Font - Bold
Italic	Home - Font - Italic
Underline	Home - Font - Underline
Align Left	Home - Alignment - Align Left
Align Center	Home - Alignment - Align Center
Align Right	Home - Alignment - Align Right
Merge & Center	Home - Alignment - Merge - Merge & Center
Currency Style	Home - Number - Accounting Number Format
Percent Style	Home - Number - Percent Style
Comma Style	Home - Number - Comma Style
Increase Decimal	Home - Number - Increase Decimal
Decrease Decimal	Home - Number - Decrease Decimal
Increase Indent	Home - Number - Increase Indent
Decrease Indent	Home - Number - Decrease Indent
Borders	Home - Font - Border
Fill Color	Home - Font - Fill Color
Font Color	Home - Font - Font Color

✳ ✳ ✳

Chapter 3

Keyboard Shortcuts

When Excel gurus hear that Microsoft changed the menu system, they are often most concerned about all of the shortcut keys that they previously learned.

In Excel 97 – Excel 2003, most menu items had a single letter underlined. If you wanted to selected Edit – Fill – Justify from the menu, you simply had to hold down the Alt key while typing the underlined letter from each menu selection. Thus, Alt+E+I+J would allow you to quickly select the Justify command.

There are a few menu commands that I have memorized and I can type those shortcuts in my sleep.

In 80% of the cases, Excel 2007 will support your knowledge of legacy shortcut keys.

All Ctrl Key Shortcuts Continue to Work

Any Ctrl key shortcuts will continue to work. Some of the popular Ctrl shortcuts:

- Ctrl+B for Bold
- Ctrl+I for Italics
- Ctrl+U for Underline
- Ctrl+A to select All
- Ctrl+C to Copy
- Ctrl+X to Cut
- Ctrl+V to Paste
- Ctrl+Z to Undo

Most Alt Shortcuts for Edit, View, Insert, Format, Tools, and Data Will Work

When you press Alt+E, Alt+V, Alt+I, Alt+O, Alt+T, or Alt+D, Excel 2007 enters a special Office 2003 compatibility mode. A box appears in the top center of the screen showing the Office 2003 access keys that you have entered so far. When you enter enough keys to invoke a menu command in Excel 2003, the command will be invoked in Excel 2007.

In Figure 3.1, two-thirds of the keystrokes for Edit-Fill-Justify have been selected. When you strike the J, Excel will invoke the Justify command.

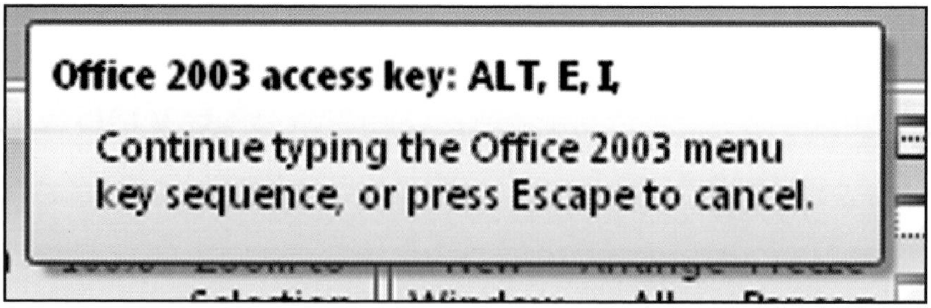

Figure 3.1
When you use the old Alt key sequences, this tip shows the keys you have pressed so far. It would have been helpful if they would have shown Edit – Fill.

Office 2003 access key: ALT, E, I,

Continue typing the Office 2003 menu key sequence, or press Escape to cancel.

Caution! While this feature is good in theory, it does not work fast enough in the beta. There is a slight delay when you press Alt+E. I find that I usually have typed the I+J before the Office 2003 access key window appears. So, to use the Alt keyboard shortcuts that you've memorized from Office 97-2003, you have to type them a bit slower than normal.

Tip: Alt+F (File), Alt+W (Window), and Alt+H (Help) behave differently. Read about these keys below.

Using the Office 2007 Keyboard Shortcuts

If you are a fan of using the keyboard, you might have noticed one problem in Excel 2003. There were often menu items that did not have a keyboard shortcut. In Excel 2007, every menu item can be selected from the keyboard.

To access the new keyboard shortcuts, press and release the Alt key on the keyboard.

Excel displays a single-character keyboard shortcut for each tab of the ribbon.

If any contextual ribbon tabs are visible, they will have a two-character shortcut key.

All of the icons on the QAT are assigned a numeric keyboard shortcut. The first nine items are assigned the keys 1 through 9. Icons after that are assigned a two-character shortcut starting with a zero.

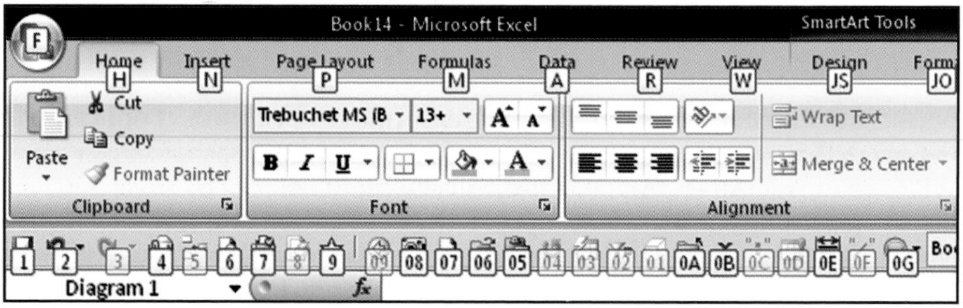

Figure 3.2
Press and release Alt to see the new shortcut keys.

When you press F, H, N, P, M, A, R, or W, Excel displays the appropriate tab of the ribbon. The original shortcut key tips are replaced with new keytips that allow you to select any of the items in the ribbon. Figure 3.3 shows the key tips for the Data ribbon.

Figure 3.3
Press a shortcut key for the Data ribbon and you will see the Data shortcut keys.

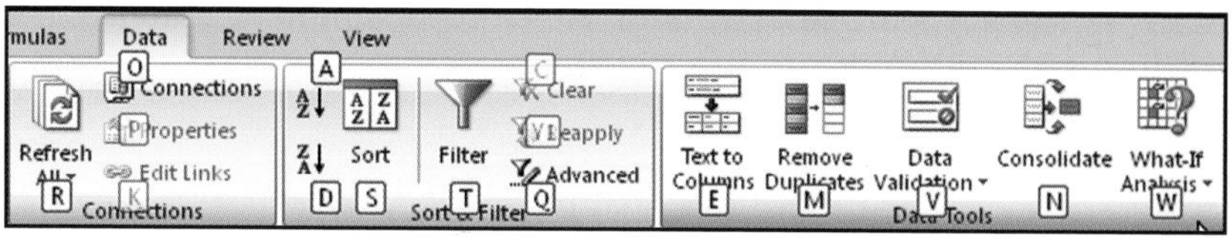

Some of the key tips make sense: A for Sort Ascending; D for Sort Descending; W for What If; V for Validation. Other shortcuts just seem to use the left over letters.

If you type W to select What If Analysis, its dropdown provides you with three new shortcut keys from which to select items.

Figure 3.4
As you type additional shortcut keys, new shortcut keys appear until you finally actually select a command.

While the keyboard shortcuts for the QAT will constantly change, depending on how your QAT is customized, you should find that the keyboard shortcuts for the ribbon will remain constant. You can memorize that Alt+A+A will sort in ascending order. Alt+A+W+G will open the Goal Seek dialog.

Accessing the Old File and Window Menus

In Excel 2003, Alt+F would open the File menu. Alt+W opened the Window menu. In Excel 2007, these keystroke combinations do not show the Office 2003 keyboard shortcut window. Instead, Alt+F opens the Office Icon menu and Alt+W opens the View ribbon.

Many of the keyboard shortcuts in the Office Icon menu match the same shortcuts as in the File menu.

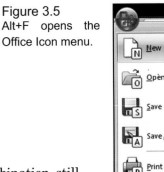

Figure 3.5
Alt+F opens the Office Icon menu.

Thus, Alt+F+S was File – Save in Excel 2003, and this combination still executes a Save in Excel 2007.

Alt+F+D+A in Excel 2003 was File – Send to – Mail Recipient as Attachment. In Excel 2007, Alt+F+D still gets you to the Send menu, but now E is used to send a file as an e-mail attachment and A is used to send a file as an XPS attachment (Microsoft's new open source file format meant to compete with Adobe PDF).

Figure 3.6
Some of the old keystrokes don't quite work. If you had memorized Alt+F+D+A, it is now Alt+F+D+E.

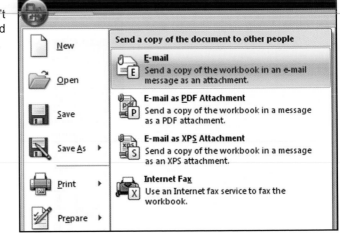

Pressing Alt+W in Excel 2003 opened the Window menu. The commands on the old Window menu were New Window, Arrange, Compare Side by Side, Hide, Unhide, Split, and Freeze Panes.

Pressing Alt+W in Excel 2007 opens the View ribbon. All of the keyboard shortcuts (N, A, B, H, U, S, and F) perform identical actions in Excel 2007.

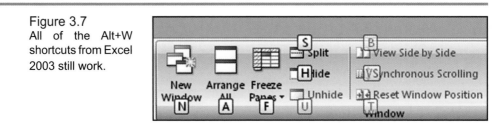

Figure 3.7
All of the Alt+W
shortcuts from Excel
2003 still work.

> Note: In Excel 2003, Alt+W+2 would switch to the next open workbook. To do this in Excel 2007, use Ctrl+Tab.

Accessing Commands on the Excel 2003 Help Menu

Microsoft has simply abandoned the Alt+H command to access commands on the Excel 2003 Help menu.

The Office 2007 paradigm is that Alt+H takes you to the Home menu.

This is not a horrible loss, since there were not many commands on the Excel 2003 Help menu that you would have accessed using Alt+H. Alt+H+H would open Help, but the F1 key did, too, and continues to be a faster way to access Help.

Bonus Tip: Using the Keyboard to Enter Formulas

This trick is not new, but it is a faster way to enter formulas. In fact, the trick originated with Lotus 1-2-3 back in the 1980s. If you are a fan of using the keyboard, you should learn this method for entering formulas.

Say that you need to enter a formula in B8 a shown in Figure 3.8.

Figure 3.8
The fastest way to enter
this formula is the arrow
key method.

	A	B	C	D
1	Davis had 7 donuts. He gave 2 to Zeke			
2	and bought 4 more at the store. How			
3	many donuts does Davis have?			
4				
5		7		
6	-	2		
7	+	4		
8				

1. Start in cell B8. Type either an equals sign or a plus sign. If you regularly use the numeric keypad, it is easier to type a plus sign.

2. Press the up arrow three times. Excel shows a flashing cursor around cell B5. The provisional formula in B8 shows =B5.

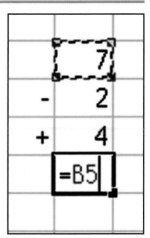

Figure 3.9
B8 is still the active cell (thick border), but you are pointing to B5 (dashed border).

3. Type a minus sign to continue the formula. The flashing box disappears. The focus returns to cell B8. If you want to point to cell B6, type the up arrow two times. The provisional formula now shows =B5-B6.

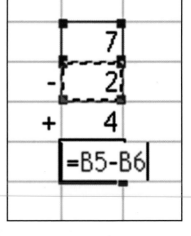

Figure 3.10
When you type a math sign, the focus returns to the original cell. It required two up arrow presses to arrive at B6.

4. Type a plus sign.

5. Type the up arrow to move to B7.

6. Type the Enter key to accept the formula.

Figure 3.11
The final formula

B8			f_x	=B5-B6+B7

	A	B	C	D	E
1	Davis had 7 donuts. He gave 2 to Zeke				
2	and bought 4 more at the store. How				
3	many donuts does Davis have?				
4					
5		7			
6	-	2			
7	+	4			
8		9			

If you try it, you will find that typing =↑↑↑-↑↑+↑<Enter> is far faster than using the mouse to enter the formula.

✳ ✳ ✳

Chapter 4

Taming the QAT &
Finding the Mini Bar

Although you now understand why Microsoft eliminated the menu and toolbars in favor of a ribbon, there is still one fundamental problem. In a toolbar system, there were certain icons that were always available at the top of your screen.

In Excel 97-2003, you always had quick access to icons for bold, italics, cut, paste, align right, decrease decimal, sort ascending, print preview, the chart wizard, and more.

With Excel 2007, these icons are spread across seven ribbon tabs, so the odds are that you will not always have access to the various icons that you might need. Microsoft addresses this problem with the Mini Toolbar and the QAT (Quick Access Toolbar).

- The Mini Toolbar is a floating toolbar that fades into view whenever you select text in Excel. This toolbar offers 17 formatting icons. Surprisingly, however, it is fairly rare in Excel to select text. Selecting an entire cell does not count – you actually have to select characters within the cell.

- The Quick Access Toolbar (QAT) is a toolbar that is always visible near the ribbon. While the QAT initially contains four icons (Save, Print Preview, Undo, and Redo), you can customize the QAT to hold all of your favorite icons. One set of customizations can apply to all workbooks opened on the computer, while a second set of icons can be defined to open for each specific workbook.

Finding the Mini Toolbar

If you have used Outlook 2003, you might be familiar with toolbars that fade in. When you receive a new Outlook message, a notifier box starts to appear in the lower right corner of the screen. This notifier shows the subject line, the first words in the message, and icons to immediately delete or open the e-mail. If you are busy working on a document and ignore the notifier, it slowly fades away. However, if you move the mouse towards the notifier, it solidifies so that you have time to hit the Delete button in order to eliminate the mail if it is junk.

The Mini Toolbar uses similar technology. I think it will appear much more frequently in Word and PowerPoint than it will appear in Excel. It is possible to use Excel 40 hours a week and never see the Mini Toolbar appear.

Note: During the beta period, Microsoft has variously called this feature a "Mini Bar", "Mini Toolbar" and a "Floaty". While I prefer visiting the "Mini Bar", it looks like "Mini Toolbar" will win out in the final version. When I write books for QUE, the editorial guidelines there state that the "T" in toolbar is never capitalized. While I generally agree with this, to me, "Mini Toolbar" is just a bad replacement for "Mini Bar", and so I will capitalize the T. After all, you wouldn't drive a "Mini cooper" automobile, would you?

The Mini Toolbar is elusive in Excel for two reasons. First, it is relatively hard to select characters within a cell in Excel. It is easier in Excel charts or SmartArt graphics to select characters, but it is relatively rare to select just a few characters inside of a cell. Second, on many computers, the Mini Toolbar initially appears in a completely invisible state! If you don't move the mouse pointer towards the completely invisible Mini Toolbar, it will never appear.

In Figure 4.1, the Mini Toolbar is just starting to appear after double clicking a chart title to select the characters in the title. The toolbar is so light that it is difficult to guess if it will even show up as this book goes through the printing press. The Mini Toolbar starts just above the "r" in Chart.

Figure 4.1
Select some text and a nearly invisible Mini Toolbar starts to appear.

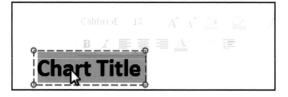

If you then hold the mouse still, the Mini Toolbar will remain in its nearly invisible state. If you move the mouse left or down, the Mini Toolbar will become completely invisible.

However, if you move the mouse right or up by a few pixels, the Mini Toolbar fades completely into view.

Figure 4.2
Move towards the Mini Toolbar and it solidifies.

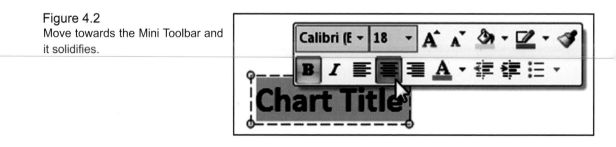

The theory behind the Mini Toolbar is that a leading reason for selecting text is that you might be planning on formatting the text. The Mini Toolbar puts sixteen popular formatting commands at your mousetip. You can do a fair amount of formatting without ever having to visit the ribbon or the QAT. In Figure 4.3, the font face, font size, fill color, line color, italics, and font color have all been changed using the QAT.

Figure 4.3
While I am not suggesting this is a good looking title, all of the changes from Figure 4.2 to Figure 4.3 were initiated using the Mini Toolbar.

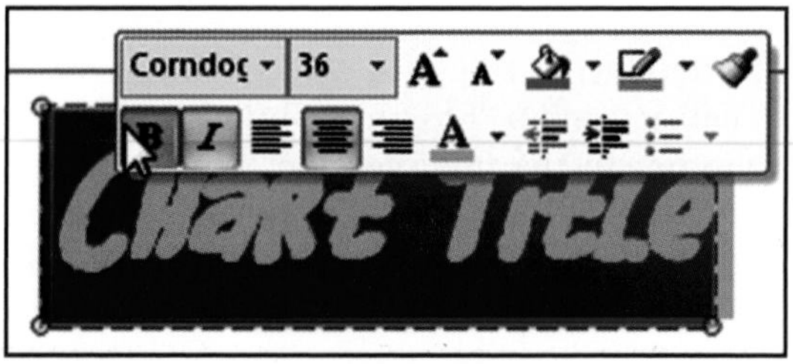

Although the Mini Toolbar only contains 16 icons, a few of those icons lead to dropdown menus with significant variations. In Figure 4.3, the gradient was added using the options under the paint bucket icon, as shown in Figure 4.4.

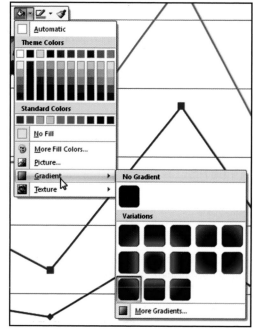

Figure 4.4
Some icons on the Mini Toolbar lead to menus with hundreds of options.

Mini Toolbar Tips and Notes

There are a couple of tips and notes for using the Mini Toolbar. The next sections discuss these tips.

Versions of the Mini Toolbar

The figures shown previously in this chapter represent the Mini Toolbar when you are formatting a chart title. If you cause the Mini Toolbar to appear when you are editing text within a cell, there are some buttons that do not apply.

Quadruple-click any non-blank cell and move the mousepointer up and to the right. An abbreviated version of the Mini Toolbar with seven icons will appear. It doesn't make sense to change the indentation of just a few characters in a cell, so Excel produces this version of the Mini Toolbar, shown in Figure 4.5.

Figure 4.5
If you select characters within a cell, an abbreviated Mini Toolbar appears.

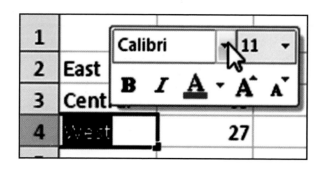

Right-Click Any Cell to Access the Mini Toolbar

If you right-click any cell, the full Mini Toolbar appears above the cell. This is by far an easier way to invoke the toolbar than by selecting characters within the cell.

Customizing the Mini Toolbar

In Excel 2007, you cannot customize the Mini Toolbar. While it would be cool if Microsoft would let you add buttons to the toolbar, they have not enabled that functionality for this release.

I can predict that the Mini Toolbar found in this book and the Mini Toolbar in your version of Excel will be slightly different. Since the first beta came out, customers have been lobbying Microsoft to add other buttons to the Mini Toolbar. Buttons have come and gone in each release of the beta. Some last minute lobbying will undoubtedly cause a button to be added after this book goes to press.

I think that the fervor with which people are discussing the Mini Toolbar suggests that it would be great if Microsoft would let you customize the Mini Toolbar. Maybe this will be available in Excel 14.

When Does the Mini Toolbar Completely Disappear?

As discussed previously, if you move towards the Mini Toolbar, it solidifies. If you move away from the Mini Toolbar, it disappears. You can move your mouse from southwest to northeast and cause the Mini Toolbar to fade into and out of view.

However, once your mouse strays a certain distance from the selection, the Mini Toolbar disappears and will not reappear until you reselect the text.

This distance is based on pixels. In general, though, if you move approximately 10 rows away from the selection in a spreadsheet with the default font and zoom, you will have hit the limit and the Mini Toolbar will permanently disappear.

I can see many situations where you would move away from the selection (for example, to respond to an incoming e-mail notification). Once you've moved too far away from the selection, you will either have to re-select the text or use the formatting icons in the Home ribbon.

Permanently Disabling the Mini Toolbar

The Mini Toolbar is fairly elusive in Excel and will rarely get in your way. However, if you would like to permanently disable the feature, you can do so.

From the Office Icon menu, choose Excel options. The very first setting in the Popular category is Show Mini Toolbar On Selection. Uncheck the box shown in Figure 4.6 to disable the Mini Toolbar.

Figure 4.6
Use this setting to permanently disable the Mini Toolbar.

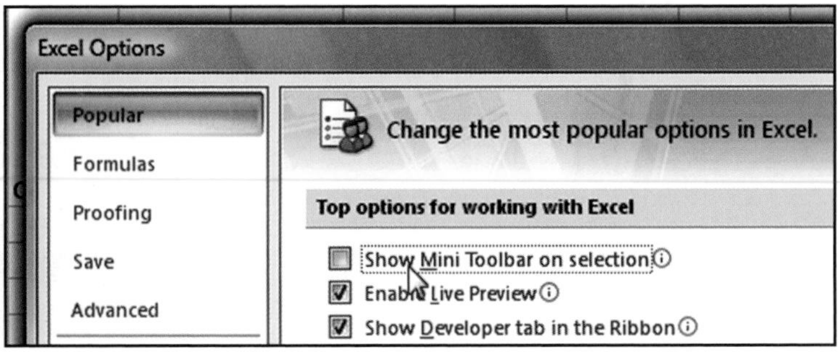

Using the QAT

The QAT is always visible in Excel. Even if you minimize the ribbon, the QAT will remain visible. This makes the QAT a great place to store icons that you use frequently. With clever customization of the QAT, you can minimize the need to access anything on the various ribbon tabs.

The QAT can either appear above or below the ribbon. While the QAT appears a little more stylistic above the ribbon, it is more functional below the ribbon. When the QAT is below the ribbon, it requires less movement of the mouse to reach the QAT. Also, when it is below the ribbon, you have more space to add buttons to the QAT before the QAT starts squeezing the area used for the file name of the currently active workbook.

To change the location of the QAT, right-click on the QAT and choose Show Quick Access Toolbar Below the Ribbon, as shown in Figure 4.7.

Figure 4.7
Right-click the QAT to change the location.

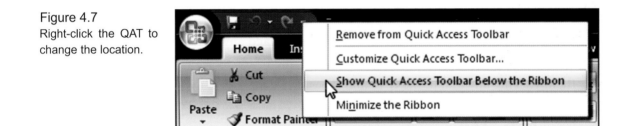

When shown below the ribbon, the QAT appears just above the Formula bar in Excel.

Figure 4.8
Moving the QAT below the ribbon gives you quicker access to the QAT.

Customizing the QAT

Initially, the QAT is a tiny toolbar with three icons. It appears to the right of the Office Icon, above the ribbon tabs, as shown in Figure 4.9.

Figure 4.9
Initially, the QAT is at the top of the window with three icons.

There are five ways of customizing the QAT:

- Using the dropdown at the right side of the QAT to add any of 11 popular icons.
- Right-clicking any icon on any ribbon and choosing to add to the QAT.
- Right-clicking any icon in the QAT and choosing Remove from Quick Access Toolbar.
- Right-clicking the QAT to access the Customize pane of the Excel Options dialog.
- Using the Excel Options button in the Office Icon menu to customize the QAT.

Quickly Customizing Using the Dropdown at the Right Side of the QAT

At the far right end of the QAT, a dropdown offers a list of 11 popular icons that you can easily add to the QAT. As shown in Figure 4.10, select any icons from this list to add them to the QAT.

Figure 4.10
Excel remembers the order in which you add icons to the QAT and shows the icons in that sequence.

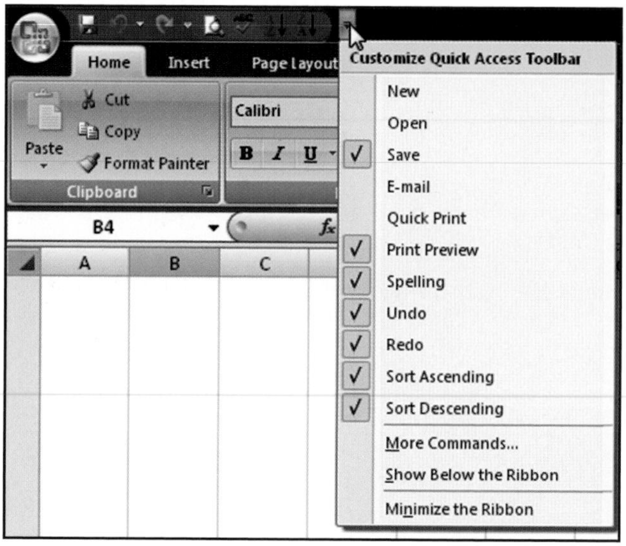

Right-Clicking Any Icon to Add to the QAT

When you find a useful icon in any ribbon, you can right-click the icon and choose Add to Quick Access Toolbar.

Figure 4.11
Right-click to add an icon to the end of the QAT.

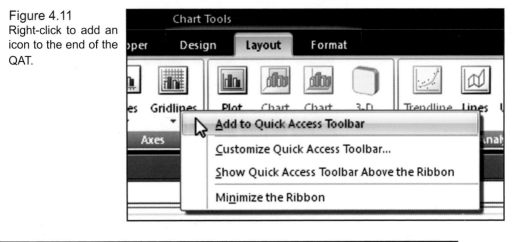

Note: You can even do this with icons that are in the context ribbons, such as the Chart Tools ribbons. Of course, if you do this, the icons will be grayed out any time that a chart is not active.

There is a minor limitation on what can be added to the QAT. While you can add the Font Size dropdown to the QAT, you cannot add an individual selection from the Font Size dropdown to the QAT. If you were to right-click on the 36 point font size, Excel would offer to allow you to add the gallery to the Quick Access Toolbar. When you add a gallery, Excel adds a single icon to the QAT with a dropdown arrow. Open the dropdown arrow and you will see the complete set of options available in the gallery. Figure 4.12 through Figure 4.15 show gallery dropdowns for font size, font face, quick chart styles, and chart gridlines.

Figure 4.12
The font size gallery dropdown offers a simple list of font sizes.

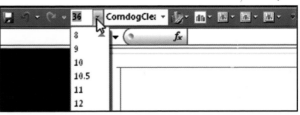

Figure 4.13
The font face gallery shows all of the installed fonts in their own font.

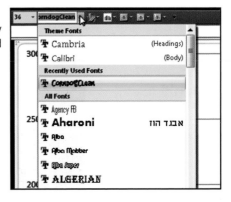

Figure 4.14
The charting quick styles icon opens to display 48 possible chart formats.

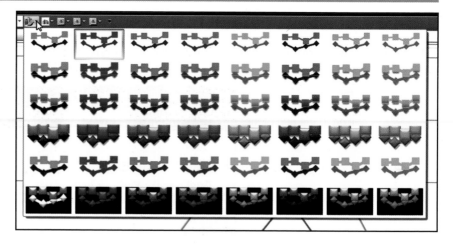

Figure 4.15
This gallery is the result of adding the large gridlines icon from the Chart Tools Layout ribbon. The two icons to the right in the QAT are the individual menus for Horizontal Gridlines and then Vertical Gridlines.

Primary Horizontal Gridlines ▶
Primary Vertical Gridlines ▶

None
Do not display Horizontal Gridlines

Major Gridlines
Display Horizontal Gridlines for Major units

Minor Gridlines
Display Horizontal Gridlines for Minor units

Major & Minor Gridlines
Display Horizontal Gridlines for Major and Minor units

More Primary Horizontal Gridlines Options...

Right-Clicking Any Existing QAT Icon to Remove from the QAT

If your QAT is becoming crowded, you can remove individual icons by right-clicking them and choose Remove From Quick Access Toolbar.

Figure 4.16
Right-click an icon on the QAT to remove it from the QAT.

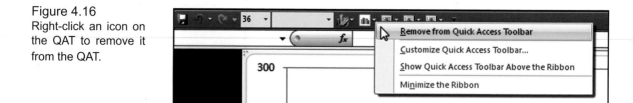

Remove from Quick Access Toolbar

Customize Quick Access Toolbar...

Show Quick Access Toolbar Above the Ribbon

Minimize the Ribbon

300

Using Excel Options to Customize the QAT

All of the previous methods show quick ways to make small customizations to the QAT. If you need to make many customizations to the QAT, you will want to use the full-featured customization tool available in Excel options.

You can reach this tool using one of three methods:

- Choose the Office Icon – Excel Options and then click on the Customize category along the left side.
- Right-click the QAT and choose Customize Quick Access Toolbar….
- Open the dropdown at the right side of the QAT and choose More Commands….

The Customize dialog box has many powerful features. Here are tips for getting the most out of the dialog.

Figure 4.17
Using the QAT
Customize tool

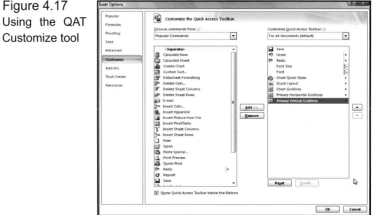

- Select any icon in the right list box and then use the up and down buttons on the right edge of the dialog to re-sequence the location of the icon.
- Select any icon in the left list box and then click the Add>> button to add this icon after the selected icon in the right list box.
- The left listbox offers dozens of popular icons, but there are 31 different versions of the left listbox. Use the top left dropdown to choose a different version of the left listbox (see Figure 4.18).

Figure 4.18
Each of these items offers dozens of icons that can be added to the QAT.

- Choose Commands Not in the Ribbon from the left listbox to locate your favorite commands that were not popular enough to make it to the ribbon. You will find over 200 icons in this list. As you might guess, adding these to the QAT is the only way to access most of these commands. A selection of these icons is shown in Figure 4.19.

Figure 4.19
A few of the 200+ icons available in the "Commands Not in the Ribbon" category.

- Choose Macros from the left listbox to add a custom VBA macro to the QAT. These icons are the only ones where you can use the Modify button. See "Adding Icons for VBA Macros to the QAT" below.
- The left listbox always starts with a <Separator> entry. This is not an actual command, but draws a vertical bar in the QAT to break your commands into groups.
- If you want to add commands to the QAT for the current workbook only, change the top right dropdown to display one of the currently open workbooks. This will start a new list of icons for the selected workbook.
- To restore the QAT to its original set of three icons, choose the Reset button.

Adding Icons for VBA Macros to the QAT

When you are customizing the Quick Access Toolbar, the left dropdown offers a setting for Macros. This will display all of the macros available in open workbooks, plus macros available from installed add-ins. Each macro has an identical icon.

Choose a macro from the list and click the Add button to add it to the QAT.

Figure 4.20
Choose a macro from the left list and add it to the QAT.

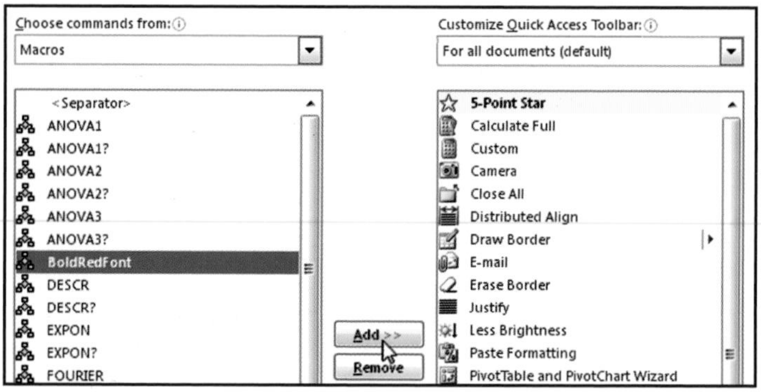

After adding the macro to the QAT, you can select the macro in the right listbox and choose Modify. The Modify Button dialog appears with 200 new icons. Try to find an icon that might work with your macro. Also, you can type a new name for the button. This name will appear as a tooltip when you hover over the icon in the QAT.

Figure 4.21
The previous version of Excel offered 4096 custom icons. Being limited to only 200 is an incredible disappointment.

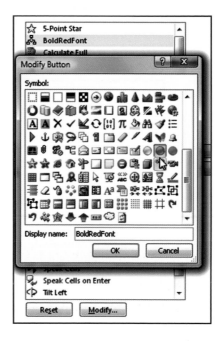

Adding Too Many Icons to the QAT

If you add too many icons to the QAT, only the first row of icons is shown on the QAT. A More Controls icon appears at the right end of the QAT. (Figure 4.22). Click the More Controls icon to see a second row of QAT icons. (Figure 4.23). If you have even more icons than will fit on the second row, a scrollbar at the right edge of the second row of the QAT will allow you to scroll through the additional icons.

Figure 4.22
If you have more than one row of icons, use the More Controls icon to see the rest.

Figure 4.23
Even the second row
doesn't show all of the icons
that have been added.

Note: Writing a book can be deceiving. In the original outline for this book, I sort of dismissed the QAT and thought that this would be a one page chapter. Even though it is easy to customize the QAT, there are a lot of different options to help make the QAT useful for you.

Caution! The previous chapter talked about using keyboard shortcuts. While it might be possible to memorize some keyboard shortcuts, it will be hard to memorize the keyboard shortcuts associated with the QAT. The QAT icons are assigned shortcut keys on the fly every time that you hit the Alt key. If you want to reliably memorize certain QAT icons, be sure to add them to the leftmost section of the QAT, before any icons that may occasionally be grayed out.

✳ ✳ ✳

Chapter 5

Unlocking the Big Grid

Excel 2007 offers more rows and columns.

That is an understatement.

This table shows the magnitude of the increase, but I am not sure that numbers do it justice.

	Excel 97-2003	Excel 2007	% Change
Rows	65,536	1,084,576	1500%
Columns	256	16,384	25500%
Cells	16.7 Million	17.2 Billion	102300%

In case you wondered how Microsoft comes up with numbers such as 16,384 and 1,084,576, these are powers of 2. There are 2^20 rows and 2^14 columns.

In the prior version of Excel, you could not have daily dates for one year stretching across the columns. In the new version, you can show weekdays for 46 years before you run into the last column (XFD).

This chart helps you to visualize how large the new grid is. The green area is the size of one worksheet in the new Excel. The tiny yellow box in the lower left corner is the size of one worksheet in the old Excel.

Figure 5.1
The yellow is the size of the old Excel grid. The green is the size of the new Excel grid.

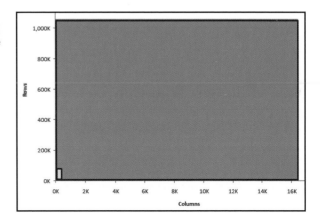

What Happened to the Big Grid?

I was excited to see this new, larger grid in Excel 2007. The first thing that I did was to open one of my old workbooks. After pressing End+Down arrow and End+Right arrow, I was disappointed to see that I was only at cell IV65536. Here, I am in Excel 2007, yet the grid only has the old limits!

This problem happens because the when you open an Excel 2003 workbook in Excel 2007, it is opened in Compatibility Mode. When you are in compatibility mode, you cannot access any rows beyond 65,536.

To exit compatibility mode, follow these steps:

1. From the Office icon menu, choose Convert.
2. Read the note that you are about to convert the file and click OK.
3. Read the note that the conversion was successful. In order to access more rows, you need to close and re-open the workbook. Click Yes to do this.

> Caution! When you perform the above steps, Excel will erase the .xls version of the file and replace it with an Excel 2007 version of the file. If you prefer to keep both versions, use File – Save As to save an Excel 2007 version of the file.

After converting the file, you can see cell XFD1048576:

Figure 5.2
The new final cell in the big grid.

Named Ranges That Can Be a Problem

It is possible to name a range in Excel. Useful names might be "Expenses" or "TaxRate". A range name cannot duplicate an existing Excel cell name.

There are a lot of three letter words that used to be safe range names that would now be problems. For example, "Tax97" or "ROI2007" would have been valid names in Excel 2003, but are now cell addresses in Excel 2007.

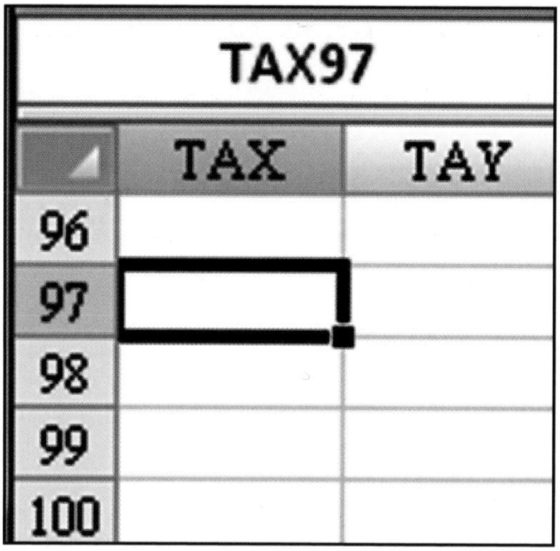

Figure 5.3
In Excel 2007, Tax97 is a
cell address.

If you attempt to convert an existing file that uses a name such as Tax97, Excel will alert you and convert the range name to _Tax97.

While all references in formulas will automatically update, you should check any VBA macros or OFFSET functions to see if they explicitly referenced the old range names.

Who Needs This Many Cells?

After using Excel 2007 for a year, I've never had an occasion to use 17 billion cells. However, I have run into datasets that filled A1:S675000. I've also run into CSV files from Quickbooks that had more than 500 columns.

So, while you may never need 17 billion cells, there are times when you will need more than 65K rows or 256 columns. Microsoft realizes that changing the grid size causes a change in the file format. The new grid size is designed to get you through the next several versions of Excel.

✳ ✳ ✳

Chapter 6

Page Layout View

When you are getting ready to print your workbook, the new page layout tools will make the job easy.

Previous versions of Excel offered two views – either Normal or Page Break Preview. Excel 2007 adds a new view called Page Layout View. There are many advantages of Page Layout View:

- Excel draws in the margins of each page as white space.

- You can edit headers and footers in Page Layout View

- You can continue to work in your worksheet, adding new data, new rows, and new columns in Page Layout View.

Look for a row of three icons in the lower right side of your Excel window. The three icons are for Normal, Page Layout View, and Page Break Preview.

Figure 6.1
While most commands are on the ribbon, these three view icons are in the lower right of the screen.

To the right of the icons, a zoom slider allows you to adjust the zoom from 10% to 400%. Figure 6.2 shows a worksheet at 50% zoom in Page Layout View.

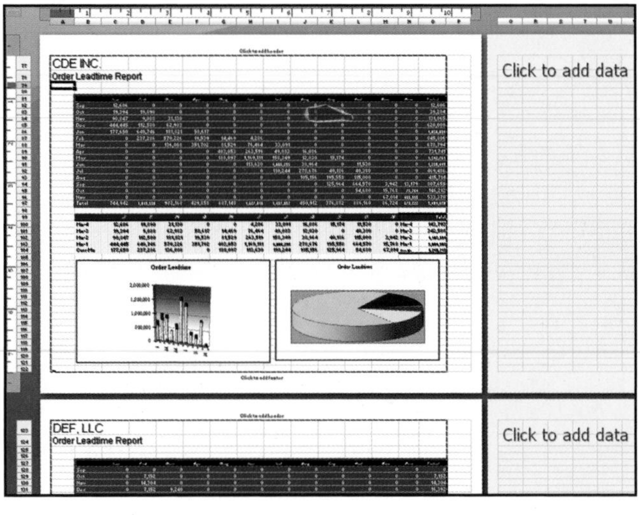

Figure 6.2
You can see margins and headings in Page Layout view.

The Page Layout ribbon offers all of the print settings. You can adjust margins, scaling, etc. and instantly see the results in Page Layout View.

Figure 6.3
Everything on the old Page
Setup dialog is on the Page
Layout ribbon.

Adding Headers and Footers

In Page Layout View, words appear in the top and bottom margin, encouraging you to Click to Add Header or Click to Add Footer. There are actually three click zones for headers and three click zones for footers. In Figure 6.4, a click would edit the left footer.

Figure 6.4
Click to add a left footer.

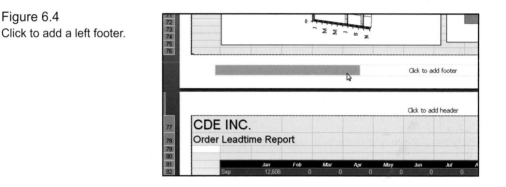

When you click in a header or footer zone, a new Header & Footer Tools Design ribbon appears, as shown in Figure 6.5.

Figure 6.5
This context ribbon
only appears when
you are editing a
header or footer.

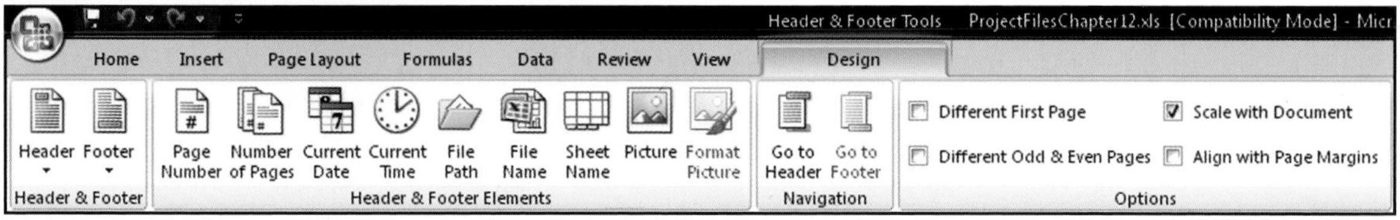

You can choose from built-in text by using the Header or Footer dropdown at the left side of the ribbon.

Figure 6.6
Built-in text for headers
or footers

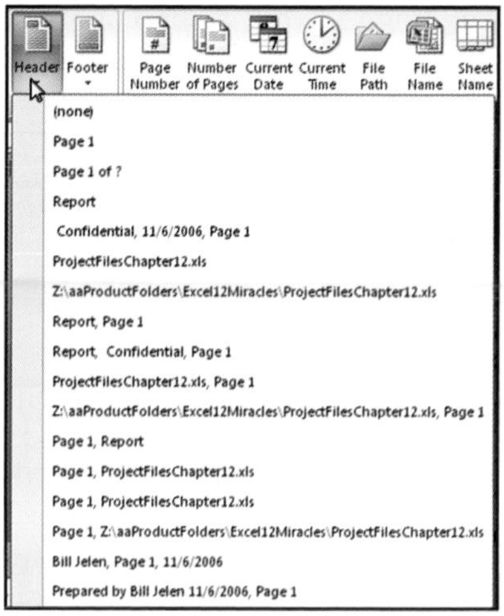

Alternatively, you can design your own footer by using the Header & Footer Elements icons.

Excel 2007 now offers the ability to have a different header on odd/even pages, or a different header on the first page.

When you click outside of the Header or Footer area, Excel returns you to the Page Layout ribbon.

What Happened to Print Preview?

Microsoft is so confident that you will like the new Page Layout View, that they have buried the Print Preview icon deep in the menu system.

To access Print Preview, use the Office Icon – Print – Print Preview.

In Print Preview mode, you have only one ribbon tab available.

Figure 6.7
The print preview ribbon

Tip: If you still like Print Preview, you can add the icon to your Quick Access Toolbar. See Chapter 4 on page 25.

Using the Zoom Slider

Use the slider in the lower right corner of the window to adjust the zoom from 10% to 400%.

At a 10% zoom, you can get a 50,000 foot view of your workbook. Figure 6.8 shows a worksheet at a 20% zoom. You can see approximately 25,344 cells at this zoom. You can't make out any of the values, but you can get an overview of your worksheet.

Figure 6.8
See your document from a 50,000 foot view.

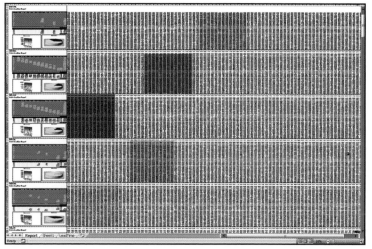

At the opposite end of the spectrum, a 400% view will show you about 40 cells.

Figure 6.9
At the maximum zoom, you can make out details in drawings and charts.

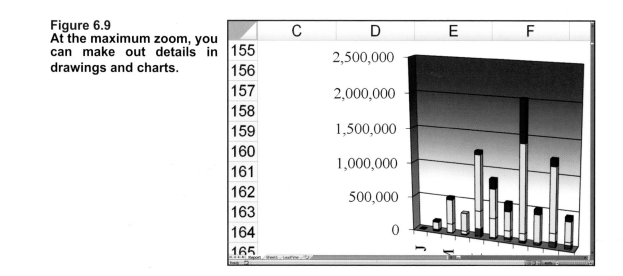

✳ ✳ ✳

Chapter 7

Tables

Many spreadsheets in Excel contain a two dimensional table of data. You have headings in the first row, and each row of the worksheet represents a different record in a table.

Because a common task in Excel is dealing with tables, Excel 2007 has added several features for dealing with tables.

Figure 7.1 shows a typical table in Excel.

Figure 7.1
You frequently encounter table-like datasets in Excel.

	A	B	C	D	E	F	G
1	Region	Product	ShipDate	Customer	Quantity	Revenue	Profit
2	East	I881	1/1/2007	Amazing Yardstick Partners	1000	22810	12590
3	Central	J690	1/1/2007	Inventive Opener Corporation	100	2257	1273
4	East	M144	1/1/2007	Magnificent Jewelry Inc.	500	10245	6010
5	Central	R543	1/2/2007	Magnificent Tackle Inc.	500	11240	6130
6	Central	P154	1/3/2007	Leading Yogurt Company	400	9204	5116
7	East	W202	1/3/2007	Excellent Doorbell Company	800	18552	10680
8	East	H385	1/3/2007	Paramount Doghouse Inc	400	9152	5064

To turn on the features, select a single cell in the dataset and type Ctrl+T. Excel will assume your table extends to either the edge of the spreadsheet or to a blank row and blank column. The Create Table dialog will ask you to confirm the range for the table.

Figure 7.2
Excel guesses the current region as the address for the table.

Note: Instead of using Ctrl+T, you can use the Format as Table dropdown on the Home ribbon.

- Excel applies a default table format. You can change to another style using the Table Styles gallery on the Table Tools Design ribbon.

- Excel turns on the Filter dropdowns on each heading (Figure 7.3). You can use these dropdowns to sort by a column (Sort by Color on page 55) or to filter a column (Finding Records with Filter on page 110).

- You can add totals to the bottom of the dataset by using the Total Row checkbox in the Table Tools Design ribbon.

The following features are not immediately visible, but will work:

- Any new data typed in the blank row below the table is made part of the table. This means that any charts, pivot tables, or formulas that refer to the table automatically incorporate the new data.

- A resize handle in the bottom right corner of the table allows you to drag to manually extend the table to include additional columns.

- You can use the Table Style Options checkboxes to turn on alternate formatting for the first column, last column, header row, or total row, or to apply alternating shading to rows or columns.

- Any formulas that point to columns in the table will be written in a new table nomenclature. Enter a formula once and Excel will copy it to all rows of the table.

Figure 7.3
Excel adds AutoFilter dropdowns as part of the table formatting.

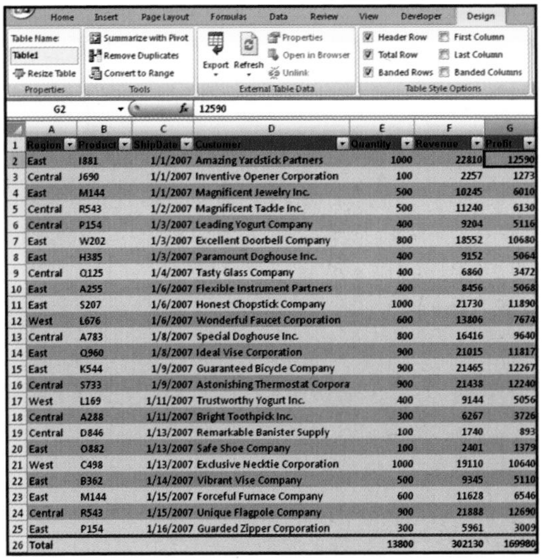

Working with Table Formulas

Excel can greatly automate the process of entering formulas for a new column in a table. Say that you want to add a profit % column to the above table. Follow these steps:

1. Enter a heading of GP% in cell H1.

2. Format cell H2 as a percentage with 1 decimal place. I realize that in Excel 2003, you would normally format the cell after entering the formula. You need to get in the habit of formatting the cell before entering the formula.

3. In cell H2, type an equals sign. Click on the Profit in G2. Type a divide sign. Click on the Revenue in F2. You will already notice something different – Excel is building a formula of =[Profit]/[Revenue].

4. Type the Enter key to complete the formula. Excel automatically copies the formula down to all of the rows in your dataset!

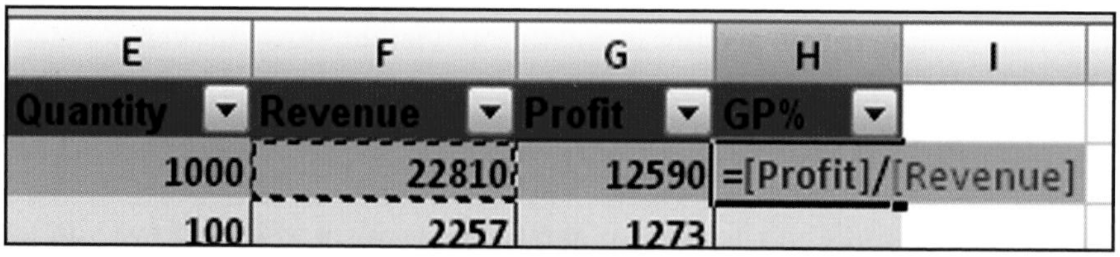

Figure 7.4
The table formula nomenclature is similar to the old Natural Language Formulas. By the way, those formulas were depreciated in Excel 2007.

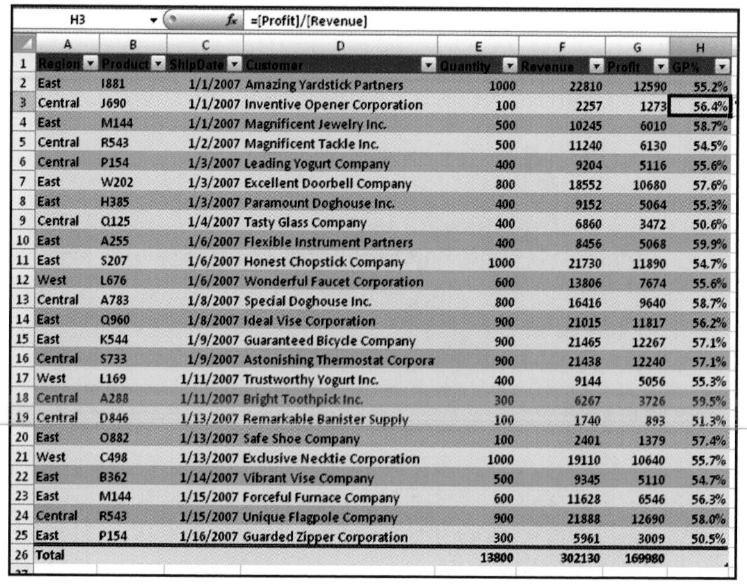

Figure 7.5
The =[Profit]/[Revenue] formula is copied to all rows.

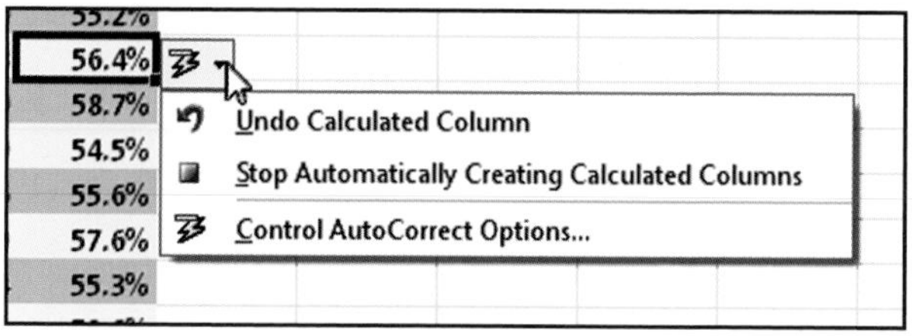

Figure 7.6
Override automatic formula copying.

The automatic copying of the formula is a great feature. However, there will be a few times where you do not want this to happen. If so, find the AutoCorrect dropdown and open it. You will have choices to turn of the calculated column or to turn off the feature permanently.

Working with Table Styles

There are 60+ built-in table styles in the gallery. The styles in the gallery will change, depending on which table style options are selected. For example, if you turn on Banded Columns and open the gallery, you will see that many of the styles support banded columns.

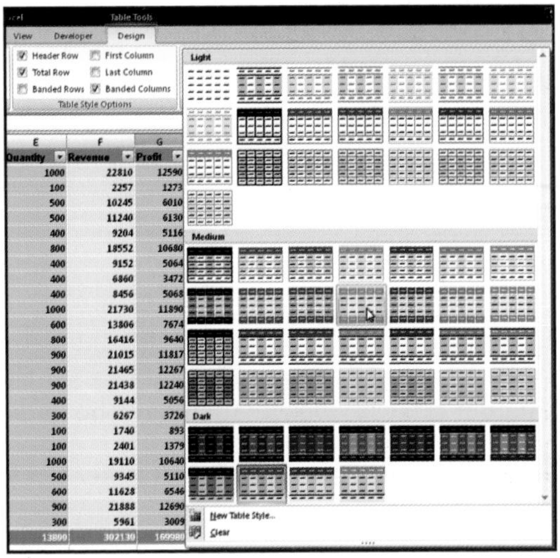

Figure 7.7
Choose Table Style Options
before opening this gallery.

If you instead turn on Banded Rows and open the Table Styles gallery, you will see that several styles support banded rows.

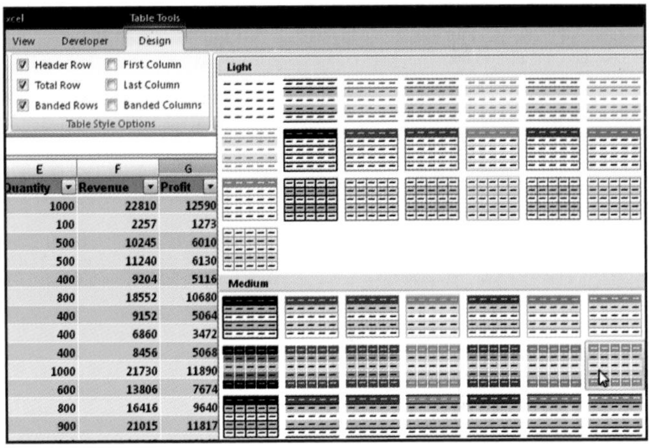

Figure 7.8
The gallery looks different when Banded Rows is turned on.

The gallery supports Live Preview – simply hover over a style in the gallery and the worksheet will redraw to show you that table style. When you find a style that you like, click the style to apply that formatting.

Choosing a Table Style as the Default

Right-click any table style and choose Set As Default to make this the default style used by Ctrl+T in the future.

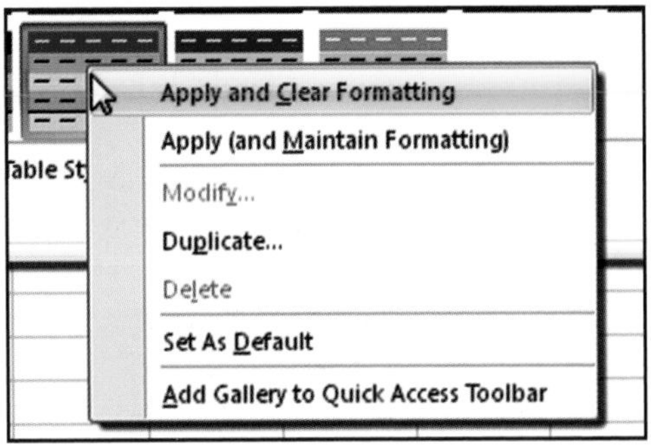

Figure 7.9
Set a style as the default table style.

Creating a Custom Table Style

You can edit any of the built-in table styles. Right-click a style and choose Duplicate…. The Modify Table Quick Style dialog appears. You can type a new name for the table style, and then micro-manage every element of the table.

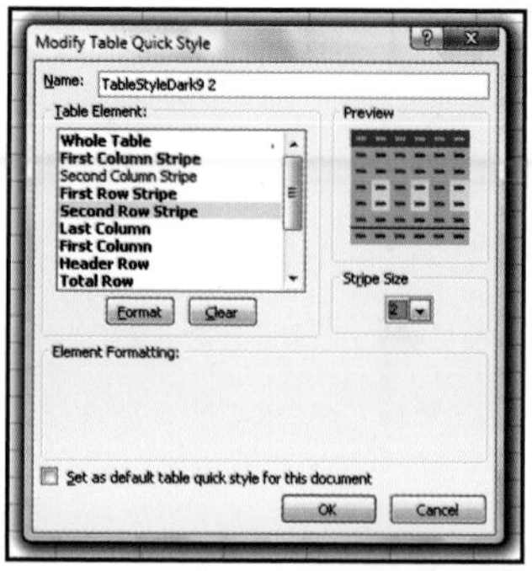

Figure 7.10
Edit the stripe size.

In Figure 7.10, the Stripe Size for the Second Row Stripe is increased from 1 to 2. After a similar change to the First Row Stripe, a new Custom table style is available in the gallery.

The table features row banding that is two rows tall.

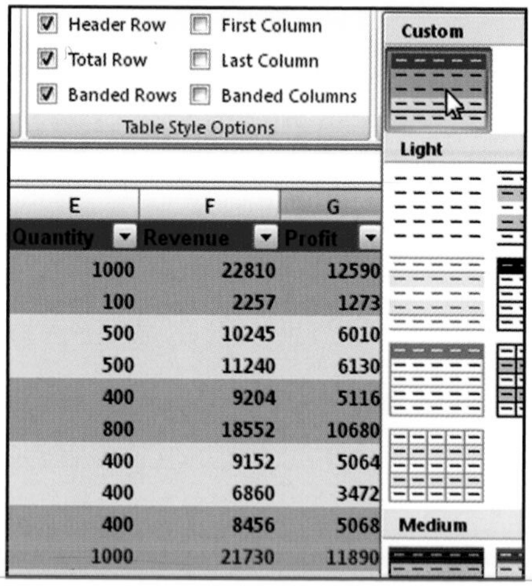

Figure 7.11
A different take on the greenbar format.

Dealing with Table Annoyances

The table functionality is pretty cool. There are two annoyances.

First, the filter dropdowns cover up some of the headings. As you can see, I actually left-aligned many headings in the previous figure so that I could read the headings. You can turn off the filter dropdowns by using Home – Sort & Filter – Filter.

Second, sometimes I just turn on the Table functionality in order to quickly apply a format to the table. It is OK to use Ctrl+T to create and format a table and then immediately use Table Tools – Convert to Range to turn the table back into a normal range. The table formatting remains!

Figure 7.12
Change a table back to a range. The table formatting remains, but the other table features go away.

＊ ＊ ＊

Chapter 8

Data Visualizations

Microsoft added a difficult-to-use conditional formatting feature to Excel in 1997. The feature gets a complete makeover in Excel 2007. It is fantastic to use.

In-Cell Data Bar Charts

Select a range of numbers. Choose Home – Conditional Formatting – Data Bars – Blue. Excel will add a tiny in-cell databar to every number in the selection. This makes it very easy to quickly focus on the largest or smallest numbers in the dataset.

Figure 8.1
The longer bars allow you to quickly see the top cells.

Tip: Do not include the total cell in your selection. If you included the $244K total in the range, that one cell would be the only cell to have a large databar. All of the other cells would appear small.

Color Scales

There are eight built-in varieties of color scales. The left four varieties in Figure 8.2 rely on variations of three colors. Some rely on the traffic light red-yellow-green color scheme and some rely on the temperature red-yellow-blue scheme. The four built-in varieties in columns H:K of Figure 8.2 are two-color schemes.

To apply a color scale, select the cells containing numbers and choose Home – Conditional Formatting – Color Scales.

Figure 8.2
Four built-in three-color
scales appear in B:E.
Four built-in two-color
scales are in H:K.

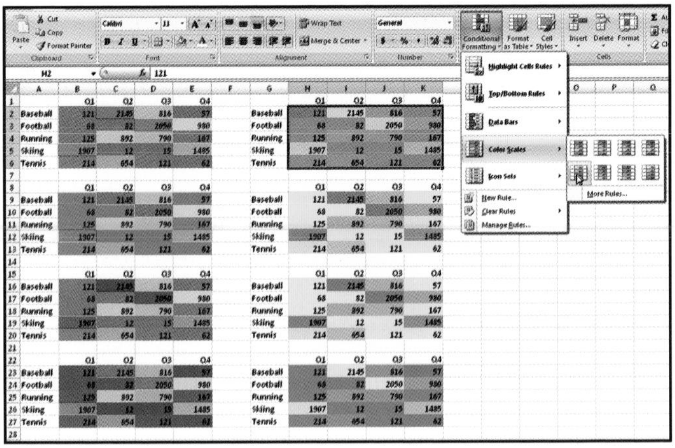

While it is easy to create the formatting, you can access dialogs where you can tweak the built-in effects. Using Conditional Formatting – Manage Rules – Edit, you can change the settings for a visualization. In Figure 8.3, the colors have been changed to a bizarre purple-orange-red color scheme and the percentile for the midpoint is shifted from 50 to 30%.

Figure 8.3
Create your own colors
for the color scale.

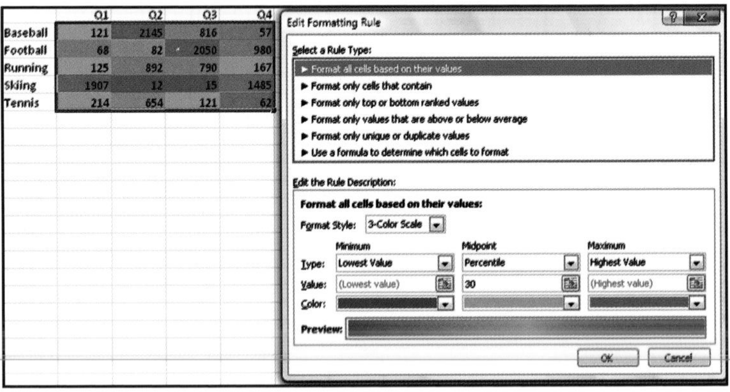

Icon Sets

Icon sets are my least favorite of the new visualizations. The icons are left-justified in the cell. The only way for the icon to appear near the number is if you center all of the numeric values.

To assign an icon set, use Home – Conditional Formatting – Icon Sets and then choose one of the 17 built-in sets.

Figure 8.4
Excel offers icon sets with 3, 4,
or 5 icons.

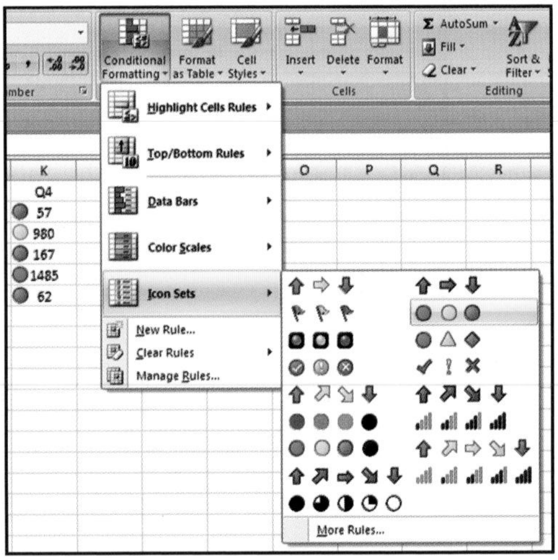

Other Conditional Formatting Rules

The Conditional Formatting dropdown offers fly-out menus for Highlight Cells Rules (Figure 8.5) and Top/Bottom Rules (Figure 8.6).

Figure 8.5
All of these are easier to use than the Excel 2003 conditional formatting.

Figure 8.6
In Lake Wobegon, all the kids are above average.

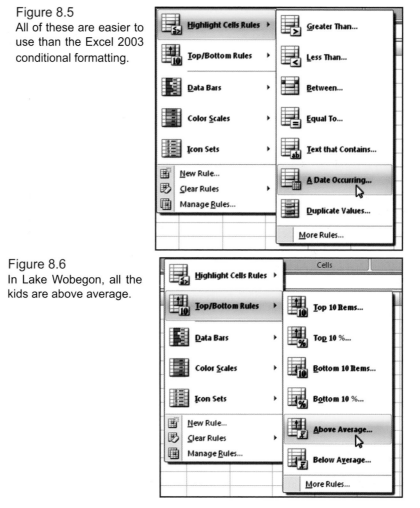

Special Tweaks for Data Visualizations

There are a couple of tricks that people have discovered with data visualization. The first trick involves highlighting the entire row when a value in a particular column meets a condition. This is easier in Excel 2007 if you turn on the Table feature, but it can still be done using a formula rule.

The other trick is making it appear that you are applying conditional formatting to only a portion of your dataset.

Highlighting the Entire Row Using Tables

In Figure 8.7, the data in columns H and I has been defined as a table (see Tables on page 44). If you apply conditional formatting to cells that are in a table, the dialog box will offer to Format the Entire Row for cells that meet the condition.

Figure 8.7
Format Entire Row is only available if you've formatted the range as a table.

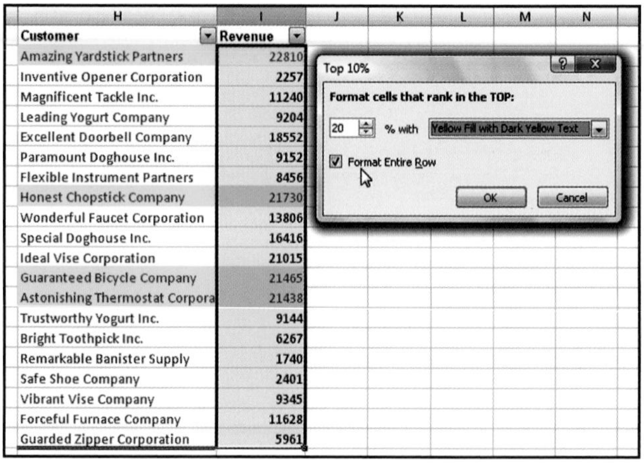

Highlighting the Entire Row Using Formulas

This is the most powerful conditional formatting trick, but it is the hardest to use. Follow these steps.

1. Select the entire range containing your data.
2. Select Home – Conditional Formatting – New Rule.
3. Select Use a Formula to Determine Which Cells to Format.
4. You now have a box where you can write a formula. In the Format values where this formula is true, you should write a formula that applies to the first cell in the selection. Some portion of the formula should have a reference where the row number is relative. The formula in this case is =$B2=MAX($B$2:$B$21). In this formula, the row number in $B2 is allowed to change as it applies to other rows in the selection. The formula checks to see if the value in column B of this row is equal to the max of all the column B values.
5. Click the Format... button. Choose a fill, font color, or numeric formatting to appear when the condition is true.

Figure 8.8
As in Excel 2003, the formula option offers powerful possibilities.

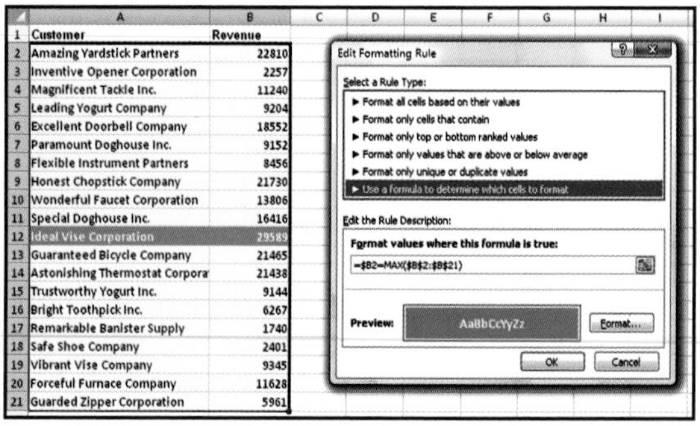

Using Formula rules, you can create visualizations where the cells highlighted in one column are based on values in other columns.

Applying Rules to a Portion of a Dataset

The Conditional Formatting Rules Manager contains a Stop if True setting. You can trick Excel into applying an icon set to a portion of a dataset. Follow these steps.

1. Highlight a range of data.
2. Add an icon set using Conditional Formatting – Icon Sets.
3. Select Conditional Formatting – Manage Rules.
4. Click on the Icon Set rule and choose Edit Rule.

Figure 8.9
You can edit, delete, or add rules here.

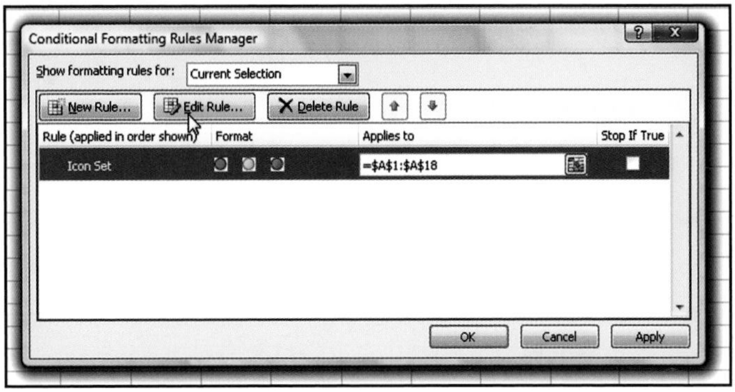

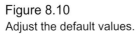

5. In the Edit Formatting Rule dialog, adjust the value for the green traffic light to appear only when the value is >=75. Click OK.

Figure 8.10
Adjust the default values.

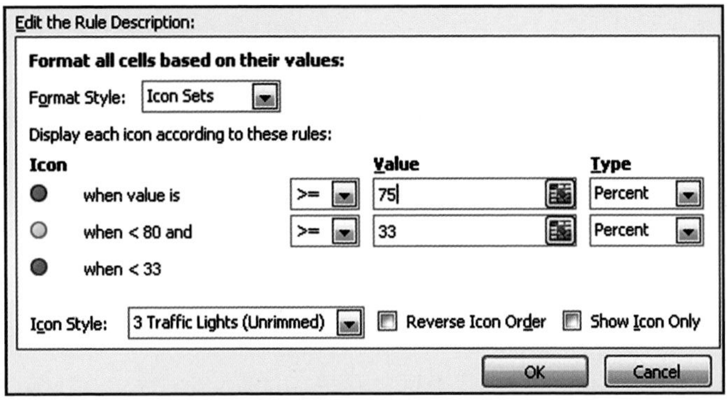

6. Back in the Conditional Formatting Rules Manager, click the New Rule... button.

7. In the New Formatting Rule dialog, choose Format Only Cells That Contain. Choose Cell Value, less than 75. Don't apply a format for this rule – leave all of the formatting plain. Click OK.

Figure 8.11
Choose no formatting.

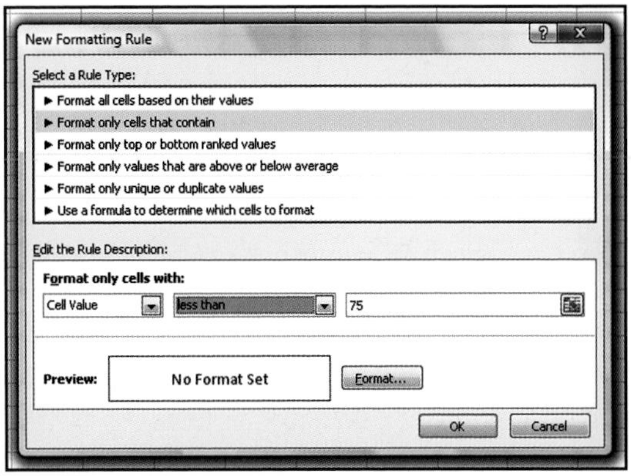

8. Back in the Conditional Formatting Rules Manager, place a checkmark next to Stop if True for the Cell Value < 75 rule. This basically tells Excel that if the cell is less than 75, it should apply no formatting and stop processing more rules. Only the values above 75 will proceed to the icon set rule, so you will only have green icons in the result.

Figure 8.12
Being able to turn on Stop if True enables the trick. Anything less than 75 will never make it to the icon set rule.

Conditional Formatting Rules Manager					? X
Show formatting rules for:	Current Selection ▾				
🖉 New Rule...	🖉 Edit Rule...	✕ Delete Rule ⬆ ⬇			
Rule (applied in order shown)	Format	Applies to			Stop If True
Cell Value < 75	No Format Set	=$A$1:$A$18	🔲	☑
Icon Set	● ○ ●	=$A$1:$A$18	🔲	☐

| | OK | Cancel | Apply |

Figure 8.13
Only cells above 75 have the icons.

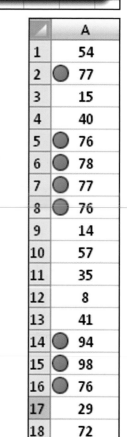

	A
1	54
2	● 77
3	15
4	40
5	● 76
6	● 78
7	● 77
8	● 76
9	14
10	57
11	35
12	8
13	41
14	● 94
15	● 98
16	● 76
17	29
18	72

You can use similar methods to only apply color scales or databars to certain ranges of data. Again, the trick is to set up a dummy rule that formats all the unwanted cells with plain formatting and to have this rule appear first in the list. By using the Stop if True setting, you prevent the other data visualization rules from running on the unwanted values.

✳ ✳ ✳

Chapter 9

Sort by Color

Do you ever use color to mark problem cells?

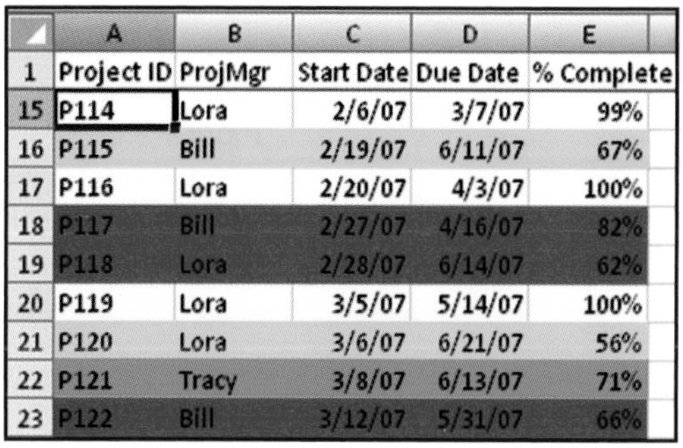

Figure 9.1
Red projects are really behind; yellow projects are a little behind.

	A	B	C	D	E
1	Project ID	ProjMgr	Start Date	Due Date	% Complete
15	P114	Lora	2/6/07	3/7/07	99%
16	P115	Bill	2/19/07	6/11/07	67%
17	P116	Lora	2/20/07	4/3/07	100%
18	P117	Bill	2/27/07	4/16/07	82%
19	P118	Lora	2/28/07	6/14/07	62%
20	P119	Lora	3/5/07	5/14/07	100%
21	P120	Lora	3/6/07	6/21/07	56%
22	P121	Tracy	3/8/07	6/13/07	71%
23	P122	Bill	3/12/07	5/31/07	66%

While it is easy to use the paint bucket icon to color cells, it is difficult to then do anything with the colors. Now, in Excel 2007, you can sort the data by color.

1. From the Data menu, click on the Sort icon.

2. In the Sort dialog, change the Sort On dropdown from Values to Cell Color.

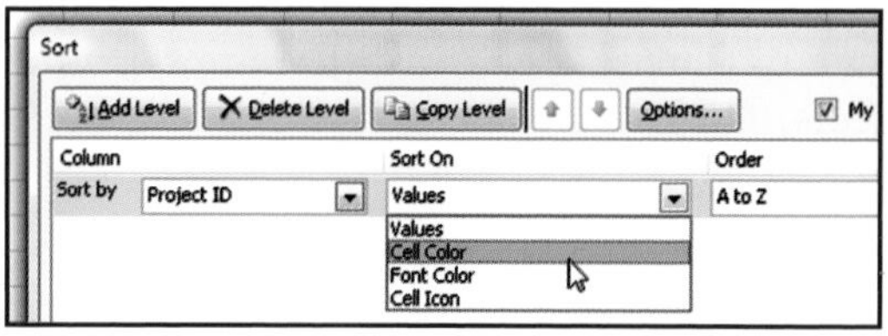

Figure 9.2
You can sort by cell color, font color, or conditional formatting icon.

3. A dropdown appears in the Order column. Choose the appropriate color from the dropdown.

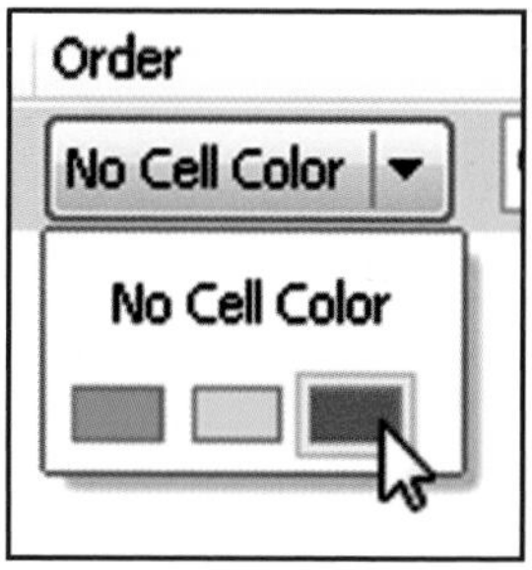

Figure 9.3
The dropdown shows colors present in the range.

4.   If you want an additional color to appear after the first color, click Add Level. Repeat steps 2 – 3 for each additional color. Your dialog might look like Figure 9.4.

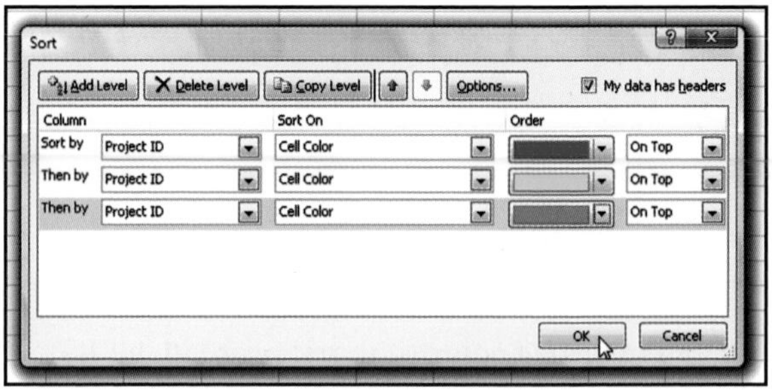

Figure 9.4
If you used 50 colors, filling out this dialog would take forever.

5.   Click OK to perform the sort. All of the red cells will come to the top.

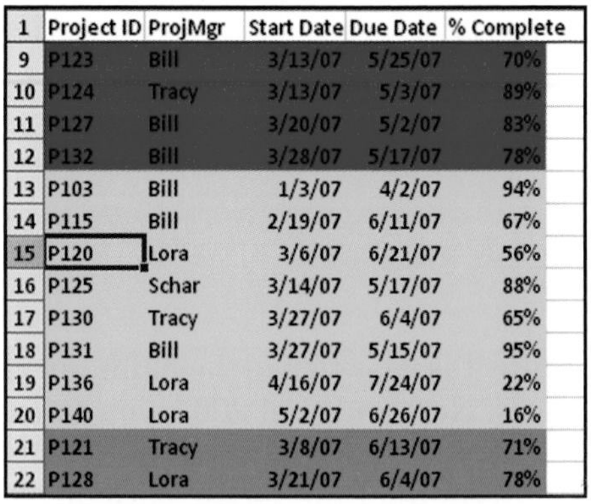

Figure 9.5
The data is sorted by color. Any cell with no fill color appears at the end of the dataset.

1	Project ID	ProjMgr	Start Date	Due Date	% Complete
9	P123	Bill	3/13/07	5/25/07	70%
10	P124	Tracy	3/13/07	5/3/07	89%
11	P127	Bill	3/20/07	5/2/07	83%
12	P132	Bill	3/28/07	5/17/07	78%
13	P103	Bill	1/3/07	4/2/07	94%
14	P115	Bill	2/19/07	6/11/07	67%
15	P120	Lora	3/6/07	6/21/07	56%
16	P125	Schar	3/14/07	5/17/07	88%
17	P130	Tracy	3/27/07	6/4/07	65%
18	P131	Bill	3/27/07	5/15/07	95%
19	P136	Lora	4/16/07	7/24/07	22%
20	P140	Lora	5/2/07	6/26/07	16%
21	P121	Tracy	3/8/07	6/13/07	71%
22	P128	Lora	3/21/07	6/4/07	78%

Quick Sort by Color

If you are interested in one particular color, you can sort that color to the top using the right-click menu. Choose a cell with the appropriate color. Right-click and choose Sort – Put Selected Cell Color On Top.

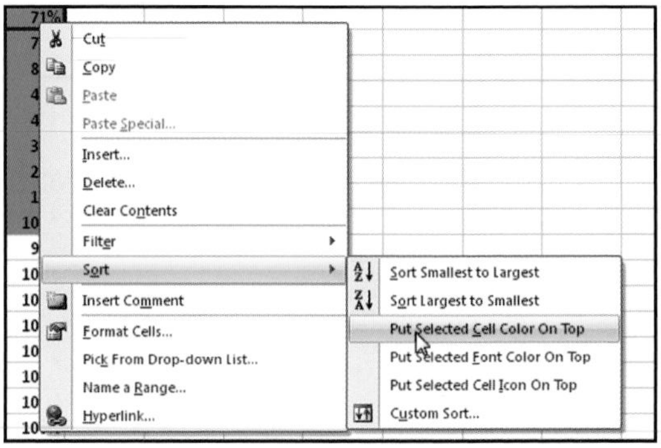

Figure 9.6
For a quick sort, just right click a cell with the color you want to bring to the top.

✳ ✳ ✳

Chapter 10

Removing Duplicates

There are many tasks in Excel where you need to remove duplicates from a data set.

Tip: This feature can also be used to find the unique list of values in a data set.

Say that you want to find the unique list of customers in this range:

Figure 10.1
Who are the unique customers in the list?

	A	B	C
1	Date	Customer	Sales
2	6/27/2007	Inventive Eggbeater Inc.	184
3	6/14/2007	Amazing Yogurt Corporation	169
4	6/12/2007	Tasty Belt Corporation	106
5	6/23/2007	Modular Thermostat Company	181
6	6/6/2007	Tasty Belt Corporation	168
7	6/9/2007	Magnificent Tripod Inc.	153
8	6/9/2007	Hip Raft Corporation	135
9	6/25/2007	Tasty Belt Corporation	105
10	6/6/2007	Inventive Eggbeater Inc.	117
11	6/27/2007	Modular Thermostat Company	143
12	6/29/2007	Succulent Paint Supply	171
13	6/18/2007	Inventive Eggbeater Inc.	153
14	6/27/2007	Best Adhesive Inc.	124
15	6/10/2007	Best Adhesive Inc.	117
16	6/15/2007	Hip Raft Corporation	184
17	6/27/2007	Alluring Shingle Inc.	190
18	6/8/2007	Inventive Eggbeater Inc.	95
19	6/5/2007	Hip Raft Corporation	143
20	6/30/2007	Modular Thermostat Company	183

Caution! Remove Duplicates is a destructive function. It is best to make a copy of your data before you use the feature!

In Figure 10.2, a copy of the customer column appears in column F. From the Data ribbon, choose Remove Duplicates.

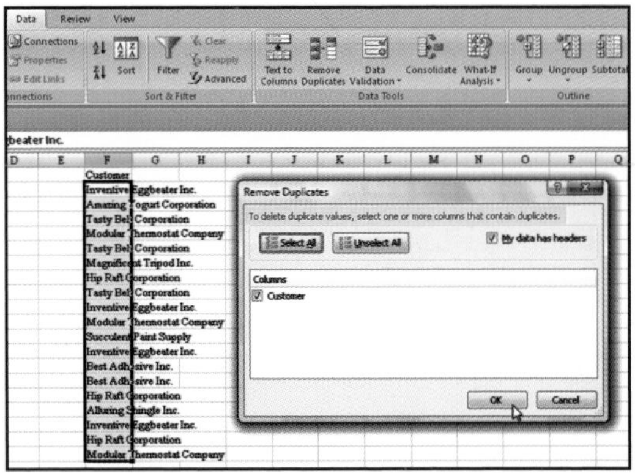

Figure 10.2
If your data set has multiple columns, you can tell Excel to base the duplicates on a subset of the columns.

Click OK and Excel will delete any duplicated values. The remaining dataset is the unique list of customers.

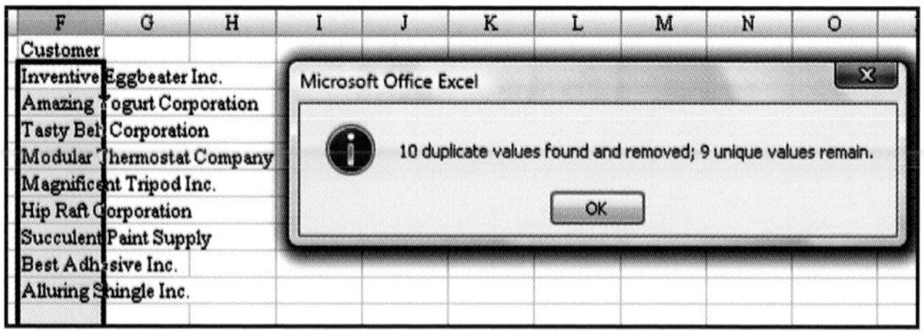

Figure 10.3
The duplicates are actually removed.

Marking Duplicates

While the Remove Duplicates button is amazing, it is also destructive. Perhaps you would like to identify the duplicates so that you can decide how to combine information from the duplicates. Select the range of values. On the Home ribbon, choose Conditional Formatting – Highlight Cells Rules – Duplicate Values. Excel will highlight the duplicates in red.

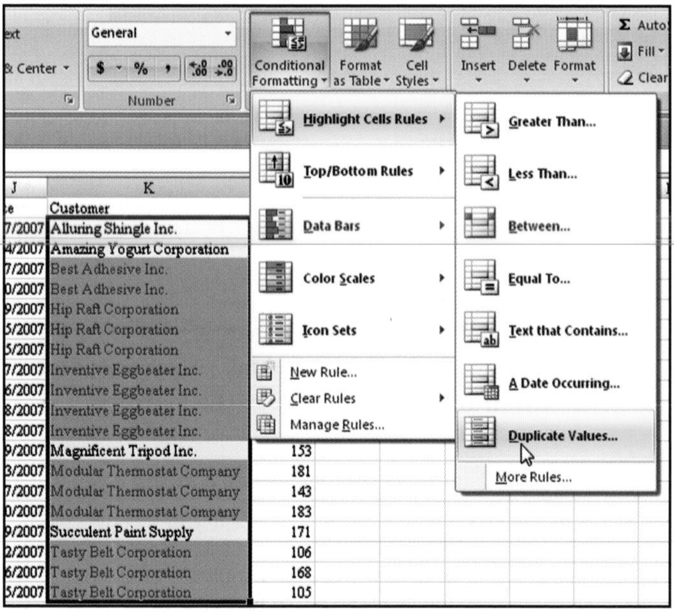

Figure 10.4
Marking the duplicates with conditional formatting is less destructive and gives you time to figure out how to combine duplicates.

* * *

Chapter 11

Seeing Totals in the Status Bar

You can figure out totals without ever entering a formula.
Simply select some cells that contain numeric data. Excel's Status bar will show you the total of the selected cells.

Figure 11.1
At the bottom of the screen, you can see the total of these cells is 1033. There are 12 cells, ranging from 22 to 210, with an average of 86.08.

Qty	Price	Merchandise	Tax	Freight	Total	M
5	42	210	12.6	9	231.6	
2	31	62	3.72	6	71.72	
5	23	115	6.9	9	130.9	
3	26	78	4.68	7	89.68	
4	40	160	9.6	8	177.6	
2	28	56	3.36	6	65.36	
3	21	63	3.78	7	73.78	
1	30	30	1.8	5	36.8	
4	23	92	5.52	8	105.52	
3	33	99	5.94	7	111.94	
1	22	22	1.32	5	28.32	
2	23	46	2.76	6	54.76	

Average: 86.08333333   Count: 12   Min: 22   Max: 210   Sum: 1033

The Status bar has been doing this for a dozen years, yet few people ever noticed. In prior versions of Excel you could choose to have the Status bar show either a total, min, max, count, or average.

Now, in Excel 2007, you can have the Status bar show you all of those statistics.

Simply right-click the Status bar and you can choose to turn on or off any of these settings.

Figure 11.2
Have Excel show you a wide range of statistics for the current selection.

Customize Status Bar

✓	Cell Mode	Ready
	Signatures	Off
✓	Information Management Policy	Off
✓	Permissions	Off
	Caps Lock	Off
	Num Lock	On
✓	Scroll Lock	Off
	Fixed Decimal	Off
✓	Overtype Mode	
✓	End Mode	
✓	Macro Recording	Not Recording
✓	Selection Mode	
✓	Page Number	
✓	Average	86.08333333
✓	Count	12
	Numerical Count	
✓	Minimum	22
✓	Maximum	210
✓	Sum	1033
✓	View Shortcuts	
✓	Zoom	100%
✓	Zoom Slider	

Average: 86.08333333   Count: 12   Min: 22   Max: 210   Sum: 1033

Note: The statistics in the Status bar only appear when more than one numeric cell is selected.

With the exception of the count statistics, Excel will ignore text cells in your selection. As soon as your selection includes one error cell, such as #N/A!, Excel will stop displaying statistics in the Status bar.

> Tip: Say that you have 5,000 rows of data and you need to know if any of the values are #N/A! errors. Select the range. If Excel will not show you the total, then you know that you have at least one error cell in the range. If you find that your range contains an error cell and don't want to sort the data, use this technique. Start in the first cell. Hold down the Shift key while repeatedly pressing Page Down. As soon as the Status bar stops showing a total, you know that an error cell was encountered in the most recent page.

✳ ✳ ✳

Chapter 12

Handling Large
Blocks of Text

Excel is great with numbers, but also has some tricks for dealing with text.

Say that you have typed some text at the bottom of a worksheet and you wish to wrap the text in order to fit a rectangular range from column B through I.

Figure 12.1
You would like to word wrap this text to fill columns B:I.

	A	B	C	D	E	F	G	H	I	J	K	L
29		Costs in year 1			1176120	0	0	0	0			
30		Bottom Line			3693144	4869264	4869264	4869264	4869264	23170200		
31												
32			Final Result	3980883.2								
33												
34												
35		Lorem ipsum dolor sit amet, consectetuer adipiscing elit. Aenean congue blandit velit. Sed scelerisque blandit sem.										
36		Sed tincidunt tincidunt felis.										
37		Morbi vel eros vel felis consectetuer accumsan. Donec a arcu eu urna lacinia dictum. Proin consectetuer elit sed nisi.										
38		Donec eleifend arcu porta tellus. Nunc feugiat lacus et nunc.										
39		Mauris scelerisque magna ac diam.										
40		Maecenas eget ipsum in augue hendrerit suscipit.										
41		Nunc tempor tortor et est. Morbi egestas neque eu nisl. Sed sit amet quam in augue pellentesque ultrices.										
42		Aenean dapibus arcu ut neque. Vestibulum interdum mattis magna. Phasellus euismod ante nec massa.										
43		Cras mattis sagittis ipsum. Praesent dignissim massa id erat. Nam facilisis diam vel nisl.										
44		Duis nonummy elit rhoncus pede.										
45												
46												
47												

Select a rectangular range that includes all of the text in B and is wide enough to fill the range that you want to fill. It is a good idea to include a few extra blank rows at the bottom in case the wrapped text needs to extend that far.

From the Home ribbon, select Fill – Justify.

Figure 12.2
Select the Justify command.

Σ AutoSum ▾

Fill ▾

Down
Right
Up
Left
Across Worksheets...
Series...
Justify

Excel will wrap the text to fill the selected area.

Figure 12.3
Fill – Justify will cause the
text to fit a certain area.

	A	B	C	D	E	F	G	H	I
35	Lorem ipsum dolor sit amet, consectetuer adipiscing elit. Aenean congue blandit velit. Sed
36	scelerisque blandit sem. Sed tincidunt tincidunt felis. Morbi vel eros vel felis consectetuer
37	accumsan. Donec a arcu eu urna lacinia dictum. Proin consectetuer elit sed nisi. Donec
38	eleifend arcu porta tellus. Nunc feugiat lacus et nunc. Mauris scelerisque magna ac diam.
39	Maecenas eget ipsum in augue hendrerit suscipit. Nunc tempor tortor et est. Morbi egestas
40	neque eu nisl. Sed sit amet quam in augue pellentesque ultrices. Aenean dapibus arcu ut
41	neque. Vestibulum interdum mattis magna. Phasellus euismod ante nec massa. Cras mattis
42	sagittis ipsum. Praesent dignissim massa id erat. Nam facilisis diam vel nisl. Duis nonummy
43	elit rhoncus pede.
44	

Using the Justify command is not perfect. It does not work when a cell contains more than 255 characters. If you resize any columns after the Justify, you will have to repeat the Justify command. If some cells have different formatting, that formatting will be lost after the Justify.

Using a TextBox

If you are dealing with long passages of text, you can insert them in a textbox in Excel. Follow these steps:

1. On the Insert ribbon, choose Text Box.
2. Draw a rectangle in your worksheet about the size and shape that you want the text to fill.
3. Paste (or type) the text.
4. Select the text in the text box and use the Mini Toolbar to format the font size to fit the text box.
5. Right-click the text box and choose Format Shape. On the Line Color category, choose No Line. In the Text Box category, you can specify the number of columns that you would like in the text box.

Figure 12.4
New in Excel 2007, text boxes
support multiple columns.

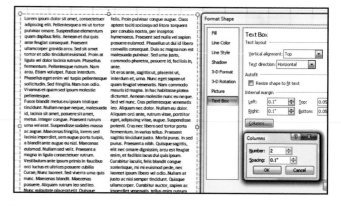

When you click out of the text box, your text will float on the worksheet.

✳ ✳ ✳

Chapter 13

Creating Business Diagrams with SmartArt

Office 2007 adds support for 80 different types of business diagrams. These diagrams include list charts, process charts, cycle charts, hierarchy and org charts, relationship charts, matrix charts, and pyramid charts.

Figure 13.1 shows a selection of SmartArt diagrams.

Figure 13.1
Communicate ideas using SmartArt diagrams.

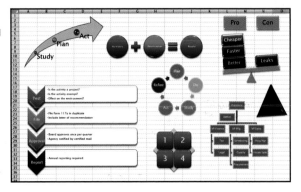

Creating SmartArt Diagrams

To create a SmartArt diagram, choose the basic layout and then type the text to build the shape. In most cases, the diagram will support Level 1 and Level 2 text. Each Level 1 bullet point translates to a new shape in the diagram. Each Level 2 bullet point appears near the Level 1 shape.

> Note: This is not a hard-and-fast rule. Some layouts support Level 1 text and some layouts add shapes for Level 2 text. Certain layouts, such as the Org Chart or Hierarchy, can support Level 3, Level 4, and Level 5 text.

1. From the Insert ribbon, choose SmartArt.

Figure 13.2
Access the SmartArt icon on the Insert ribbon.

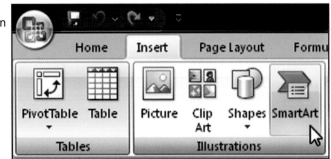

2. Choose a layout from the dialog.

Figure 13.3
Click on a layout thumbnail in
the center to see a description
on the right.

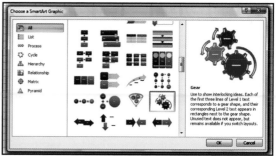

Excel displays a default diagram, usually with three place holders for text in the Text pane.

Figure 13.4
The [Text] entries are
placeholders, waiting for
you to add your own text.

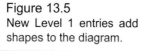

3. Type your text in the text pane. Press Tab to demote the current entry from Level 1 to Level 2. Press Shift+Tab to promote Level 2 text to Level 1 text. Press Enter to add a new entry at the current level. Adding a new Level 1 entry will add a shape to the diagram. As you add text, Excel automatically resizes the fonts in the diagram. (Figure 13.5)

Figure 13.5
New Level 1 entries add
shapes to the diagram.

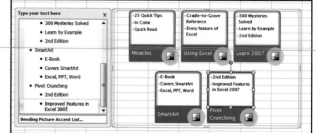

4. On the SmartArt Tools Design ribbon, choose the Change Colors dropdown to choose from 32 different color variations for the graphic.

Figure 13.6
The dark yellow box is the
current color. The light yellow
box is the color shown in Live
Preview.

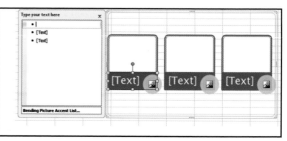

5. Choose the SmartArt Styles gallery to add one of 14 built-in styles to the diagram. There are five 2-D styles and 9 3-D styles. The styles go from fairly plain, to stylish, to impossible to read. Something from the middle of this list, such as Polished or Inset adds sufficient effect while still making the diagram easy to read. If you go with the final choices, either Sunset or Bird's Eye, it will be very difficult to read the diagram.

Figure 13.7
The left box in each pair shows the name of the style applied to the diagram.

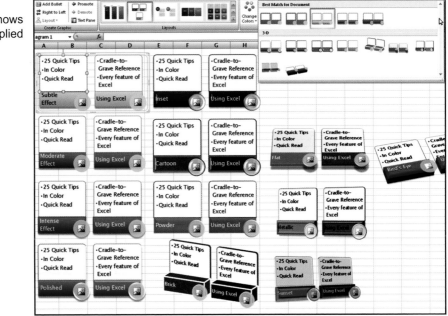

Changing to a New Layout

Once you have built your diagram, you can easily change it to any of the other layouts. From the SmartArt Tools Design ribbon, open the Layout gallery and choose a different layout.

Figure 13.8
Excel does a fairly good job when you change diagram types.

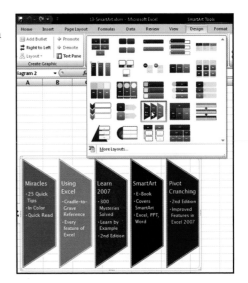

Micro-Managing Setting

In general, Excel will try to keep your SmartArt diagram looking consistent. If you add a lot of text to one shape, Excel will make the text smaller in all shapes so that the diagram has identical fonts in all shapes.

You can micro-manage these settings using the SmartArt Tools Format ribbon. Select an individual shape and use the tools on the Format ribbon to add effects. As you can see in Figure 13.9, you can make horrible looking SmartArt diagrams using the tools on the Format ribbon.

Figure 13.9
Customize the fill, reflection, and so forth for a single shape using the Format ribbon.

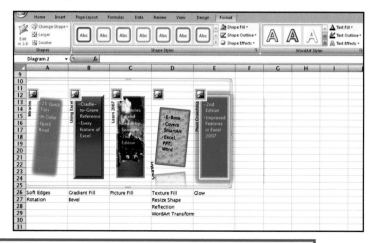

> Tip: Get your SmartArt diagram as close to finished as possible before venturing over to the Format ribbon.

Adding Images to Shapes

There are a handful of styles that offer accent pictures as part of the layout. You should get your SmartArt completely finished before adding images. If you decide to switch to a new layout after specifying images, your images will be lost. (I think this is a bug. Microsoft calls it a feature.)

To specify an image, click on the picture placeholder icon.

Figure 13.10
Clicking the circle won't work. You have to click the picture icon.

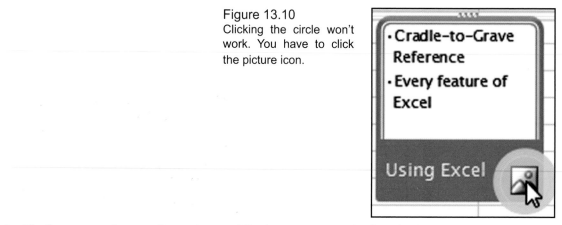

Excel will allow you to browse for an image. The images are resized to fit the accent shape.

Adding Formulas to Shapes

For Excel fans, the biggest disappointment with SmartArt diagrams is that their text is static. You cannot have the text for a SmartArt diagram dynamically calculated by Excel. Also, Microsoft did not expose the SmartArt object model to VBA, so you cannot use macros to dynamically build SmartArt.

Excel has been able to apply a formula to a shape for over a decade. It is very disappointing that the Excel team could not hook up this 10-year-old feature for the shiny new SmartArt diagrams.

The only work-around is to use the SmartArt tools to build a diagram and then convert the diagram to shapes. You can then apply formulas to the shapes.

In Figure 13.11, a database query feeds individual sales figures in columns A:C. SUMIF formulas in G4:G6 show the current sales for each rep. RANK formulas in E4:E6 figure out which rep is in the lead. VLOOKUP formulas in F8:H10 combine the associate name and their sales total. This report is functional, but it lacks visual interest.

Figure 13.11
My eyes glaze over just trying to write the caption.

	A	B	C	D	E	F	G	H	I	J
1	Sales Log					Summary by Associate				
2										
3	Associate	Ticket	Revenue							
4	Ted	1891	33.6		3	Ted	377.7			
5	Bob	1892	63.77		1	Mary	718.22			
6	Mary	1893	105.2		2	Bob	559.6			
7	Ted	1894	10.76							
8	Mary	1895	210.47		1	Mary	718.22	1. Mary is the daily star with $718		
9	Ted	1896	13.84		2	Bob	559.6	2. Bob has sales of $560		
10	Bob	1897	95.85		3	Ted	377.7	3. Ted has sales of $378		
11	Bob	1898	137.73							

1. Build a SmartArt diagram with three shapes. Use dummy text of about the right length. Use the SmartArt Tools to format the diagram. In Figure 13.12, the Format ribbon was used to resize the individual shapes.

Figure 13.12
The text is still static text as this point. It is there to help with sizing the boxes.

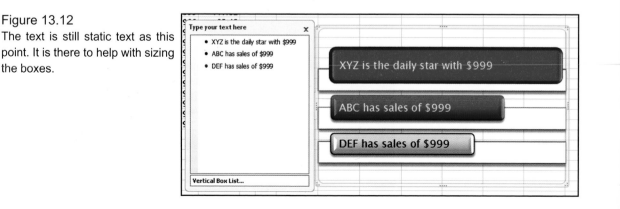

2. Click inside the SmartArt but not on any shape. Press Ctrl+A to select all of the shapes in the SmartArt diagram.

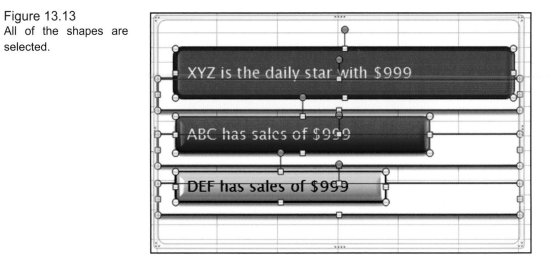

Figure 13.13
All of the shapes are selected.

3. Press Ctrl+C to copy the shapes.

4. Click outside of the SmartArt and press Ctrl+V to paste the shapes onto the worksheet.

5. You can now delete the original SmartArt diagram.

6. Click on the first shape in the worksheet. Drag to select the text in the shape. Click in the Formula bar and type =H8 and press Enter. The text in the selected shape changes to reflect the result of the formula in H8.

7. Repeat Step 6 to assign =H9 to the second shape and =H10 to the third shape.

You now have something that looks like a SmartArt diagram, but the text for the shapes comes dynamically from the worksheet.

Figure 13.14
Now the text in the diagram is a live result from the data.

	A	B	C	D	E	F	G	H	I	J	K
1	Sales Log					Summary by Associate					
2											
3	Associate	Ticket	Revenue								
4	Ted	1891	33.6			3 Ted		377.7			
5	Bob	1892	63.77			1 Mary		718.22			
6	Mary	1893	105.2			2 Bob		559.6			
7	Ted	1894	10.76								
8	Mary	1895	210.47			1 Mary		718.22	1. Mary is the daily star with $718		
9	Ted	1896	13.84			2 Bob		559.6	2. Bob has sales of $560		
10	Bob	1897	95.85			3 Ted		377.7	3. Ted has sales of $378		
11	Bob	1898	137.73								
12	Bob	1899	117.82								
13	Bob	1900	82.42			1. Mary is the daily star with $718					
14	Bob	1901	23.33								
15	Ted	1902	102.45								
16	Ted	1903	29.85								
17	Mary	1904	70.05			2. Bob has sales of $560					
18	Mary	1905	242.74								
19	Bob	1906	20.06								
20	Mary	1907	89.76								
21	Bob	1908	18.62			3. Ted has sales of $378					
22	Ted	1909	43.22								
23	Ted	1910	143.98								

As the query in A:C updates with new sales, the formulas in E:H, and thus the text in the diagram, will automatically update. While Mary was on a break, Ted made a large $395 sale. The worksheet updates as shown in Figure 13.15.

Figure 13.15
Add a record, and the
graphic changes.

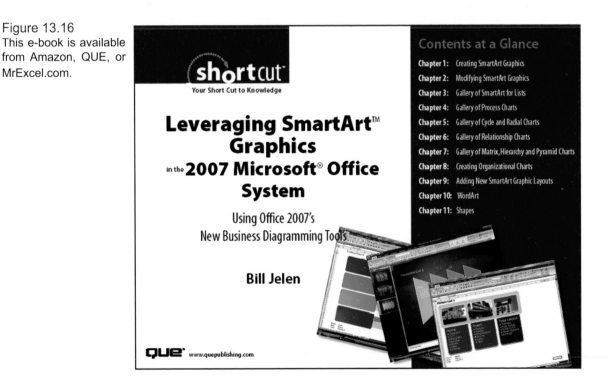

Tip: The case study above was adapted from ideas in Ron Martin's Retail Selling Made Easy. If you manage a retail store and want to motivate your sales staff, Ron's book is invaluable. Order it from http://www.ronmartin.net/books/rsme01.html.

For more information about using SmartArt, check out the e-book that I wrote for QUE: "Leveraging SmartArt Graphics in the 2007 Microsoft Office System".

Figure 13.16
This e-book is available
from Amazon, QUE, or
MrExcel.com.

* * *

Chapter 14

Charting

The Excel 2003 charting engine looked tired and old. Little had changed in 15 years in charting. I think it will take two complete versions before we have all of the changes planned for the charting engine.

In Excel 2007, the core engine was rebuilt. You will find it easier to make good looking charts. In Excel 2009, you will start to find more chart types appear.

Creating a Chart in Excel 2007

Creating a chart involves four broad steps:

1. Prepare your data. Make sure that you have headings above and to the left of the data to be charted. If one of the headings has date or numeric fields, leave the top-left corner cell blank. Select the range of data to be charted.

Figure 14.1
Leave the top left cell blank when your headings are dates.

	A	B	C	D
1		Jan-07	Feb-07	Mar-07
2	East	75748	90879	99540
3	Central	65897	72487	79736
4	West	82974	66379	73017

2. Choose one of the broad chart types from the gallery on the Insert ribbon. Although there are 70+ chart types, there are often three or four variations of each type. The four types of 3-D Column charts are illustrated in Figure 14.3.

Figure 14.2
Choose a subtype from the dropdown menu.

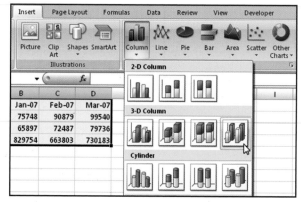

The thumbnails often use a light blue and dark blue element arranged to suggest one of these four chart types:

- In a clustered column chart, each region will have its own bar for each month. This allows you to compare each region to the others, and also to compare the growth of one region from month to month. (See top left of Figure 14.3.)

- In a stacked column chart, the individual regions are stacked on top of each other. This allows you to compare the height of the total bar, but makes it very hard to discern if the West region increased from month 1 to month 2. (See bottom left of Figure 14.3.)

- In a 100% stacked column chart, the regions are stacked and every month's bar is exactly the same height. This would allow you to see the relative contribution of each region from month to month. (See lower right chart of Figure 14.3.)

- The 3D chart actually stacks the columns behind each other. You often have to rotate this chart in order to see the smaller series. (See top right of Figure 14.3.)

Figure 14.3
Most chart types come in variations where series are plotted side by side, stacked, or 100% stacked.

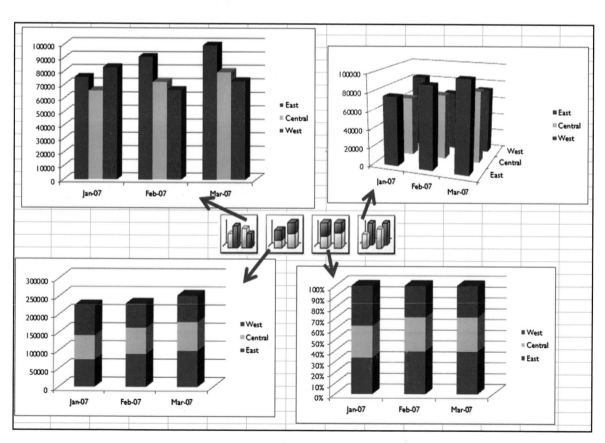

3. Visit the Chart Tools Design ribbon to choose a Chart Layout and a Chart Style. Chart Layouts offer up to a dozen different views of the same chart. In Figure 14.4, the formerly difficult process of creating a histogram is now one click away.

Figure 14.4
The layouts offer 6-12 built-in presets that vary from chart type to chart type.

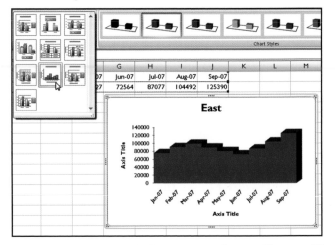

The Chart Styles gallery offers 48 color combinations built around the current theme. If you will be copying the chart to PowerPoint, you can use the new darker layouts to match the background of your slide.

Figure 14.5
It is easy to re-color the chart.

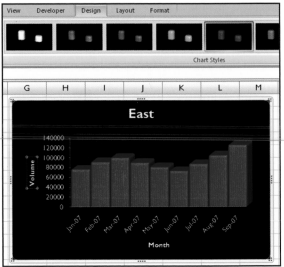

4. If the built-in style didn't perfectly provide axis titles, legends, etc., visit the Layout ribbon to have easy editing choices for all chart elements.

Figure 14.6
Icons for every chart element allow easy formatting of the chart.

nulas	Data	Review	View	Developer	Design	Layout	Format

| Chart Title ▾ | Axis Titles ▾ | Legend ▾ | Data Labels ▾ | Data Table ▾ | Axes ▾ | Gridlines ▾ | Plot Area ▾ | Chart Wall ▾ | Chart Floor ▾ | 3-D Rotation | Trendline ▾ | Lines ▾ | Up/Down Bars ▾ | Error Bars ▾ |

| Labels | Axes | Background | Analysis |

For more granular control, visit the Format ribbon, where you can apply an effect to any particular element in the chart.

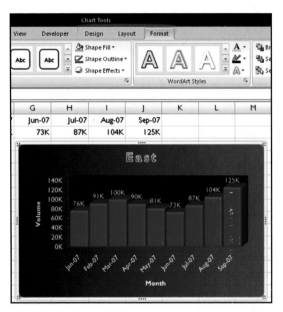

Figure 14.7
Use the Format ribbon to apply an effect to a particular chart element.

Using Other Chart Types

In a Scatter chart, your data should contain pairs of numbers. Excel will find the first number along the horizontal access and the second number along the vertical axis and add plot a marker at the intersection of those values. This chart works well for seeing if two variables are related.

Figure 14.8
Each point represents the intersection of an X, Y pair.

	A	B	C
1		Lat	Jan Temp
2	Anchorage, AK	61	13
3	Austin TX	30	49.1
4	Bismark ND	47	6.7
5	Charleston WV	38	32.9
6	Grand Rapids, MI	43	22
7	Honolulu HI	21	72.6
8	Los Angeles CA	34	56
9	Madison WI	43	15.6
10	Minneapolis MN	45	11.2
11	Olympia WA	47	37.2
12	San Francisco CA	38	48.5
13	Tampa FL	28	59.8

For the Stock Charts, your data must be in the exact order specified by the name of the chart type. In Figure 14.9, a high-low-close chart requires columns sequenced in high, low, close sequence.

Figure 14.9
The High-Low-Close chart
is one of four stock charts
available.

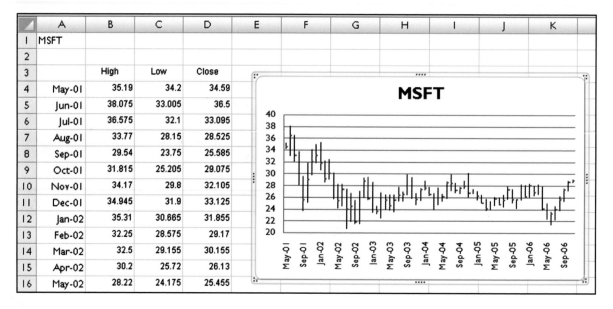

A bubble chart is like a scatter chart, but a third column of numbers controls the size of the data marker. In Figure 14.10, used car prices are plotted to show age, mileage, and price.

Figure 14.10
The third column is used to figure
the relative size of each circle.

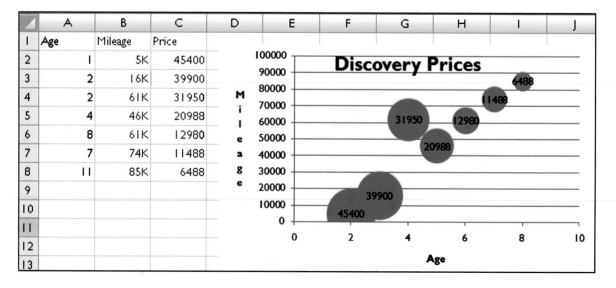

Adding New Data to a Chart

Say that you have produced a series of charts last month and now you need to update all of those charts to reflect a new month of data. Follow these steps:

1. Open the workbook from last month. Type the new month's data adjacent to the old month's data in the workbook.

2. Click on the plot area of the chart. A blue rectangle appears around the range of data currently plotted on the chart. Notice that there are blue square handles in each corner of the range.

Figure 14.11
Drag the handle to the right to include the new October data.

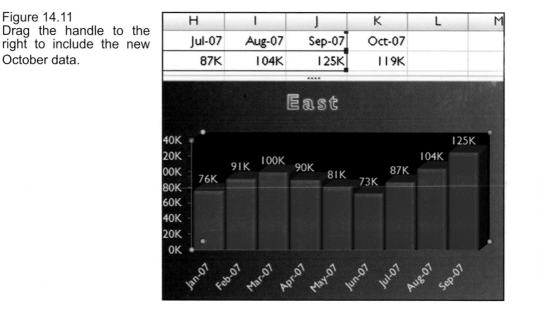

Figure 14.12
After dragging the handle, the chart updates to include the new month.

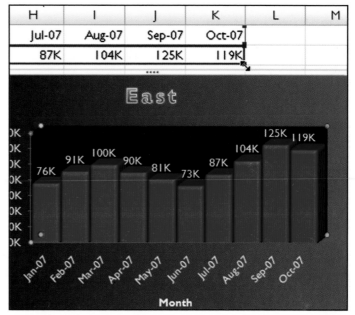

Creating a Chart with One Keystroke

To create a chart with one keystroke, select your data to be charted and press Alt+F1 to embed a default chart on the current sheet. Or, use the F11 key to create a default chart on a new chart sheet.

> Tip: The keystroke creates a default chart. To change the default chart type, click Chart Tools Design – Change Chart Type. Select a chart type from the dialog, and click the Set As Default Chart button.

* * *

Chapter 15

All Text Can Be WordArt

Here is a nice looking chart with a really boring looking title.

Figure 15.1
Spice up the title.

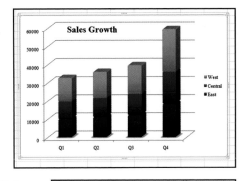

Any text in Excel can now become WordArt. Follow these steps.

Figure 15.2
The colors are based on the selected theme.

1. Select the text in the title.

2. From the Chart Tools Format ribbon, use the WordArt Styles group to format the title. Choose the first gallery to choose from 20 different styles.

3. Use the Text Effects dropdown to add glow, shadow, reflection, etc.

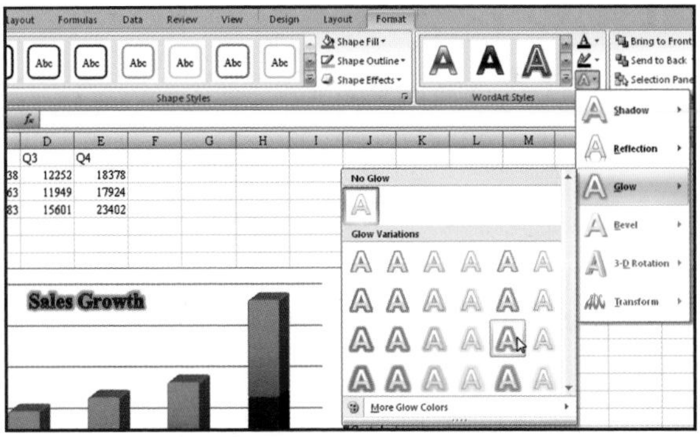

Figure 15.3
The classic WordArt effect – Transform – is not available inside a chart.

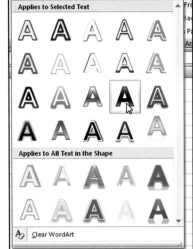

Note: The best WordArt feature, transform is not available for chart titles. To work around this, remove the chart title. Use the Text Box icon on the Insert menu to draw a new text box on the chart. Type your title. Click on the border of the text box. Use the font size icons on the Home ribbon to enlarge the text. Use Format – Shape Outline – No Outline to remove the outline from the text box. Select the characters in the text box and use Format - Text Effects – Transform to twist the type.

Using WordArt as a Title in a Worksheet

If you were a fan of WordArt in Excel 2003, the process of creating WordArt has changed a bit in Excel 2007. Follow these steps.

1. From the Insert ribbon, open the WordArt dropdown. Choose from 30 different styles. These styles will be different, depending on your selected theme.

2. WordArt appears as "Your Text Here". Type new text to replace "Your Text Here".

3. The Drawing Tools Format ribbon offers a WordArt Styles gallery similar to above, but you have full access to Bevel, 3-D Rotation, and Transform. Figure 15.4 shows the Bevel options. Figure 5 shows the Transform options.

Figure 15.4
Built-in Bevel options
For more, click the 3-D
Options choice.

Figure 15.5
Most Excel 97 – 2003
WordArt made liberal use of
Transforms.

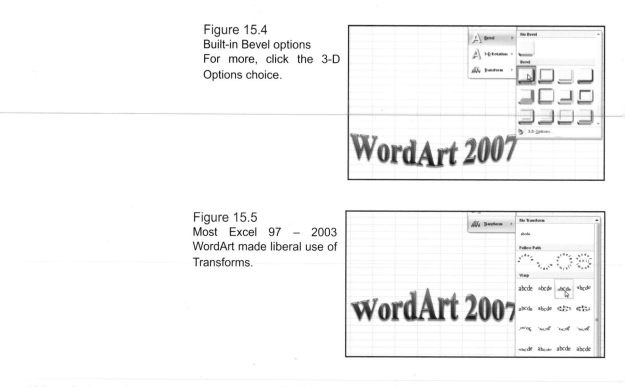

Although it requires more steps to create WordArt, there are fantastic options available in Excel 2007. Use WordArt to add visual interest to your worksheet titles.

* * *

Chapter 16

Using Picture Tools

There is a new set of picture tools in Excel 2007. Use the Picture icon on the Insert ribbon to add a picture to your worksheet.

When the picture is selected, you can access the Picture Tools Format ribbon.

With today's digital cameras, it is likely that your picture will appear too large. Use the Size group to resize your image. To cut out unnecessary background, click the Crop button. Eight crop handles will appear on the edge of the picture. Drag any handle inwards to crop out portions of the photo.

Figure 16.1
Use the Crop icon and then drag the handles inward to crop.

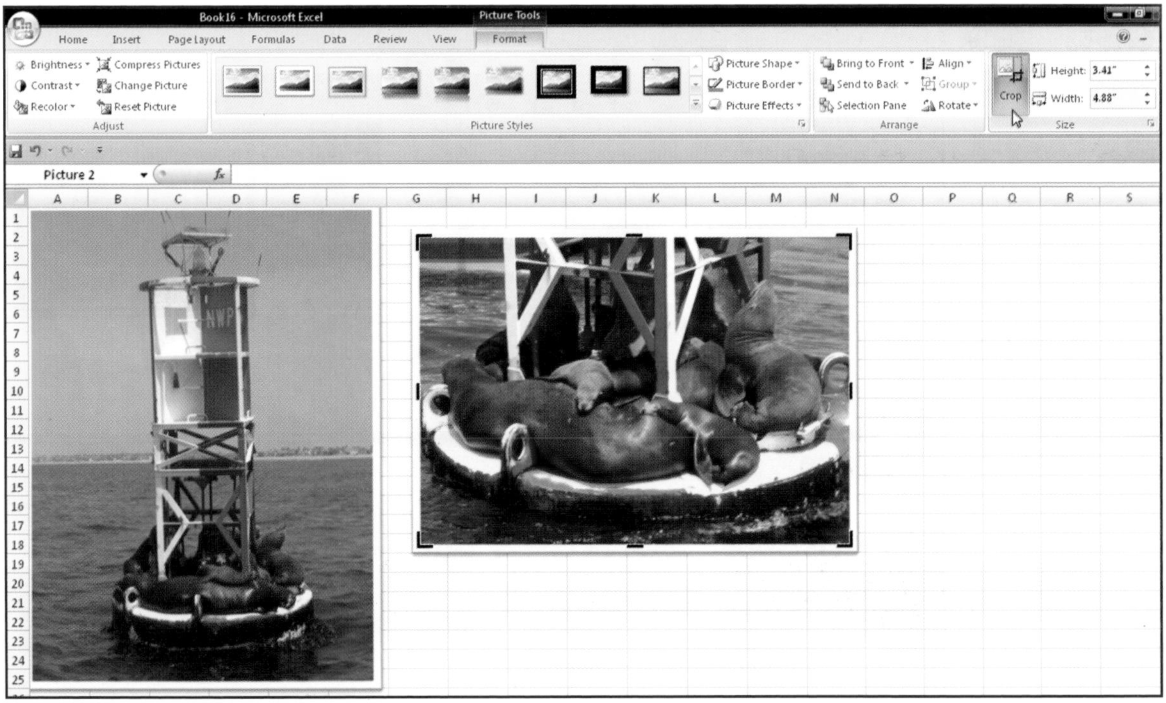

The Adjust group offers settings for Brightness, Contrast, and the ability to Recolor the picture.

Figure 16.2
Easily apply sepia
or other formatting.

The Picture Styles gallery offers 30 different built-in style effects for your picture.

Figure 16.3
The built-in styles
change the frame,
bevel, tilt, etc.

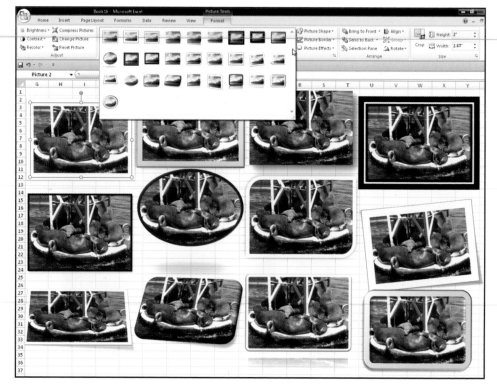

If you don't like the built-in styles, use the Picture Shape, Picture Border, or Picture Effects dropdowns to apply a wide variety of effects to your pictures.

Figure 16.4
Apply a variety of effects using the flyout menus under the Picture Effects dropdown.

Compressing Pictures

If you are not planning on printing the spreadsheet in a glossy magazine, you can save file size by using the Compress Pictures icon. After pressing Compress Pictures, choose the Options button to access the Compression Settings. You can choose if the pictures should be compressed for Print, Display, or E-mail quality.

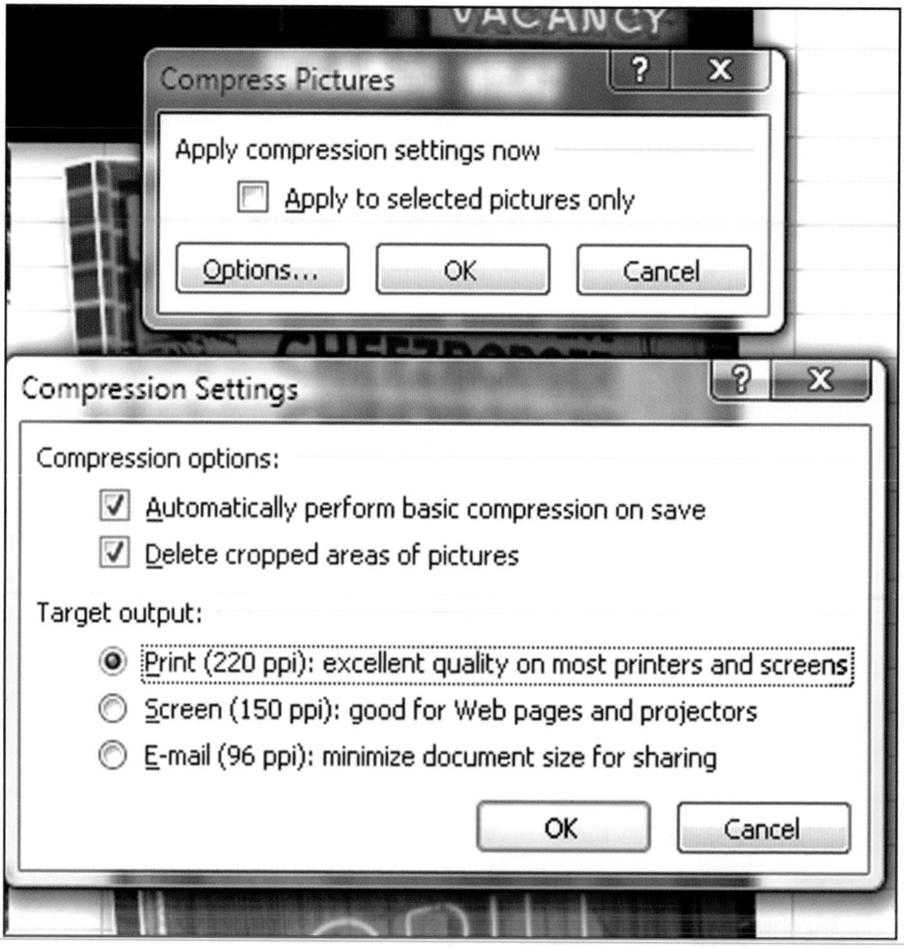

Figure 16.5
Important compression
options   are   hiding
behind   the   Options
button.

Adding a Background for Display

Excel can display a picture behind your spreadsheet. Choose Background from the Page Layout ribbon. Browse and select any picture.

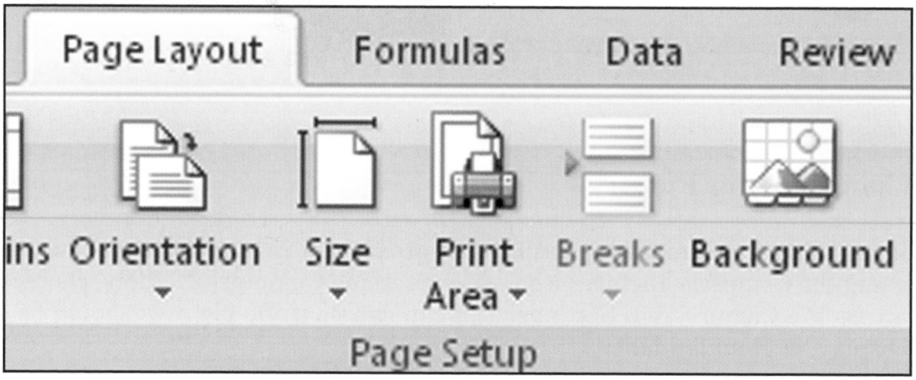

Figure 16.6
The background icon
is on the Page Layout
ribbon.

Excel will tile that picture behind your spreadsheet cells. Be sure to choose a contrasting color for the text in the spreadsheet.

Figure 16.7
Excel will tile the picture behind your spreadsheet.

Adding a Picture Background for Printing

Unfortunately, the background as described above does not print! To create a printable picture background, follow these steps.

1. On the Insert ribbon, choose Shapes and then a rectangle shape.
2. Click and drag in your worksheet to draw a solid background of the proper size.
3. Right-click the shape and choose Format Shape.
4. On the Fill tab, choose Picture or Texture Fill.
5. Use Insert From File....

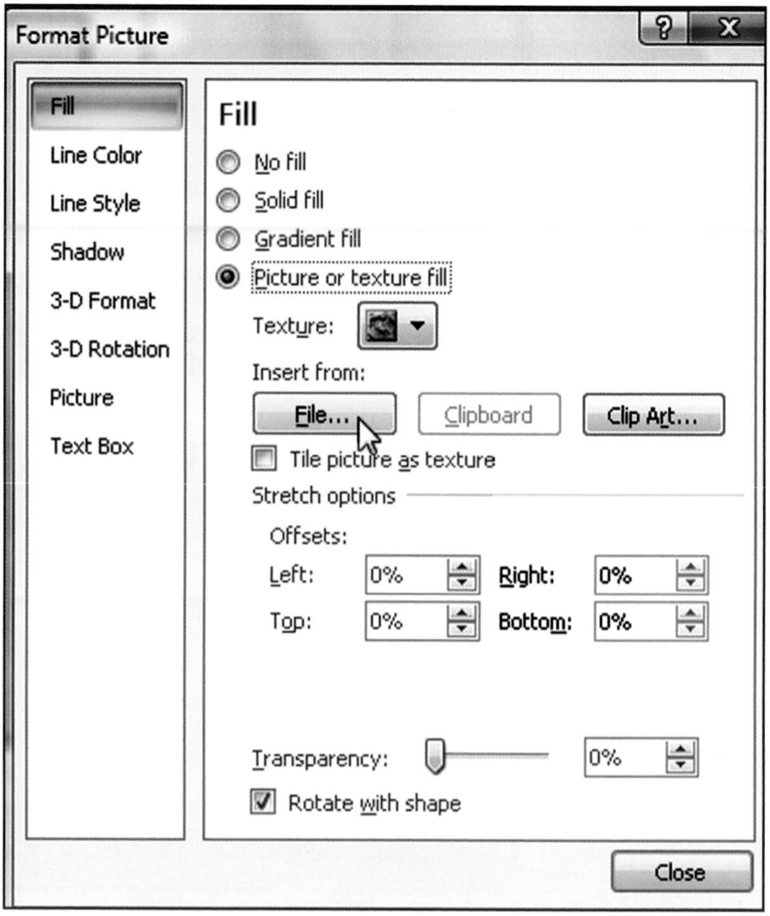

Figure 16.8
When you want to print the
background picture, use a
regular picture instead of a
background picture.

Format Picture

Fill

Fill

- ○ No fill
- ○ Solid fill
- ○ Gradient fill
- ● Picture or texture fill

Texture:

Insert from:

File...   Clipboard   Clip Art...

☐ Tile picture as texture

Stretch options

Offsets:

Left: 0%   Right: 0%

Top: 0%   Bottom: 0%

Transparency: 0%

☑ Rotate with shape

Close

6. Use the Transparency slider at the bottom of the dialog. Move the transparency up to about
    60%. This allows the text in the cells behind the shape to show through.

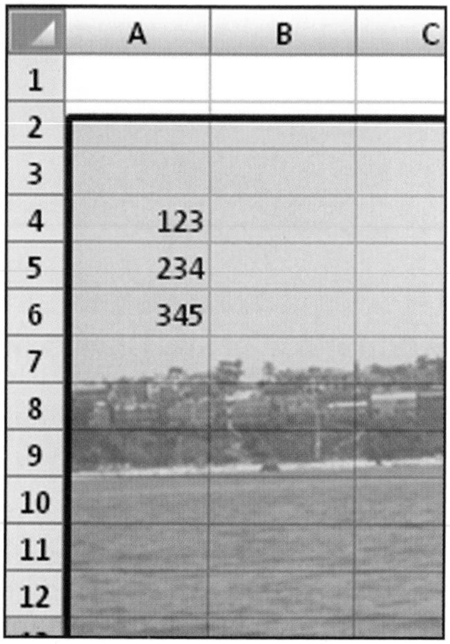

Figure 16.9
By adjusting the transparency, you
can see the cells behind the picture.
Unlike the background picture, this
one will print.

	A	B	C
1			
2			
3			
4	123		
5	234		
6	345		
7			
8			
9			
10			
11			
12			

✳ ✳ ✳

Chapter 17

Handling Error Formulas Using IfError Function

Error values are occasionally returned in Excel spreadsheets. In Figure 17.1, a Divide by 0 error occurs in cell C4 and an N/A error occurs in the VLOOKUP formula in C12.

Figure 17.1
Error cells interrupt the flow of the worksheet.

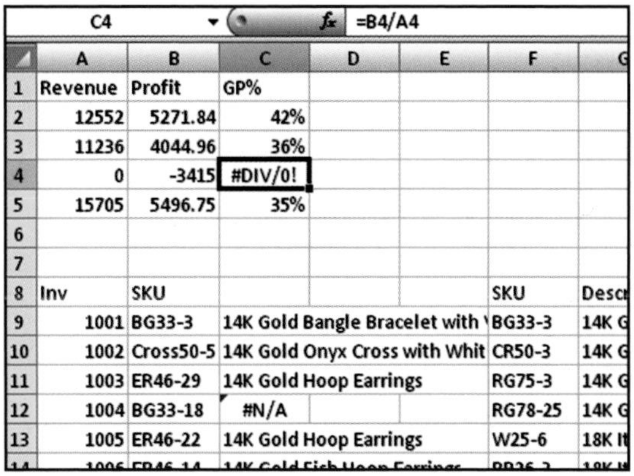

In prior versions of Excel, people would write complicated formulas to prevent the error values. For example, to prevent a divide by 0 error, you could first check to see if the divisor was zero.

Figure 17.2
Use the IF function to prevent division by 0.

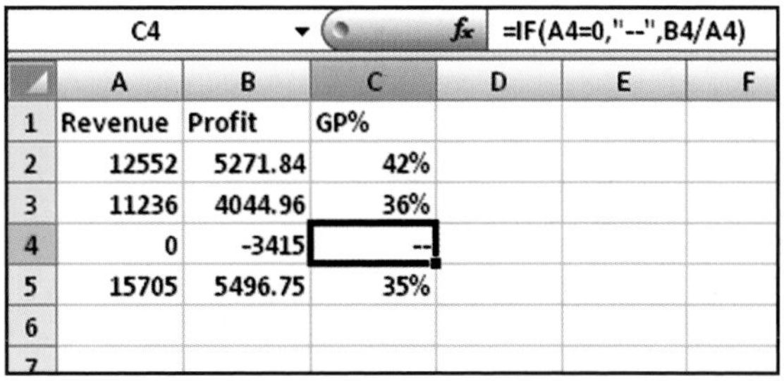

To prevent an error in the VLOOKUP formula, you had to enter an absolutely insane formula that actually performed the VLOOKUP twice. The IF function first tested to see if the result was #N/A and if so, it provided alternate text. If the original result was not #N/A, then Excel would calculate the VLOOKUP again, resulting in the function taking twice as long to calculate.

Figure 17.3
This painful formula prevented the #N/A error in VLOOKUPs.

Excel 2007 offers a new function to help handle errors. If you have a calculation that you think might generate an error, enter the calculation as the first argument in the =IFERROR() function. For the second argument, enter a value that should be used in case the first argument generates an error.

=IfError(Value, Value If Error)

The advantage of this function is that the original calculation is performed only once. The function in Figure 17.4 is simpler than the formula in Figure 17.3.

Figure 17.4
While still unwieldy, this is an improvement over the formula in Figure 17.3.

	A	B	C	D	E	F	G	H	I	J
C12				f_x	=IFERROR(VLOOKUP(B12,$F$9:$G$36,2,FALSE),"New Product")					
10		1002	Cross50-5	14K Gold Onyx Cross with Whit		CR50-3	14K Gold Cross with Onyx			
11		1003	ER46-29	14K Gold Hoop Earrings		RG75-3	14K Gold RAY OF LIGHT Onyx Men's R			
12		1004	BG3	New Product		RG78-25	14K Gold Ballerina Ring w/ Blue & Wh			
13		1005	ER46-22	14K Gold Hoop Earrings		W25-6	18K Italian Gold Women's Watch			

✳ ✳ ✳

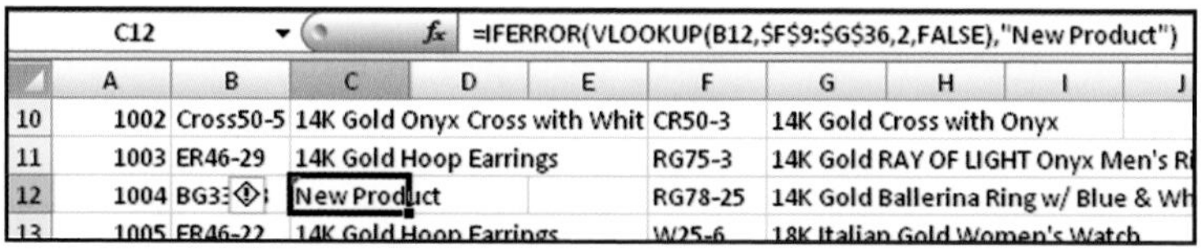

New Conditional Sum Functions

Excel has provided SUMIF and COUNTIF functions for a decade. These functions allow you to count or total records that meet one criterion.

Figure 18.1
The SUMIF function allows you to total records that meet one condition.

	A	B	C	D	E	F	G	H	I	J
						fx	=SUMIF($A$2:$A$20,E3,$C$2:$C$20)			
1	Region	Product	Quantity							
2	East	XYZ	1000		Region					
3	Central	DEF	100		East	6000	=SUMIF($A$2:$A$20,E3,$C$2:$C$20)			
4	East	ABC	500		Central	3500				
5	Central	XYZ	500		West	1000				
6	Central	XYZ	400							
7	East	DEF	800		Product					
8	East	XYZ	400		ABC	2500	=SUMIF($B$2:$B$20,E8,$C$2:$C$20)			
9	Central	ABC	400		DEF	1900				
10	East	ABC	400		XYZ	6100				
11	East	DEF	1000							
12	West	XYZ	600			ABC	DEF	XYZ		
13	Central	ABC	800		East	???				
14	East	XYZ	900		Central					
15	Central	XYZ	900		West					
16	East	XYZ	900							
17	Central	ABC	300							
18	West	XYZ	400							
19	Central	ABC	100							
20	East	XYZ	100							

COUNTIF and SUMIF are "easy" functions to replace the complicated SUMPRODUCT or array formula solutions to performing conditional sums.

Once someone learns about SUMIF, they often wonder how to sum the records that meet two conditions. In Figure 18.1, you might want a function in F13 to find the units of ABC sold in the East. This was not possible with SUMIF.

In Excel 2007, Microsoft has added three plural "S" versions, specifically SUMIFS, COUNTIFS, and AVERAGEIFS. These functions allow you to enter up to 127 different criteria. The syntax is slightly reversed from SUMIF. You start with the range of numbers to be summed, and then enter pairs of arguments, such as Criteria Range, Criteria Value, etc.

=SUMIFS(Sum Range, Criteria Range 1, Criteria 1, ...)

For example, here is how to build the formula in F13:

1. You want to sum the quantity in C2:C20. Since you will later copy this formula, press the F4 key to make it $C$2:$C$20.
2. The first criteria range is comprised of the regions in $A$2:$A$20.
3. The first criteria value is the word East in E13. Since you need to be able to copy the formula to the rest of the table, type the F4 key three times to make the reference be $E13.
4. The second criteria range is comprised of the products in $B$2:$B$20.
5. The second criteria value is the word ABC in F12. Since you need to be able to copy the formula to the rest of the table, type the F4 key twice to make the reference be F$12.

If there were additional conditions, you could continue entering additional pairs of criteria range and criteria. However, in this case, the formula is:

=SUMIFS($C$2:$C$20,$A$2:$A$20,$E13,$B$2:$B$20,F$12)

6.   Copy the formula to the rest of the table in order to find total sales by region and product.

Figure 18.2
The SUMIFS function makes it simpler to create a sum based on two conditions.

	A	B	C	D	E	F	G	H	I	J
					F13		=SUMIFS($C$2:$C$20,$A$2:$A$20,$E13,$B$2:$B$20,F$12)			
1	Region	Product	Quantity							
2	East	XYZ	1000		Region					
3	Central	DEF	100		East	6000	=SUMIF($A$2:$A$20,E3,$C$2:$C$20)			
4	East	ABC	500		Central	3500				
5	Central	XYZ	500		West	1000				
6	Central	XYZ	400							
7	East	DEF	800		Product					
8	East	XYZ	400		ABC	2500	=SUMIF($B$2:$B$20,E8,$C$2:$C$20)			
9	Central	ABC	400		DEF	1900				
10	East	ABC	400		XYZ	6100				
11	East	DEF	1000							
12	West	XYZ	600				ABC	DEF	XYZ	
13	Central	ABC	800		East	900	1800	3300		
14	East	XYZ	900		Central	1600	100	1800		
15	Central	XYZ	900		West	0	0	1000		
16	East	XYZ	900							
17	Central	ABC	300							
18	West	XYZ	400							
19	Central	ABC	100							
20	East	XYZ	100							

COUNTIFS and AVERAGEIFS work in the same manner.

Using the new AVERAGEIF Function

While the addition of SUMIFS is a great thing, I am not quite as impressed with the new AVERAGEIF.

Excel has offered SUMIF and COUNTIF for a while. If you needed to calculate a conditional average, such as in Figure 18.3, you could either use =F3/F8 or =SUMIF()/COUNTIF().

Figure 18.3
In Excel 2003, it was simple enough to build a conditional average based on SUMIF / COUNTIF.

	A	B	C	D	E	F	G	H	I	J
1	Region	Product	Quantity							
2	East	XYZ	1000		Region	Sum				
3	Central	DEF	100		East	6000	=SUMIF($A$2:$A$20,E3,$C$2:$C$20)			
4	East	ABC	500		Central	3500				
5	Central	XYZ	500		West	1000				
6	Central	XYZ	400							
7	East	DEF	800		Region	Count				
8	East	XYZ	400		East	9	=COUNTIF($A$2:$A$20,E8)			
9	Central	ABC	400		Central	8				
10	East	ABC	400		West	2				
11	East	DEF	1000							
12	West	XYZ	600		Region	Average				
13	Central	ABC	800		East	666.6667	=F3/F8			
14	East	XYZ	900		Central	437.5				
15	Central	XYZ	900		West	500				
16	East	XYZ	900							
17	Central	ABC	300							
18	West	XYZ	400							
19	Central	ABC	100							
20	East	XYZ	100							

In Excel 2007, you can now use the new AVERAGEIF function to calculate the average directly

Figure 18.4
The AVERAGEIF function is a bit simpler to use than SUMIF/COUNTIF.

	A	B	C	D	E	F	G	H
					F3	=AVERAGEIF($A$2:$A$20,E3,$C$2:$C$20)		
1	Region	Product	Quantity					
2	East	XYZ	1000		Region	Average		
3	Central	DEF	100		East	666.6667		
4	East	ABC	500		Central	437.5		
5	Central	XYZ	500		West	500		
6	Central	XYZ	400					

Tip: All of the new functions in this chapter are designed to make a difficult task simpler. Excel gurus will point out that the SUMPRODUCT function has been able to do the multiple conditional sums made possible by SUMIFS.

＊ ＊ ＊

Almost New Functions

In previous versions of Excel, you could install an add-in called the Analysis ToolPak in order to enable 90 new functions in Excel. Many of these functions were specific to engineers or bond traders. However, there are a couple of really useful functions among the 90 functions in the Analysis ToolPak (ATP).

If you tried to use a function from the ATP and shared the workbook with someone who had not installed the ATP, the formula would return the NAME! error. Subsequently, some companies had rules against using the ATP functions.

In Excel 2007, all of the ATP functions have been included in the core Excel function list. It is safer to use these functions and share the workbook with other people using Excel 2007.
A few examples of useful ATP functions appear below. At the end of this chapter, you will see the complete list of functions that have been promoted from the Analysis ToolPak to be true members of the Excel function fraternity.

Converting Units with CONVERT

The CONVERT function can convert between different units of measurement. This versatile function can handle mass, distance, time, pressure, force, energy, power, magnetism, temperature, and volume.

=CONVERT(Number, From Unit, To Unit)

Excel Help provides a complete list of abbreviations available for the CONVERT function. A few sample conversions are shown in Figure 19.1.

Figure 19.1
The CONVERT function makes conversions simple.

	D4			f_x =CONVERT(A4,B4,C4)	
	A	B	C	D	E
1	Quantity	From	To	Result	Notes
2	1 kg		lbm	2.204623	kilograms to pounds
3	180 lbm		kg	81.64662	pounds to kilograms
4	1 mi		ft	5280	feet in a mile
5	1 mi		yd	1760	yards in a mile
6	1 mi		km	1.609344	kilometers in a mile
7	5 km		mi	3.106856	miles in a 5K run
8	100 yd		m	91.44	meters in an American football field
9	1 Nmi		mi	1.150779	miles in a nautical mile
10	1 yr		hr	8766	hours in a year
11	1 mi		Pica	4561920	Picas in a mile
12	98.6 F		C	37	Convert Farenheit to Celsius
13	1 qt		tsp	192	teaspoons in a quart
14	1 tbs		tsp	3	teaspoons in a tablespoon
15	2 l		qt	2.112917	quarts in a 2 liter bottle
16	2 l		oz	67.61333	ounces in a 2 liter bottle
17	1 lbf		N	4.448222	Newtons in 1 pound force
18	1 BTU		kev	6.59E+18	kiloelectron volts in a BTU
19	455 HP		kW	339.294	kilowatts in a 455 horsepower engine

Helping Your Kids with Their Math Homework

When your middle school student brings home homework where they have to calculate greatest common denominators, least common multiples, or Roman numerals, Excel has functions to make checking this homework a breeze.

Figure 19.2
This brings back memories of junior high math.

	A	B	C	D	E
				D3	▼ fx =GCD(B3:C3)
1					
2		Greatest Common Denominator (GCD)			
3		312	456	24	=GCD(B3:C3)
4		306	204	102	
5		289	323	17	
6					
7		Least Common Multiple (LCM)			
8		13	7	91	=LCM(B8:C8)
9		54	90	270	
10		36	250	4500	
11					
12		Roman Numerals (ROMAN)			
13			2007	MMVII	=ROMAN(C13)
14			2008	MMVIII	
15			2009	MMIX	
16			41	XLI	
17			42	XLII	
18			43	XLIII	
19			44	XLIV	
20			45	XLV	

Tip: The ROMAN function is useful for filmmakers who want to figure out the proper copyright date for the end of the film credits and for NFL commissioners who need to figure out the names of upcoming Super Bowls.

Converting Color Codes from Hex to Decimal

The ATP functions include functions to convert from Hexadecimal to Octal to Decimal to Binary. If you are building a web page, you will often see colors expressed as a hexadecimal code, such as #FF9007. That code defines the mixture of red, green, and blue used to make up the color.

To create a similar color in Excel using Home – Fill Color – More Colors – Custom, you need to be able to enter the decimal equivalents of the hex numbers FF, 90, and 07.

The HEX2DEC function will perform this conversion.

Figure 19.3
This brings back memories of junior high web design class.

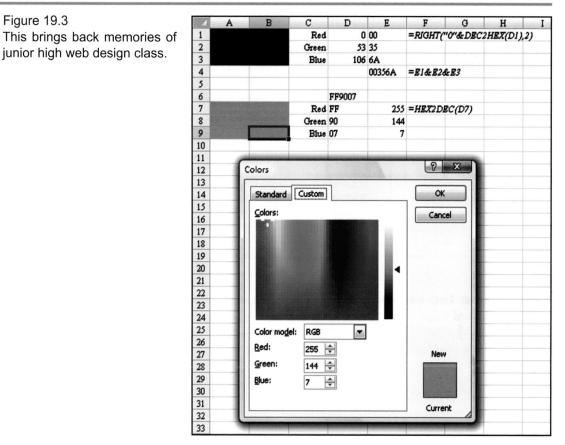

Calculating Work Days

The former ATP functions include a couple of functions that will help any human resources department. These functions can be used to calculate how many work days have elapsed between two dates, or to figure out when a certain number of work days have elapsed.

Both of these functions assume that your employees work Monday through Friday. Both functions allow you to customize them by entering a range that contains work holidays.

=WORKDAY(Start Date, Days, Holidays) – calculates a date that is a certain number of workdays away from a start date.

=NETWORKDAYS(Start Date, End Date, Holidays) – calculates how many work days have elapsed between two dates.

For example, say that new employees are given a 60 work-day probationary period. You can calculate how many work days have elapsed since their start date using NETWORKDAYS or calculate the day their probationary period will end using WORKDAY.

In Figure 19.4, both functions rely on the list of company holidays in J4:J11.

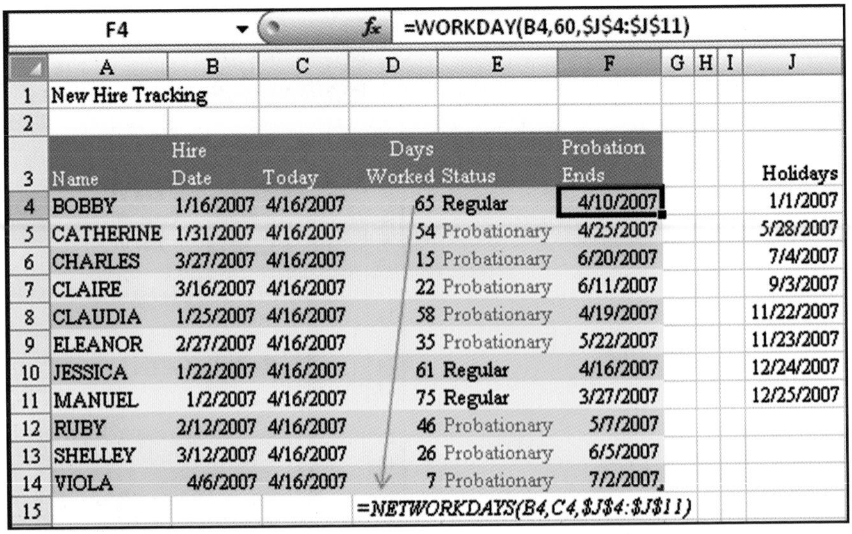

Figure 19.4
An IF function fills in
column E, while conditional
formatting is used to turn the
word "Probationary" to red.

	fx	=WORKDAY(B4,60,$J$4:$J$11)

	A	B	C	D	E	F	G	H	I	J
1	New Hire Tracking									
2										
3	Name	Hire Date	Today	Days Worked	Status	Probation Ends				Holidays
4	BOBBY	1/16/2007	4/16/2007	65	Regular	4/10/2007				1/1/2007
5	CATHERINE	1/31/2007	4/16/2007	54	Probationary	4/25/2007				5/28/2007
6	CHARLES	3/27/2007	4/16/2007	15	Probationary	6/20/2007				7/4/2007
7	CLAIRE	3/16/2007	4/16/2007	22	Probationary	6/11/2007				9/3/2007
8	CLAUDIA	1/25/2007	4/16/2007	58	Probationary	4/19/2007				11/22/2007
9	ELEANOR	2/27/2007	4/16/2007	35	Probationary	5/22/2007				11/23/2007
10	JESSICA	1/22/2007	4/16/2007	61	Regular	4/16/2007				12/24/2007
11	MANUEL	1/2/2007	4/16/2007	75	Regular	3/27/2007				12/25/2007
12	RUBY	2/12/2007	4/16/2007	46	Probationary	5/7/2007				
13	SHELLEY	3/12/2007	4/16/2007	26	Probationary	6/5/2007				
14	VIOLA	4/6/2007	4/16/2007	7	Probationary	7/2/2007				
15				=NETWORKDAYS(B4,C4,$J$4:$J$11)						

Calculating the End of the Month

Finding the last date of a month is always a challenging proposition. It is difficult to nest a series of IF functions that can figure out if this month has 31, 30, 28, or 29 days.

Without the Analysis ToolPak, the best way to produce the end of the month of a date in cell B4 was =DATE(YEAR(B4),MONTH(B4)+1,1)-1. This formula finds the first of the next month and subtracts one, which is somewhat counter-intuitive.

Instead, you can use the ATP function EOMONTH. This function finds a month ending date. You can specify that you want to find the date for something that is n months away.

=EOMONTH(Starting Date, # Months)

To calculate the end of the current month for the date stored in B4, use =EOMONTH(B4,0). To calculate the date for the month ending six months after the date in B4, use =EOMONTH(B4,6)

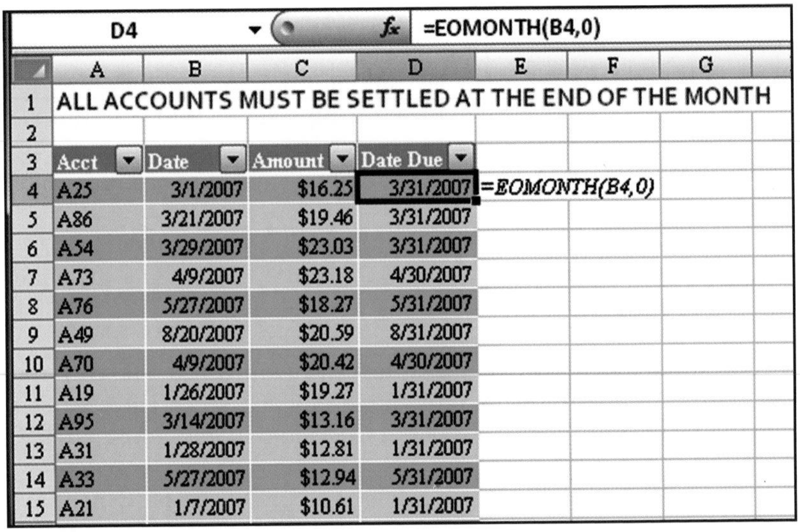

Figure 19.5
EOMONTH will calculate the
end of a month.

	fx	=EOMONTH(B4,0)

	A	B	C	D	E	F	G
1	ALL ACCOUNTS MUST BE SETTLED AT THE END OF THE MONTH						
2							
3	Acct	Date	Amount	Date Due			
4	A25	3/1/2007	$16.25	3/31/2007	=EOMONTH(B4,0)		
5	A86	3/21/2007	$19.46	3/31/2007			
6	A54	3/29/2007	$23.03	3/31/2007			
7	A73	4/9/2007	$23.18	4/30/2007			
8	A76	5/27/2007	$18.27	5/31/2007			
9	A49	8/20/2007	$20.59	8/31/2007			
10	A70	4/9/2007	$20.42	4/30/2007			
11	A19	1/26/2007	$19.27	1/31/2007			
12	A95	3/14/2007	$13.16	3/31/2007			
13	A31	1/28/2007	$12.81	1/31/2007			
14	A33	5/27/2007	$12.94	5/31/2007			
15	A21	1/7/2007	$10.61	1/31/2007			

New Analysis ToolPak Functions

This chapter describes just a few of the new functions now in the core Excel product. There are 90 functions in all that have been promoted from the ATP to Excel 2007.

The following is the complete list of functions that are now part of the core Excel functions:

ACCRINT	COUPDAYSNC	EFFECT	IMCOS	MDURATION	RANDBETWEEN
ACCRINTM	COUPNCD	EOMONTH	IMDIV	MROUND	RECEIVED
AMORDEGRC	COUPNUM	ERF	IMEXP	MULTINOMIAL	SERIESSUM
AMORLINC	COUPPCD	ERFC	IMLN	NETWORKDAYS	SQRTPI
BESSELI	CUMIPMT	FACTDOUBLE	IMLOG10	NOMINAL	TBILLEQ
BESSELJ	CUMPRINC	FVSCHEDULE	IMLOG2	OCT2BIN	TBILLPRICE
BESSELK	DEC2BIN	GCD	IMPOWER	OCT2DEC	TBILLYIELD
BESSELY	DEC2HEX	GESTEP	IMREAL	OCT2HEX	WEEKNUM
BIN2DEC	DEC2OCT	HEX2BIN	IMSIN	ODDFPRICE	WORKDAY
BIN2HEX	DELTA	HEX2DEC	IMSQRT	ODDFYIELD	XIRR
BIN2OCT	DISC	HEX2OCT	IMSUB	ODDLPRICE	XNPV
COMPLEX	DOLLARDE	IMABS	INTRATE	ODDLYIELD	YEARFRAC
CONVERT	DOLLARFR	IMAGINARY	ISEVEN	PRICE	YIELD
COUPDAYBS	DURATION	IMARGUMENT	ISODD	PRICEMAT	YIELDDISC
COUPDAYS	EDATE	IMCONJUGATE	LCM	QUOTIENT	YIELDMAT

✳ ✳ ✳

Chapter 20

AutoSum Tricks

Almost everyone knows how to use the AutoSum button to add a total to the bottom of a column of numbers. In Figure 20.1, select cell D14 and click the AutoSum button from either the Formulas or Home ribbon. (The AutoSum button (∑) is a Greek letter Sigma). Excel will propose a formula of =SUM(D2:D13).

Figure 20.1
Click AutoSum, and Excel proposes a sum formula.

	A	B	C	D	E	F
1	Region	Product	Customer	Quantity	Revenue	Profit
2	East	I881	Amazing Yardstick Partners	1000	22810	12590
3	Central	J690	Inventive Opener Corporation	100	2257	1273
4	East	M144	Magnificent Jewelry Inc.	500	10245	6010
5	Central	R543	Magnificent Tackle Inc.	500	11240	6130
6	Central	A288	Bright Toothpick Inc.	300	6267	3726
7	Central	D846	Remarkable Banister Supply	100	1740	893
8	East	O882	Safe Shoe Company	100	2401	1379
9	West	C498	Exclusive Necktie Corporation	1000	19110	10640
10	East	B362	Vibrant Vise Company	500	9345	5110
11	East	M144	Forceful Furnace Company	600	11628	6546
12	Central	R543	Unique Flagpole Company	900	21888	12690
13	East	P154	Guarded Zipper Corporation	300	5961	3009
14				=SUM(D2:D13)		
15				SUM(number1, [number2], ...)		
16						

You can then type Enter to accept the formula.

Alternatives to AutoSum

The AutoSum button has a dropdown attached to it. If you select the dropdown, you can instead choose to insert a formula that will find the Average, Count, Max, or Min value.

Figure 20.2
The dropdown next to AutoSum allows for other functions.

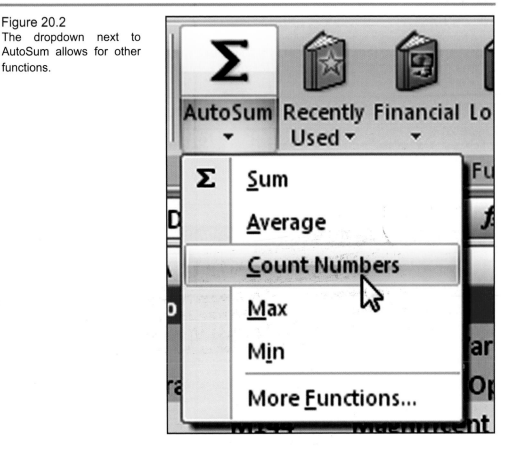

Using AutoSum to Sum a Row

The AutoSum button works to total across as well as down. If you have the cellpointer in H2 and press the AutoSum button, Excel will sum D2:G2.

Figure 20.3
AutoSum can detect data to the left of the current cell.

	C	D	E	F	G	H	I	J
1	Customer	Q1	Q2	Q3	Q4	Total		
2	Amazing Yardstick Partners	500	400	400	400	=SUM(D2:G2)		
3	Inventive Opener Corporation	500	100	300	100	SUM(**number1**, [number2], ...)		
4	Magnificent Jewelry Inc.	400	400	500	100			

The AutoSum also works fine in cell H3.

However, if you try the AutoSum in H4, Excel has to choose between summing H2+H3 or D4:G4. In this particular case, Excel's desire to sum a column wins out and Excel proposes a formula of =SUM(H2:H3).

Figure 20.4
When given a choice, AutoSum prefers to sum a column.

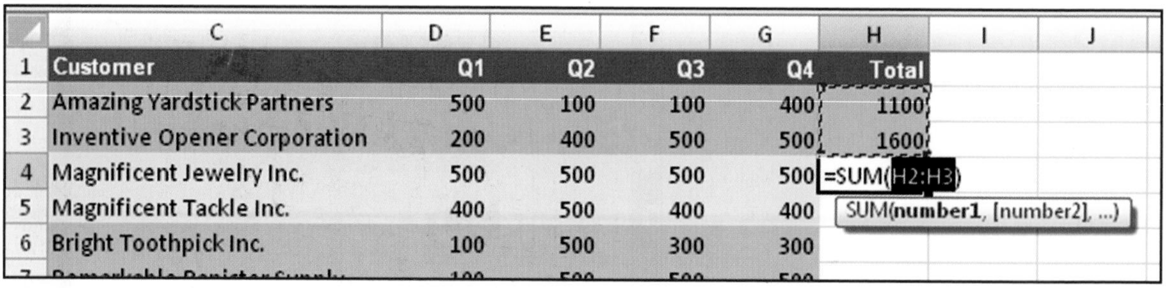

	C	D	E	F	G	H	I	J
1	Customer	Q1	Q2	Q3	Q4	Total		
2	Amazing Yardstick Partners	500	100	100	400	1100		
3	Inventive Opener Corporation	200	400	500	500	1600		
4	Magnificent Jewelry Inc.	500	500	500	500	=SUM(H2:H3)		
5	Magnificent Tackle Inc.	400	500	400	400	SUM(number1, [number2], ...)		
6	Bright Toothpick Inc.	100	500	300	300			
7	Remarkable Canister Supply	100	500	500	500			

If Excel proposes the wrong formula, simply use your mouse to highlight the correct range for the SUM.

Figure 20.5
Override Excel's guess by using the mouse to select the proper range.

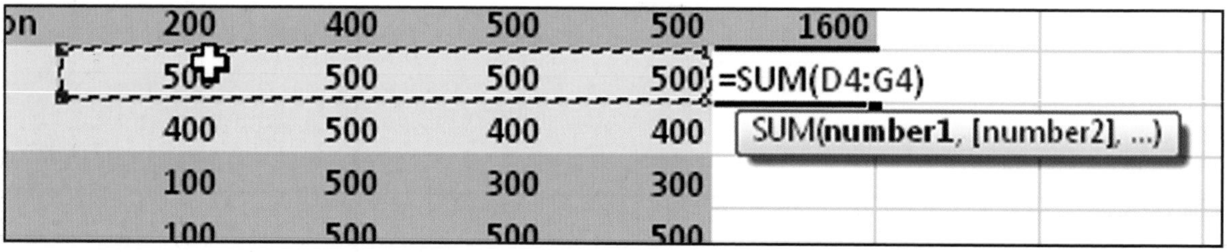

on	200	400	500	500	1600	
	50	500	500	500	=SUM(D4:G4)	
	400	500	400	400	SUM(number1, [number2], ...)	
	100	500	300	300		
	100	500	500	500		

Tip: Use Alt+= (that is, hold down Alt while typing an equals sign) as an alternative to clicking the AutoSum icon.

Entering Many SUM Formulas at One Time

The AutoSum button has some amazing tricks available. In Figure 20.6, we've selected the numeric range plus one extra row and one extra column.

Figure 20.6
The selection includes
the numbers in D:G plus
an extra row and column.

D	E	F	G	H
Q1	Q2	Q3	Q4	Total
100	500	500	200	
300	500	400	500	
200	200	300	400	
500	400	100	200	
200	200	300	100	
200	200	400	500	
100	100	500	500	
100	100	300	400	
500	400	100	400	
300	500	400	300	
300	100	300	100	
500	500	400	500	

Clicking the AutoSum button will add totals in the 17 total cells.

Figure 20.7
Except for the botched
formatting in H8:H9, the
formulas are perfect.

D	E	F	G	H
Q1	Q2	Q3	Q4	Total
400	100	100	400	1000
100	200	500	400	1200
200	200	400	500	1300
300	200	100	400	1000
100	200	200	100	600
200	200	500	100	1000
200	100	200	200	700
500	200	300	100	1100
300	400	300	300	1300
400	300	100	300	1100
200	200	200	400	1000
300	200	100	100	700
3200	2500	3000	3300	12000

In Figure 20.8, there are many holes in the dataset. Select the data as shown.

Figure 20.8
Can Excel fill all the blanks with totals?

	A	B	C
1	29	23	21
2	27	61	54
3		68	
4	53		96
5	59	52	96
6	97	63	
7		94	37
8	14		91
9	98	36	
10	29	17	91
11	86	11	40
12		70	38
13	37	13	
14	81		53
15	90	54	65
16	96	69	82
17			

From the Home ribbon, choose Find & Select – Go To Special – Blanks.
Click the AutoSum button. Excel will fill all of the missing cells with totals of the cells above.

Figure 20.9
Select the blank cells within the selection first and AutoSum will populate them all with one click.

A3			f_x	=SUM(A1:A2)
A	B	C	D	E
29	23	21		
27	61	54		
56	68	75		
53	152	96		
59	52	96		
97	63	192		
209	94	37		
14	209	91		
98	36	128		

* * *

Chapter 21

Investigating Formulas

When someone sends you a new worksheet, it is difficult to figure out how all of the formulas work, or even which cells contain formulas.

Figure 21.1
Someone else created this worksheet. How does it work?

	D33		f_x	=(E31/C4)^(D4/D5)+D14-E21*E16+Sheet2!C5					
	A B	C	D	E	F	G	H	I	J
1			Section 1: Historical Trends (Per Month)						
2									
3	Store Type	Size	Rent	Sales	Profit	Labor	Net		
4	Regular	1200	2400	12456	6228	6480	-2652		
5	BigBox	2600	5200	34500	17250	8640	3410		
6									
7	Section 2: Number of Stores								
8									
9	Regular	81							
10	BigBox	184							
11									
12	Section 3: Analysis of Profitability of Current Store Mix								
13		Sales	Net Profit	NP%					
14	Total Chair	88283232	4951536	5.6%					
15	Regular	12107232	-2577744	-21.3%					
16	Big Box	76176000	7529280	9.9%					
17									
18	Section 4: Profit Projections with a New Mix of Stores								
19			Sales	Profit	NP%				
20	Regular	0	0	0					
21	BigBox	240	99360000	9820800					
22	New Mix	240	99360000	9820800	10%				
23									
24	Cost of Closing Stores								
25	Labor	787320							
26	Lost Rent	388800							
27									
28				Year 1	Year 2	Year 3	Year 4	Year 5	Total
29	Increased Profit from New Stores			4869264	4869264	4869264	4869264	4869264	
30	Costs in year 1			1176120	0	0	0	0	
31	Bottom Line			3693144	4869264	4869264	4869264	4869264	23170200
32									
33		Big Formula	3,980,883						

Excel 2007 has the same Formula Auditing tools as Excel 2003, but they are a little more evident on the Formulas ribbon.

Figure 21.2
The Formula Auditing tools are in the Formulas ribbon.

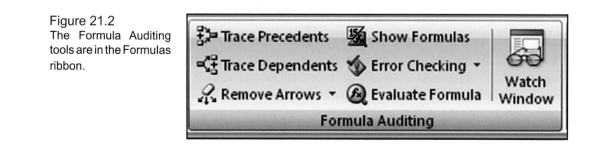

Using Show / Hide Formulas

If you want to figure out which cells have formulas, you can click the Show Formulas icon in the Formulas ribbon. All of the columns are made a little wider, and you see the formula instead of the result.

Figure 21.3
See formulas in Show
Formulas mode. Ctrl+`
is the shortcut for this
mode.

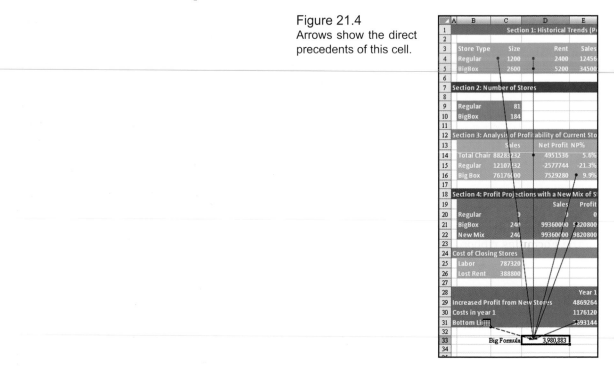

Return to normal mode by clicking the Show Formulas button again.

Finding Which Cells Are Used to Calculate the Current Cell

A formula will usually refer to other cells. In order to visually see those cells, you can click the formula and type F2 to put the formula in Edit mode. The cell addresses in the formula will turn colors, and colored boxes in the worksheet will appear to match the various formulas in the worksheet.

For something a bit more permanent, click the Trace Precedents button in the Formulas ribbon. Excel will draw arrows to all of the cells mentioned in the current formula. Note the icon in B31. This means that the formula points to at least one cell on another worksheet.

Figure 21.4
Arrows show the direct
precedents of this cell.

If you click Trace Precedents again, you will see all of the precedents of the precedents. Click a few more times, and you will see all of the cells used to calculate this cell.

Figure 21.5
After clicking Trace Precedents several times, you realize that this cell is based on many of the cells in the worksheet.

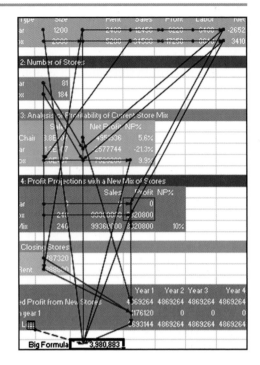

Click Remove All Arrows to remove the arrows.

Finding Which Cells Rely on the Current Cell

Many times, you might be tempted to delete a section of a worksheet. You might think, "I wonder if any cells are using the numbers in this cell?" The Trace Dependents button will show you all of the cells that reference the active cell.

In Figure 21.6, you can see the cells that reference cell H5.

Figure 21.6
Select cell H5 and press Trace Dependents several times to see all of the cells that rely on H5.

	A	B	C	D	E	F	G	H
1				Section 1: Historical Trends (Per Month)				
2								
3		Store Type	Size		Rent	Sales	Profit	Labor	Net
4		Regular	1200		2400	12456	6228	6480	-2652
5		BigBox	2600		5200	34500	17250	8640	3410
6								
7		Section 2: Number of Stores						
8								
9		Regular	81					
10		BigBox	184					
11								
12		Section 3: Analysis of Profitability of Current Store Mix						
13			Sales		Net Profit	NP%		
14		Total Chair	88283232			5.6%		
15		Regular	12107232		2577744	-21.3%		
16		Big Box	76176000			9.9%		
17								
18		Section 4: Profit Projections with a New Mix of Stores						
19					Sales	Profit	NP%	
20		Regular	0			0		
21		BigBox	240		9931000	5320800		
22		New Mix	240		9936000	5320800	10%	

Calculating a Formula in Slow Motion

The Evaluate Formula tool was added in Excel 2003. There are many times that you might have a complex formula that you feel is delivering the wrong answer. You can use Evaluate Formula in order to watch the formula be calculated one step at a time.

1. Choose a cell with a formula. Click the Evaluate Formula button on the Formulas ribbon. Excel will display the formula in the Evaluate Formula dialog. Note that one term in the formula is underlined. This is the portion of the formula that Excel will calculate first.

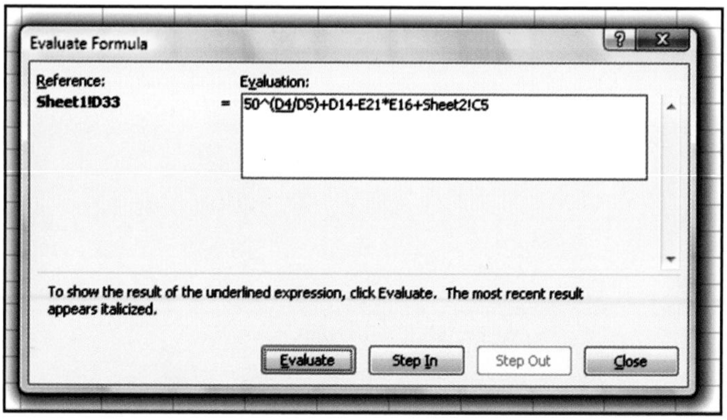

Figure 21.7
Based on the order of operations, Excel has to evaluate the terms inside the parentheses first.

2. In Figure 21.7, Excel will calculate cell D4 first. You have two choices at this point. If you click Evaluate, Excel will replace the underlined expression with the current value in D4, which is 2400 as shown in Figure 21.8.

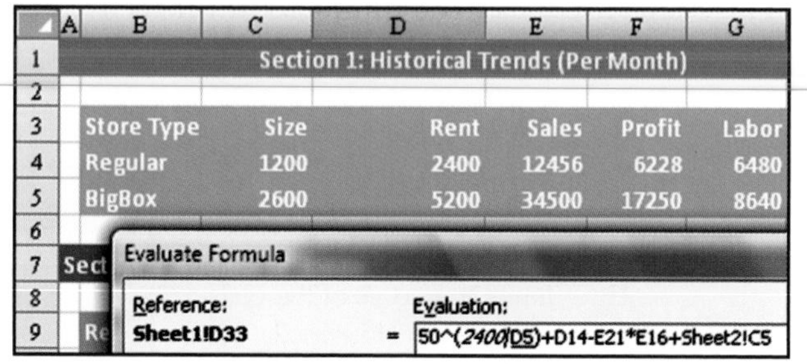

Figure 21.8
If you click Evaluate, Excel calculates the underlined expression.

3. Instead of clicking Evaluate, you can click Step In. Excel opens a new pane in the dialog and shows you the formula in the underlined cell. In Figure 21.9, you can see the results after clicking Step In for D14 and then D15.

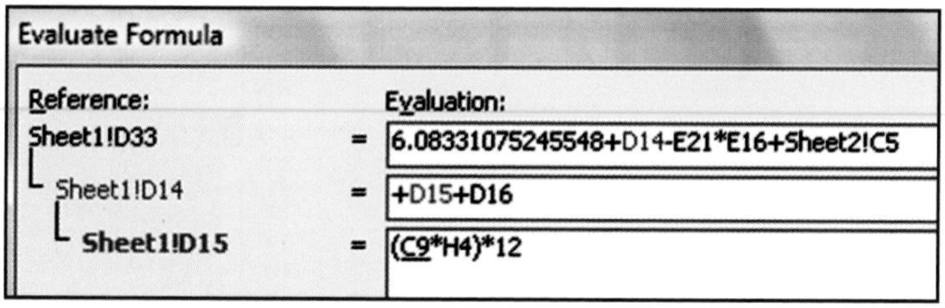

Figure 21.9
For any reference, you can choose to Step In to see the formula for any reference. You can now Evaluate those formulas or Step Out to return to the previous level.

Many students never really understand the order of operations. Using Evaluate Formula is a great way to slowly see exactly how a formula is being calculated.

Watching the Value in a Distant Cell

In a large workbook with many worksheets, you might be working in supporting worksheets and need to constantly switch over to a summary worksheet to see how your changes affect an overall total.

The Watch Window solves the problem of constantly switching back and forth between worksheets. You can set up Watch to always show you the value of a certain cell.

1. From the Formulas ribbon, choose Watch Window. Excel floats an empty Watch Window above your spreadsheet.

2. Click the Add Watch button in the Watch Window.

3. Click on any cell and choose Add.

4. Repeat Steps 2 and 3 to watch additional cells.

Figure 21.10
The Watch Window will float above your workbook, showing you the value of the watches cells.

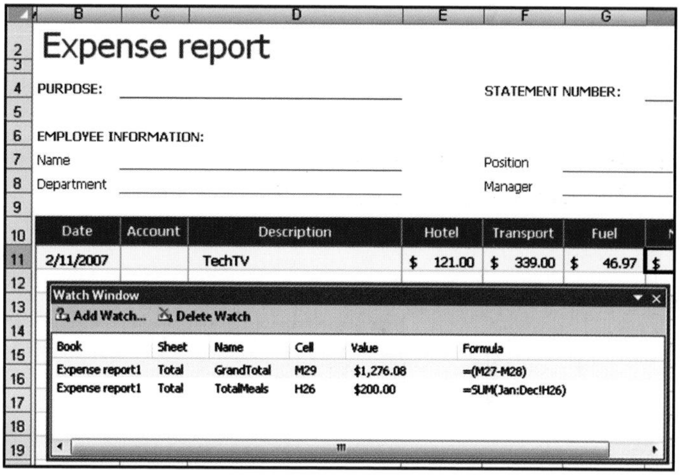

Tip: When the Watch Window is displayed, you can double-click any cell in the Watch Window to instantly navigate to that cell.

✳ ✳ ✳

Chapter 22

Formula Bar Tricks

Long formulas were frustrating in Excel 2003. Figure 22.1 shows a screen shot from Excel 2003. When you select cell Q2, the formula for Q2 is so long, it spills over from the Formula bar, and you can no longer see the result of Q2!

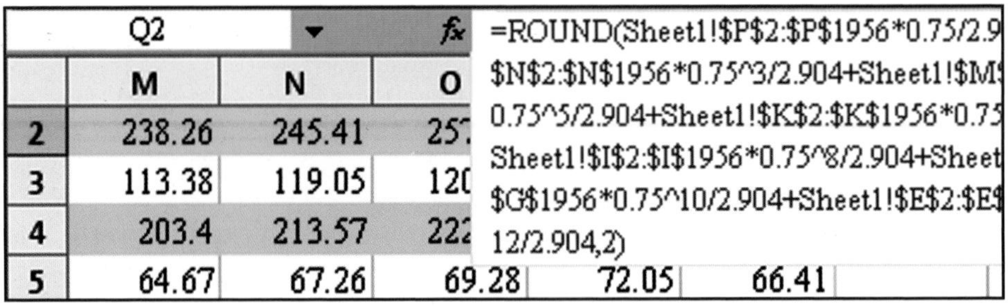

Figure 22.1
In Excel 2003, a long formula would cover the grid, often obscuring the cell you were trying to see.

	Q2	▼	*fx*	=ROUND(Sheet1!$P$2:$P$1956*0.75/2.9
	M	**N**	**O**	$N$2:$N$1956*0.75^3/2.904+Sheet1!M
2	238.26	245.41	257	0.75^5/2.904+Sheet1!$K$2:$K$1956*0.75
3	113.38	119.05	120	Sheet1!$I$2:$I$1956*0.75^8/2.904+Sheet
4	203.4	213.57	222	$G$1956*0.75^10/2.904+Sheet1!$E$2:E
5	64.67	67.26	69.28	12/2.904,2)
			72.05	66.41

Figure 22.2 shows a similar formula in Excel 2007. Initially, Excel only shows you the first part of the formula.

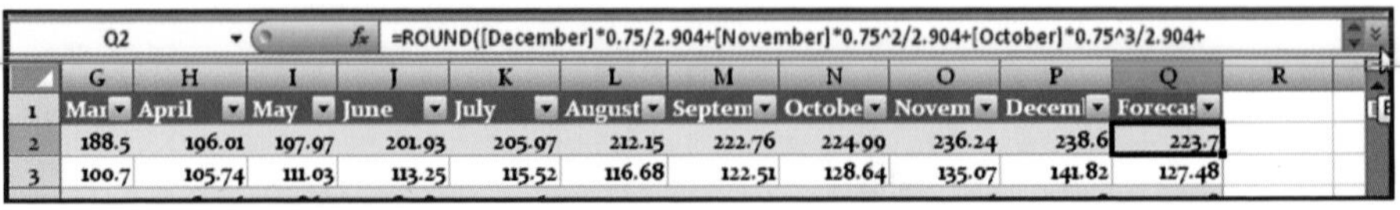

Figure 22.2
Initially, you see just the first line of the Formula bar.

Three buttons at the right end of the Formula bar allow you to either scroll the formula one line at a time, or to show the complete formula, as shown in Figure 22.3.

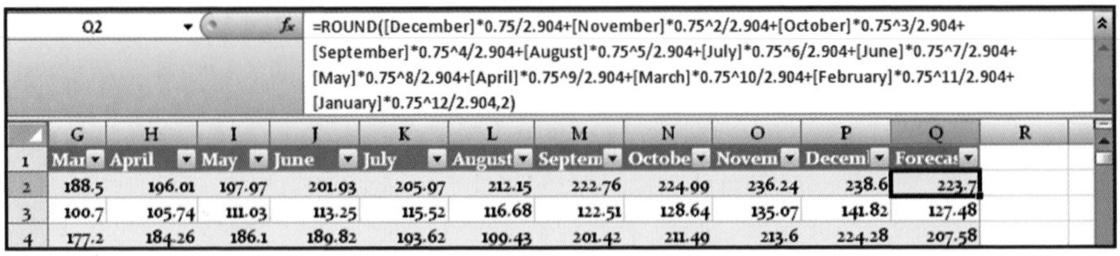

Figure 22.3
Click the expand button to open the Formula bar pane.

Notice that the Formula bar expands without covering the Excel grid. You can also drag the horizontal bar to just below the Formula bar to allow more or less room for the formula.

✳ ✳ ✳

Chapter 23

Back into an Answer Using Goal Seek

Figure 23.1 shows a simple worksheet to calculate the monthly loan payment on a car loan. If you don't like the answer, you could start adjusting values in D1:D3 until you find a suitable monthly payment.

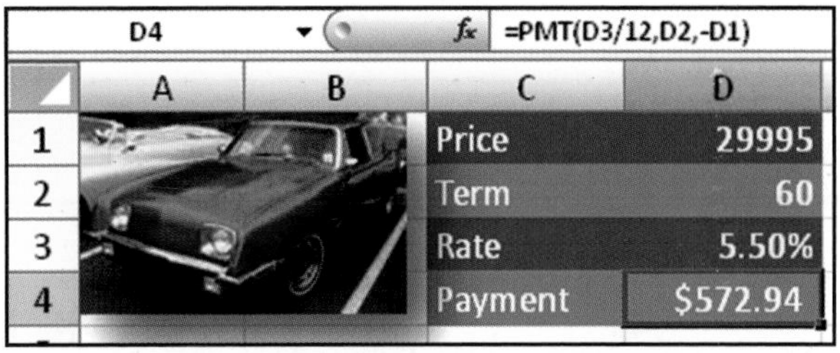

Figure 23.1
The PMT function calculates a monthly loan payment.

	D4	▼	f_x =PMT(D3/12,D2,-D1)
	A	B	C	D
1			Price	29995
2			Term	60
3			Rate	5.50%
4			Payment	$572.94

However, it can be frustrating to start guessing higher and lower in order to hone in on an answer. If you feel like Bob Barker of The Price is Right is making you play the Higher/Lower game, try using the Goal Seek command to instantly find an answer.

1. Select cell D4.
2. On the Data ribbon, choose What-If Analysis – Goal Seek….

Figure 23.2
The powerful Goal Seek command is hidden behind the What-If dropdown.

3. Fill in the goal that you are trying to find. Indicate one cell that Excel can change. Click OK.

Figure 23.3
Goal Seek is simpler than Solver, but it can only change one cell at a time.

Goal Seek

Set cell: D4
To value: 495
By changing cell: $D$1

OK   Cancel

4. In moments, Excel will propose an answer. Click OK to accept the answer. Note that the formula in D4 is still a live formula.

Figure 23.4
Click OK to accept the proposed value.

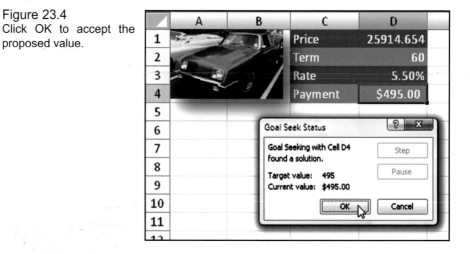

* * *

Chapter 24

Quick Translations

The Review ribbon now offers a translation feature in Excel. Choose any cell and click Translate on the Review ribbon.

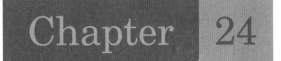

Figure 24.1
Select a cell to be translated and click Translate.

The Research pane will appear along the left side. Choose the From and To languages. Excel will send the phrase out to WorldLingo.com and return a translation of the phrase.

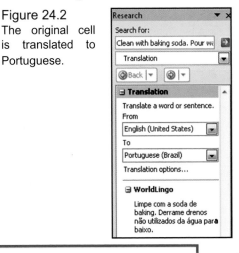

Figure 24.2
The original cell is translated to Portuguese.

Caution! This translation service is great for getting a loose understanding of text in a foreign language. Automated translations are not perfect. Hire a human translator if the task is important.

Currently, the translation service offers translations to and from Arabic, Chinese, Dutch, English, French, German, Greek, Italian, Japanese, Korean, Portuguese, Russian, Spanish, and Swedish.

✳ ✳ ✳

Chapter 25

Preventing Distribution of Hidden Information

There have been some embarrassing gaffes in the news where government agencies distributed white papers that were actually written by lobbying firms. Anyone with a casual understanding of Office can understand how to search the Properties dialog box to find the person who originally wrote the document and oftentimes to even discover the e-mail chain of who sent the document and when.

If you want to make sure to remove any personal data from your documents, you can use the new Document Inspector in Office 2007. To inspect the current workbook, use the Office Icon menu – Prepare – Inspect Document.

Figure 25.1
Excel 2007 can search for hidden content in a workbook.

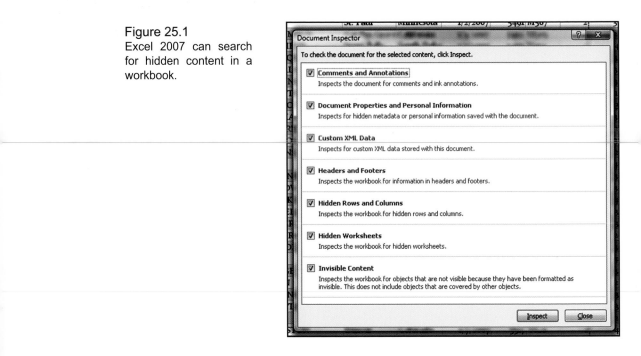

After you run the inspector, Excel will identify potential sources of hidden data. The Document Inspector dialog offers to remove all of the hidden content, but certainly removing hidden worksheets, rows, or columns could cause calculation problems with the remaining content. You should use care when removing anything using this dialog.

Figure 25.2
The inspector found many potential sources of hidden data in the workbook.

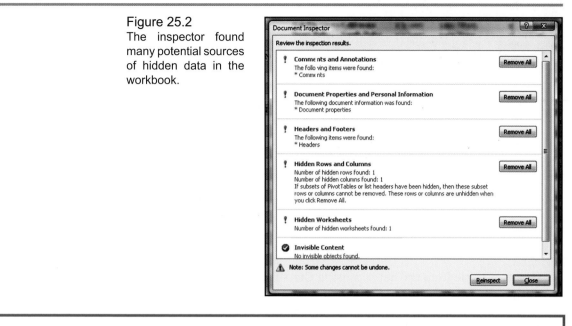

Caution! While the document inspector searches many common places for personal information, it is not perfect. The workbook also includes some cells formatted with a white font, cells formatted with the ;;; custom formatting code and personal information in the Manage Names dialog box. Excel did not find any of these items.

✳ ✳ ✳

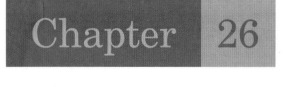

Finding Records
with Filter

The old AutoFilter feature in Excel has been improved for Excel 2007. If you have a dataset with headings in the top row, you can turn on the Filter feature using any of these methods:

- Choose Home – Sort & Filter – Filter.

- Choose Data – Filter.

- Create a Table from the dataset using Ctrl+T. By default, all new tables have their AutoFilter dropdowns turned on.

When the Filter feature is turned on, each heading in the dataset includes a dropdown next to the heading.

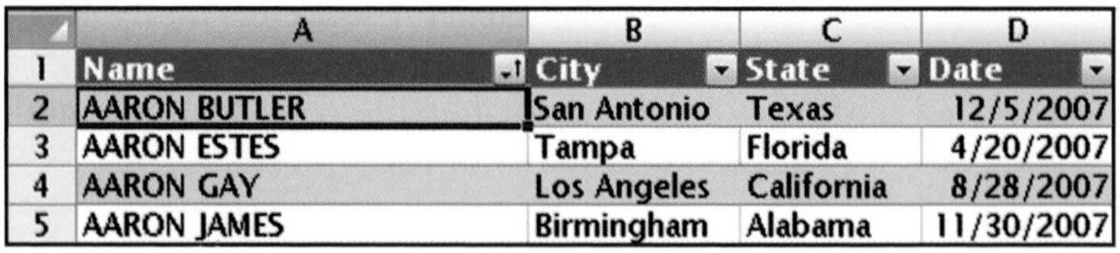

Figure 26.1
The filter dropdowns appear at the right edge of each heading.

	A	B	C	D
1	Name	City	State	Date
2	AARON BUTLER	San Antonio	Texas	12/5/2007
3	AARON ESTES	Tampa	Florida	4/20/2007
4	AARON GAY	Los Angeles	California	8/28/2007
5	AARON JAMES	Birmingham	Alabama	11/30/2007

Figure 26.2
The Excel 2007 dropdown for State offers far more options than previous versions of Excel.

In previous versions of Excel, your choices were limited to only one or two items from the filter dropdown. Now, in Excel 2007, more options are available:

- By unchecking the Select All item, you can check multiple items from the dropdown.

- For text fields, you can build filters to find cells that start with, end with, or contain certain text.

- For date fields, you can build filters to identify records from this month, next quarter, last year, year to date, etc.

- For numeric columns, you can find cells that are in a certain range, above average, or in the top 10.

- If you have applied a color to certain cells, you can filter by color.

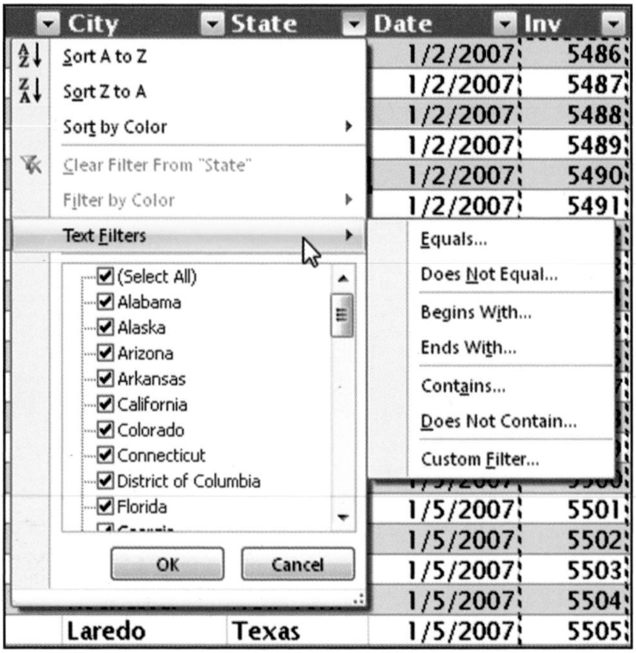

Filter Case Study

Say that you want to find the large customers from the last quarter of 2007 who live in the states of California, Texas, Arizona, New Mexico, or Nevada. You can find these records using the new Filter command. Follow these steps.

1. If the Filter dropdowns are not already visible, choose Data – Filter to add the filter dropdowns to the data set.

2. Choose the State dropdown. Remove the checkmark from Select All. Add checkmarks to Arizona, California, Nevada, New Mexico, and Texas. Click OK to close the filter.

3. Choose the Date dropdown. Choose Date Filters – All Dates in the Period – Quarter 4.

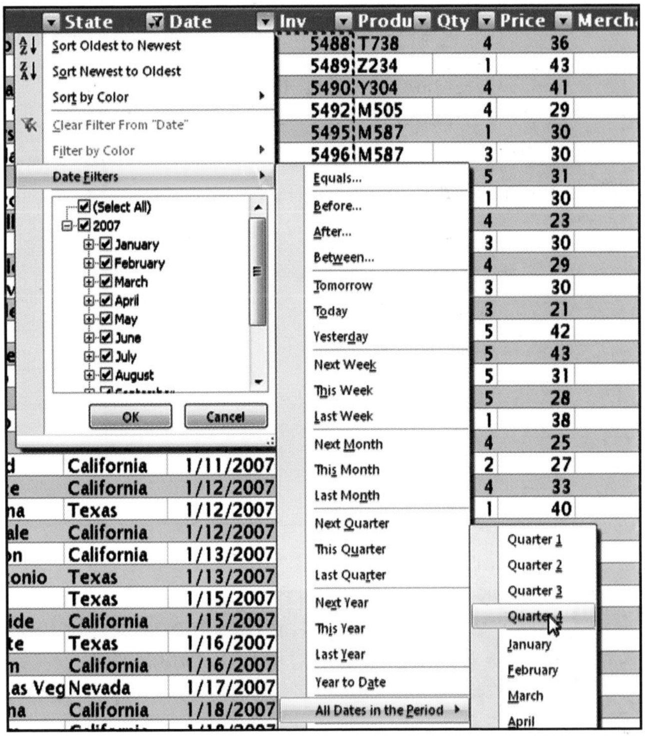

Figure 26.3
When a field contains mostly dates, date filters that are similar to the choices in QuickBooks are available.

4. Choose the Merchandise dropdown. Choose Number Filters – Greater Than... – 200.

Excel will display the records that match all three criteria. The row numbers appear in blue to indicate that a filter has been applied. Icons in cells C1, D1, and I1 indicate that filters have been applied to those columns.

Figure 26.4
Six records match the criteria.

	Name	City	State	Date	Inv	Produ	Qty	Price	Merchandise
1504	CATHERINE ROMERO	Fremont	California	10/13/2007	6988	Y304	5	41	205
1522	JASON CAIN	Albuquerque	New Mexicc	10/16/2007	7006	Z234	5	43	215
1733	TINA YORK	Sunnyvale	California	11/24/2007	7217	Z234	5	43	215
1802	EUNICE GREENE	Stockton	California	12/6/2007	7286	Y620	5	42	210
1860	CLARA COOK	Houston	Texas	12/17/2007	7344	Y620	5	42	210
1864	CONNIE HINES	Chandler	Arizona	12/17/2007	7348	Y620	5	42	210
1877	JENNY DALTON	San Francisco	California	12/19/2007	7361	Y620	5	42	210
1957									

Totaling Filtered Records

While the SUM function will total both visible and hidden rows, the SUBTOTAL function will exclude rows that are hidden in a filtered dataset.

The AutoSum button will automatically use the SUBTOTAL function if both of these conditions are true:

- At least one column in your dataset has a filter applied.

- The cell pointer is in the blank row immediately below the dataset.

The trick is to apply a filter first, and then to use the AutoSum button. Excel will use the SUBTOTAL function instead of the SUM function and provide a total of the visible records.

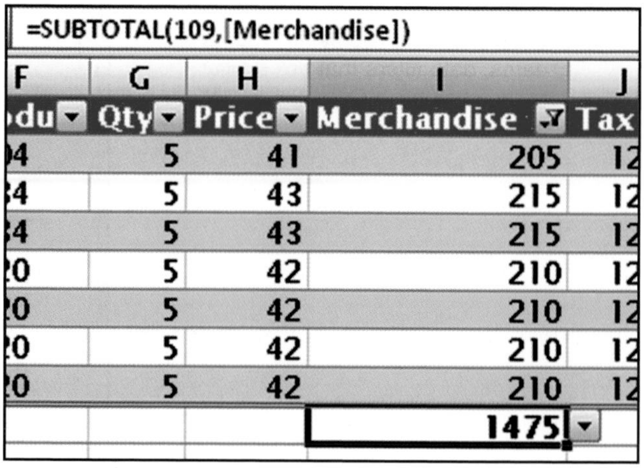

Figure 26.5
This formula was automatically entered using the AutoSum button.

=SUBTOTAL(109,[Merchandise])				
F	G	H	I	J
du ▼	Qty ▼	Price ▼	Merchandise ▼	Tax
4	5	41	205	12
4	5	43	215	12
4	5	43	215	12
0	5	42	210	12
0	5	42	210	12
0	5	42	210	12
0	5	42	210	12
			1475 ▼	

Caution! In Excel 2003, you could use the AutoSum button in any blank cell that was located on the same screen as the filtered data. If your Excel 2007 data contains a table, you must be in the first blank cell below the dataset in order for the AutoSum button to enter a SUBTOTAL function.

✳ ✳ ✳

Chapter 27

Pivot Tables

A pivot table report allows you to analyze and summarize a million rows of data in Excel 2007 without entering a single formula.

Pivot tables are incredibly flexible, and there are hundreds of different styles of reports you can create. This chapter will show you how to create a basic pivot table in Excel 2007 and then show off some of the new features available. Note that a complete book on pivot tables would be larger than this volume. If you want to learn about pivot tables, the best-selling pivot table book is Pivot Table Data Crunching by Michael Alexander and Bill Jelen.

Creating a Pivot Table

Start with a transactional dataset. You should have unique headings in the first row, and then no blank rows or blank columns in the data. For best results, keep your numeric columns filled with numeric data – replace any blank cells with a zero. A typical data set will look like Figure 27.1.

Figure 27.1
This dataset is appropriate for summarizing with a pivot table.

	A	B	C	D	E	F	G	H
1	Customer	Region	Product	Date	Quantity	Revenue	COGS	Profit
83657	Fascinating Banister Inc	SoCal	H897	31-Dec-08	36	1476	720	756
83658	Dependable Shingle Cor	SoCal	A681	31-Dec-08	108	1188	540	648
83659	Tasty Meter Partners	SoCal	L117	31-Dec-08	12	852	420	432
83660	Succulent Oven Traders	Northwest	L776	31-Dec-08	120	9720	4800	4920
83661	Honest Furnace Corpora	Texas	A681	31-Dec-08	132	1452	660	792

Figure 27.2
Initially, a blank pivot table has no fields.

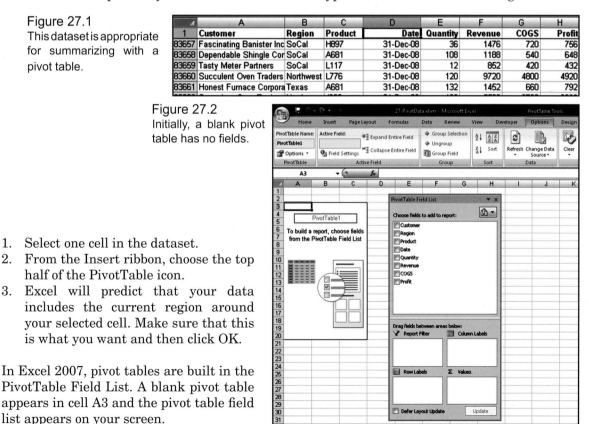

1. Select one cell in the dataset.
2. From the Insert ribbon, choose the top half of the PivotTable icon.
3. Excel will predict that your data includes the current region around your selected cell. Make sure that this is what you want and then click OK.

In Excel 2007, pivot tables are built in the PivotTable Field List. A blank pivot table appears in cell A3 and the pivot table field list appears on your screen.

4. To include a field in the pivot table summary, simply checkmark the field in the PivotTable Field List.

5. To create the report shown in Figure 27.3, click the Region field, the Customer field, and then the Revenue field.

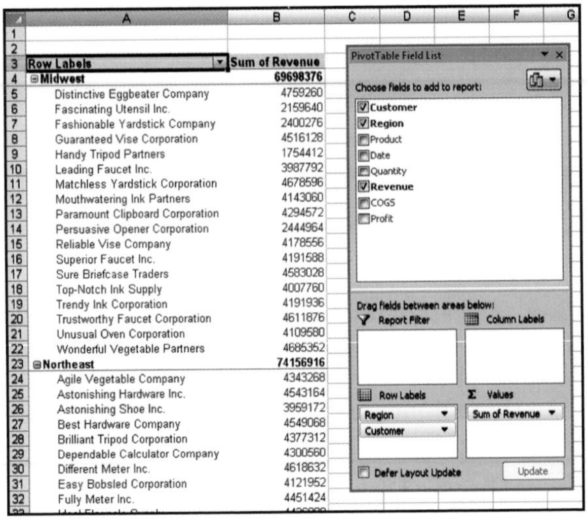

Figure 27.3
Excel uses the field types to determine where to display the fields.

6. When a pivot table has multiple fields in the Row Labels area, you can use the Collapse or Expand buttons to produce summaries of the data.

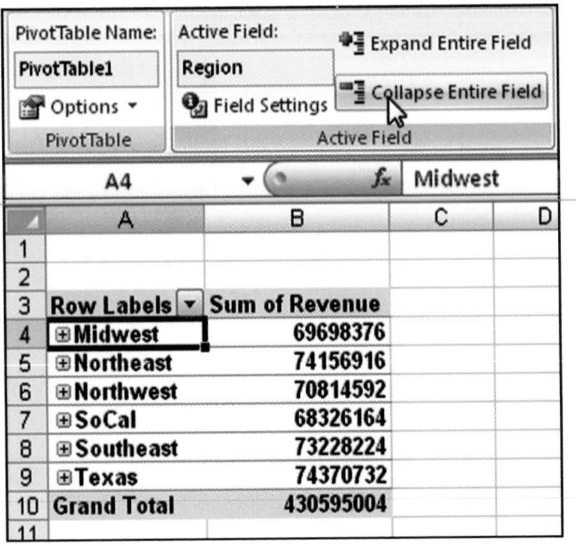

Figure 27.4
After collapsing, the customer information is temporarily hidden.

Row Labels ▼	Sum of Revenue
⊞ Midwest	69698376
⊞ Northeast	74156916
⊞ Northwest	70814592
⊞ SoCal	68326164
⊞ Southeast	73228224
⊞ Texas	74370732
Grand Total	430595004

Rearranging a Pivot Table Report

It is easy to change a pivot table report. Simply check or uncheck fields in the top half of the PivotTable Field List. You can always rearrange the order of fields by dragging the fields around the bottom half of the Field List.

Say that you want to add Product to the summary report. If you click the Product checkbox, the report would grow vertically. The Product field might be a good field to add to the Column Labels area to produce a crosstab analysis.

Grab the Product field from the top half of the PivotTable Field List, drag it, and drop it in the Column Labels section at the bottom of the PivotTable Field List. Excel creates a summary with Region and Customer down the side and Products across the top.

Figure 27.5
Product fields stretch across the columns at the top of the report.

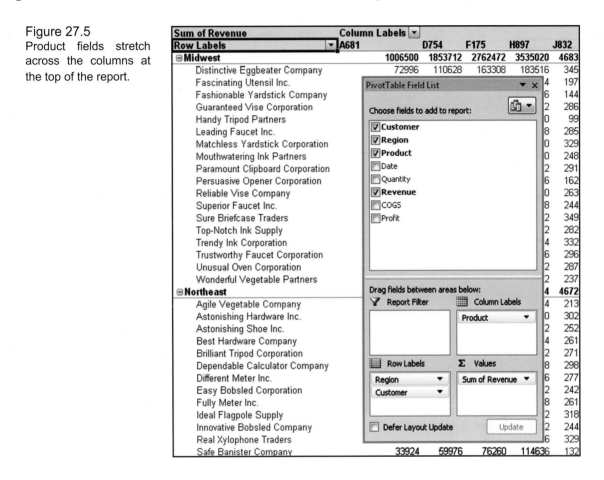

Filtering or Sorting Data in a Pivot Table

Initially, values in a pivot table will be sorted in ascending sequence. Click any field in the top portion of the field list to access a menu.

Figure 27.6
It is unintuitive, but a powerful menu appears when you hover and the click in this section of the pivot table.

The menu offers choices where you can sort or filter the field. Figure 27.7 shows the various options available in the Label filters for the Customer field.

Figure 27.7
A variety of value, date, and label filters is available.

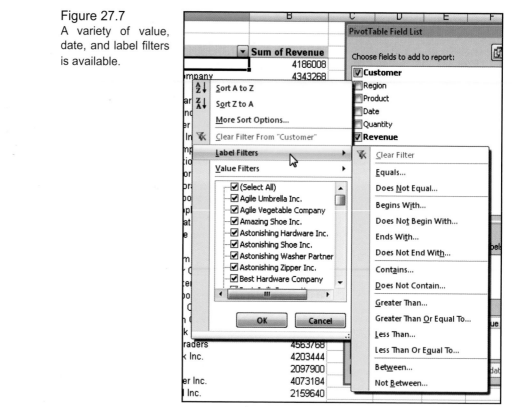

Say that you want to sequence the customers in high-to-low sequence and to show only the top 12 customers. Follow these steps.

1. Click the Customer field in the top half of the Pivot Table Field List. Use the dropdown arrow to open a menu.

2. Choose More Sort Options.

3. In the Sort (Customer) dialog, choose to sort descending by Sum of Revenue.

Figure 27.8
You are sorting one field (Customer) by the results in another field (Revenue).

4. Repeat Step 1 to access the menu again.

5. Choose Value Filters – Top 10.

6. In the Top 10 Filter dialog, choose to show the top 12 items by Sum of Revenue.

Figure 27.9
The filter can also show the
specified number of Bottom
customers.

The result is a report of the top 12 customers.

Figure 27.10
Note that the Grand
Total excludes the
hidden customers.

Row Labels	Sum of Revenue
Hip Ink Supply	4905000
Distinctive Eggbeater Company	4759260
Unique Notebook Company	4694760
Wonderful Vegetable Partners	4685352
Matchless Yardstick Corporation	4678596
Special Scooter Company	4656156
Fascinating Washer Company	4645536
Guaranteed Vegetable Company	4643592
Well-Suited Shovel Inc.	4621308
Different Meter Inc.	4618632
Effortless Adhesive Company	4614432
Trustworthy Faucet Corporation	4611876
Grand Total	**56134500**

Grouping Daily Dates into Months or Years

In Figure 27.11, the pivot table shows daily dates in the Row Labels area. Select one of the cells with a date and choose Group Field from the PivotTable Tools Options ribbon.

Figure 27.11
Select a Date field and
then choose the Group
Field icon.

Row Labels	Sum of Revenue
1-Jan-07	764604
2-Jan-07	928296
3-Jan-07	905736
4-Jan-07	784536
5-Jan-07	889260
8-Jan-07	859608
9-Jan-07	883872
10-Jan-07	782820
11-Jan-07	804912

Never group a field only by Month. Always include Months and Years in the Grouping dialog. (Otherwise, Excel will add January of 2007 and January of 2008 into a single value called January!)

Figure 27.12
Group daily dates up to months, quarters, and/or years.

The result is a summary by month and year.

Figure 27.13
Excel replaces the daily dates with monthly dates.

Row Labels	Sum of Revenue
⊟2007	
Jan	19026348
Feb	16301508
Mar	18148164
Apr	17378844
May	18719760
Jun	17187084
Jul	18311520
Aug	19169940
Sep	16522584
Oct	19429164
Nov	18229224
Dec	16929696
⊟2008	
Jan	18967380
Feb	17462196
Mar	17201376
Apr	18327120
May	18266508
Jun	17310180
Jul	19321968
Aug	17324772
Sep	17843148
Oct	18632004
Nov	16133868
Dec	18450648
Grand Total	430595004

Grouping the Date field actually adds a new virtual field to the PivotTable Field List. Move Years from Row Labels to Column Labels to produce a report showing year-to-year comparisons.

Figure 27.14
December 2008 is up over December 2007.

Sum of Revenue	Column Labels		
Row Labels	2007	2008	Grand Total
Jan	19026348	18967380	37993728
Feb	16301508	17462196	33763704
Mar	18148164	17201376	35349540
Apr	17378844	18327120	35705964
May	18719760	18266508	36986268
Jun	17187084	17310180	34497264
Jul	18311520	19321968	37633488
Aug	19169940	17324772	36494712
Sep	16522584	17843148	34365732
Oct	19429164	18632004	38061168
Nov	18229224	16133868	34363092
Dec	16929696	18450648	35380344
Grand Total	215353836	215241168	430595004

Drag fields between areas below:

Report Filter   Column Labels
                       Years

Row Labels   Σ Values
Date   Sum of Revenue

☐ Defer Layout Update   Update

More Pivot Table Tricks

In Figure 27.14, select any cell with Revenue. In the ribbon, choose the Field Settings icon. Use the Show Values As tab to change the calculation. Here, the pivot table shows the percentage of each column.

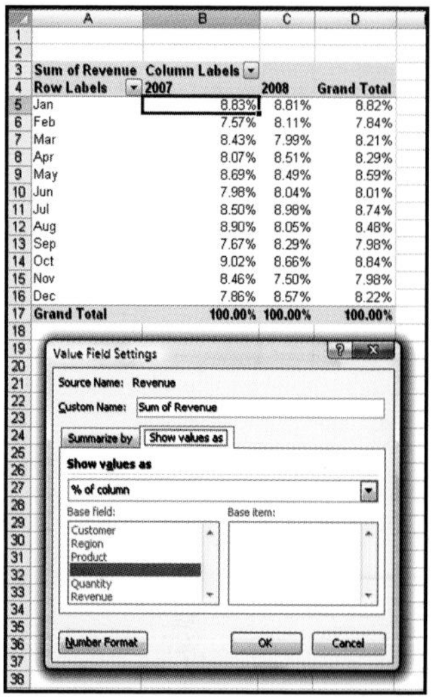

Figure 27.15
The percentages will total to 100% down the column.

Formatting a Pivot Table

The Design ribbon offers a gallery where you can quickly apply a format to the pivot table.

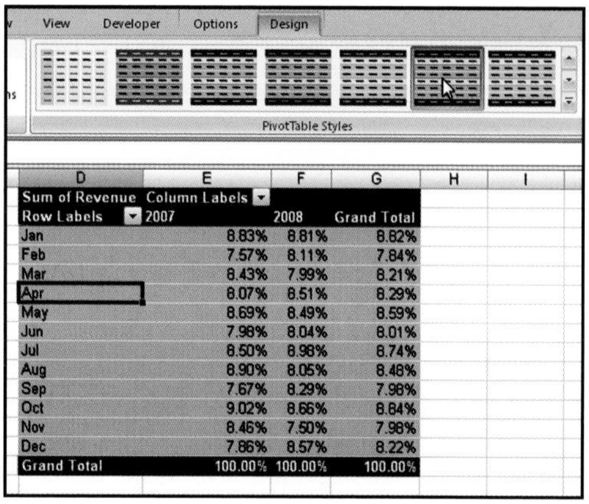

Figure 27.16
The galleries offer different styles based on the currently selected theme.

Creating a Report for Every Region

Drag a field such as Region to the Report Filter section of the Pivot Table Field List. You now have a dropdown in cell B1 where you can choose to filter the report to a particular region.

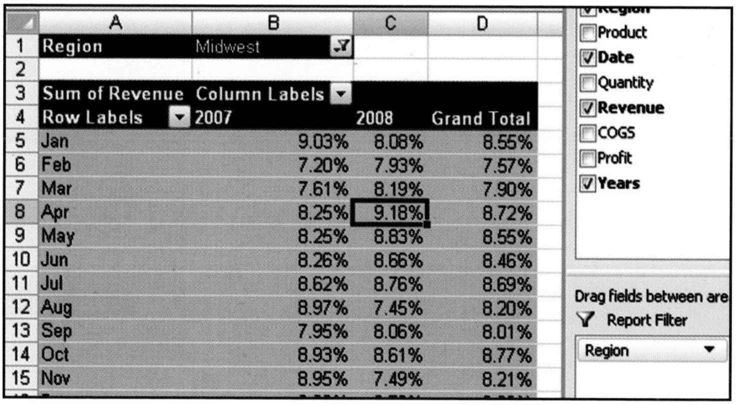

Figure 27.17
Create a report with one field in the Filter area.

Once you have a field in the Report Filter section, you can quickly replicate the report for every value in the Filter field. Follow these steps:

1. Add at least one field to the Filter area of the report.
2. On the PivotTable Tools Options ribbon, look for the Options icon on the left side of the ribbon. Do not press the Options button, but click the dropdown arrow to the right of the button.
3. From the dropdown, choose Show Report Filter Pages....

Figure 27.18
Show Report Filter Pages is a powerful command.

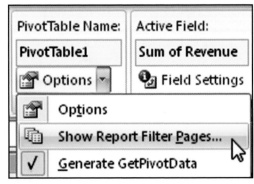

4. Choose to Show all report filter pages of Region and click OK.

Figure 27.19
If you have multiple fields in the Filter area, you have to select just one here.

Excel quickly adds new worksheets for each value in the Region dropdown.

Figure 27.20
Excel added five new worksheets with copies of the pivot table in less than a second. Notice the worksheet tabs at the bottom of this figure.

	A	B	C	D
1	Region	Northeast		
2				
3	Sum of Revenue	Column Labels		
4	Row Labels	2007	2008	Grand Total
5	Jan	8.76%	9.18%	8.97%
6	Feb	7.89%	7.64%	7.77%
7	Mar	8.84%	8.41%	8.63%
8	Apr	7.88%	8.15%	8.01%
9	May	8.95%	8.14%	8.55%
10	Jun	7.70%	7.83%	7.76%
11	Jul	8.83%	9.34%	9.08%
12	Aug	9.22%	7.71%	8.48%
13	Sep	7.77%	8.29%	8.03%
14	Oct	8.37%	9.17%	8.77%
15	Nov	8.63%	7.43%	8.04%
16	Dec	7.14%	8.72%	7.92%
17	Grand Total	100.00%	100.00%	100.00%
18				

Northeast / Northwest / SoCal / Southeast / Texas

* * *

Chapter 28

Fill Handle Tricks

If you need to quickly fill a range with days, months, dates, or numbers, you can fill just the first cell of the range and then drag the fill handle to extend the series. The fill handle is the square dot in the lower right corner of the selection rectangle. Figure 28.1 shows the fill handle.

Figure 28.1
Hover over the square dot to use the fill handle.

If you type a value in a cell and drag the fill handle to the right or down, Excel will extend the series. This trick works with days of the week, months, quarters, periods, and dates.

In Figure 28.2, "Mon" is typed in cell A2. After you the drag the fill handle to the right to H2, Excel fills in Tue, Wed, Thu, Fri, Sat, Sun, etc.

The items in rows 2 through 13 all show series that can easily be created using the fill handle.

Figure 28.2
The data in columns B:H was created by dragging the fill handle for the individual cells in column A to the right.

	A	B	C	D	E	F	G	H	I
1	Enter a value in column A and drag the fill handle to extend the series...								
2	Mon	Tue	Wed	Thu	Fri	Sat	Sun	Mon	
3	Monday	Tuesday	Wednesday	Thursday	Friday	Saturday	Sunday	Monday	
4	9:00	10:00	11:00	12:00	13:00	14:00	15:00	16:00	
5	Jan	Feb	Mar	Apr	May	Jun	Jul	Aug	
6	Jan-07	Feb-07	Mar-07	Apr-07	May-07	Jun-07	Jul-07	Aug-07	
7	2/17/2007	2/18/2007	2/19/2007	2/20/2007	2/21/2007	2/22/2007	2/23/2007	2/24/2007	
8	Q1	Q2	Q3	Q4	Q1	Q2	Q3	Q4	
9	Qtr 1	Qtr 2	Qtr 3	Qtr 4	Qtr 1	Qtr 2	Qtr 3	Qtr 4	
10	Quarter 1	Quarter 2	Quarter 3	Quarter 4	Quarter 1	Quarter 2	Quarter 3	Quarter 4	
11	Text 1	Text 2	Text 3	Text 4	Text 5	Text 6	Text 7	Text 8	
12	1st Period	2nd Period	3rd Period	4th Period	5th Period	6th Period	7th Period	8th Period	
13	1	1	1	1	1	1	1	1	
14									
15	Ctrl+Drag the fill handle to extend the series...								
16	1	2	3	4	5	6	7	8	
17	2/17/2007	2/17/2007	2/17/2007	2/17/2007	2/17/2007	2/17/2007	2/17/2007	2/17/2007	

Note that Excel does not automatically extend a "1" to be "1, 2, 3". This is annoying and a little bit inconsistent. To force Excel to extend 1 to 1, 2, 3, you can Ctrl+Click the fill handle and drag. Holding down Ctrl reverses the normal behavior of the fill handle; using Ctrl when dragging the fill handle for the date in A17 causes Excel to copy the date without extending the series.

Right-click to Fill Weekdays

This technique is excellent if you work Monday through Friday. You can ask Excel to fill in only the weekdays when you extend a series.

Right-click the fill handle and drag. Initially, the tool tip looks as if Excel will fill in the weekends as normal.

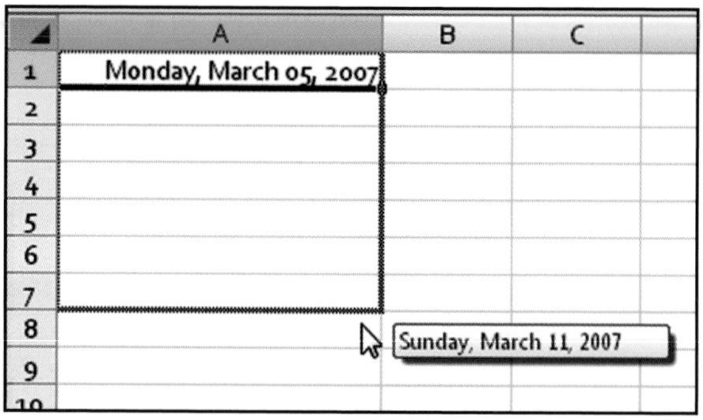

Figure 28.3
Initially, the fill handle tooltip indicates that Excel will fill in the days, just like normal.

	A	B	C
1	Monday, March 05, 2007		
2			
3			
4			
5			
6			
7			
8		Sunday, March 11, 2007	
9			

However, when you release the fill handle, a context menu appears allowing you to choose Fill Weekdays, as well as other options.

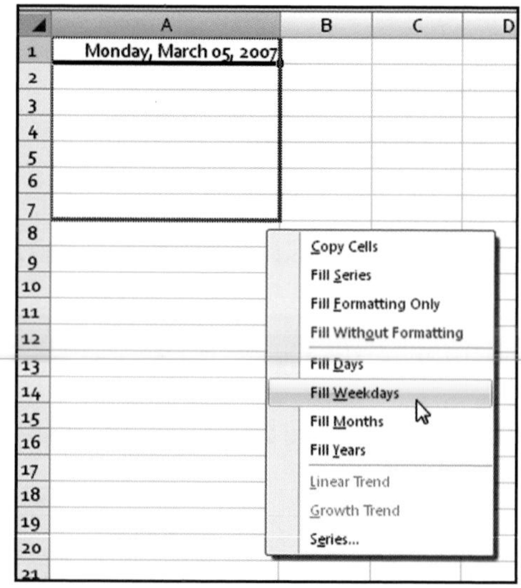

Figure 28.4
Release the right mouse button to reveal more choices.

	A	B	C	D
1	Monday, March 05, 2007			
2				
3				
4				
5				
6				
7				
8				

Context menu:
- Copy Cells
- Fill Series
- Fill Formatting Only
- Fill Without Formatting
- Fill Days
- Fill Weekdays
- Fill Months
- Fill Years
- Linear Trend
- Growth Trend
- Series...

Choose Fill Weekdays to only fill in Monday through Friday dates.

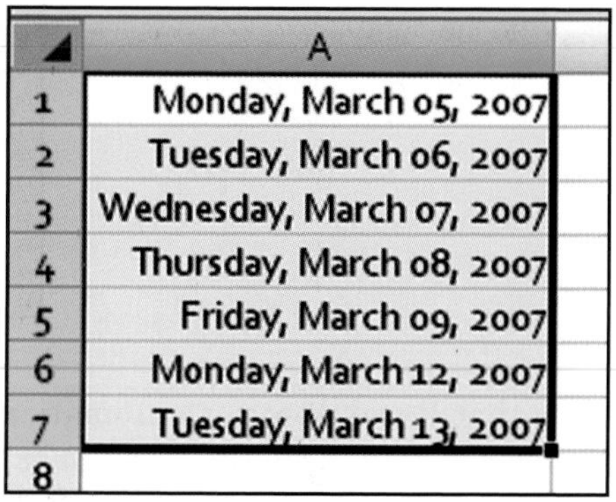

Figure 28.5
A list of weekdays generated by right-dragging the fill handle.

	A
1	Monday, March 05, 2007
2	Tuesday, March 06, 2007
3	Wednesday, March 07, 2007
4	Thursday, March 08, 2007
5	Friday, March 09, 2007
6	Monday, March 12, 2007
7	Tuesday, March 13, 2007
8	

✳ ✳ ✳

Chapter 29

Creating and Using Custom Lists

The fill handle offers a cool way to extend a series like January, February, March... – but what if you need to fill a series unique to your business?

You can set up a custom list that is unique to your job. Once you have a custom list, you can:

- Extend a series by typing the first entry and then dragging the fill handle to extend the series.
- Sort a database into a custom sequence.

There are many situations where custom lists can be useful.

- Accountants can create a custom list of cost centers or accounts.
- Teachers can create a custom list of the students in your class.
- Marketers can create a custom list of model numbers in a product line.

Creating a Custom List

To set up a custom list, follow these steps:

1. Type your list in a column of a spreadsheet. If you want to use the list for sorting into a custom sequence, be sure to type the list in the proper sequence.
2. Select the range containing the list.
3. From the Office Icon menu, choose Excel options.
4. In the Popular category of the Excel options dialog, choose the Edit Custom Lists... button (see Figure 29.1)

Figure 29.1
The custom lists button is in the first category of the Excel options dialog.

Excel Options

Popular
Formulas
Proofing
Save
Advanced
Customize
Add-Ins
Trust Center
Resources

Change the most popular options in Excel.

Top options for working with Excel

☑ Show Mini Toolbar on selection ⓘ
☑ Enable Live Preview ⓘ
☑ Show Developer tab in the Ribbon ⓘ

Color scheme: Black ▾

ScreenTip style: Show feature descriptions in ScreenTips ▾

Create lists for use in sorts and fill sequences: **Edit Custom Lists...**

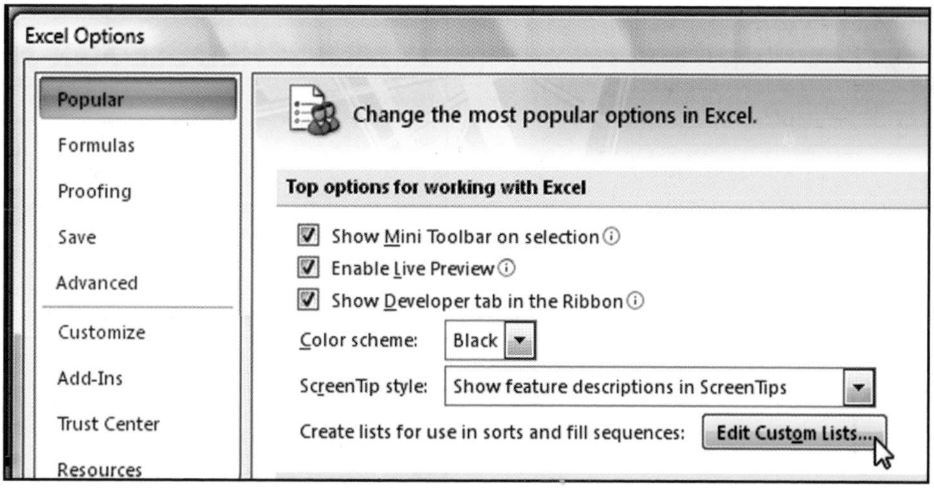

5. Because you selected the range in Step 2, that range is already entered in the Import reference box of the Custom Lists dialog (see Figure 29.2). Simply click Import to add your entries as a new custom list.

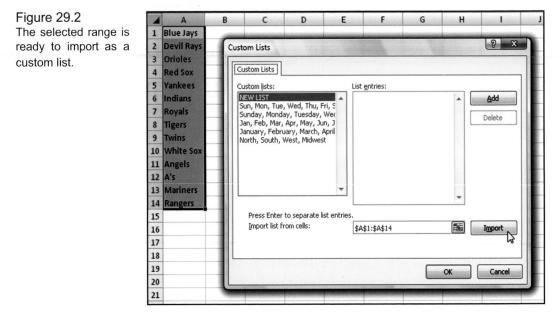

Figure 29.2
The selected range is ready to import as a custom list.

6. Click OK to close the Custom Lists dialog. Click OK to return to Excel.

Using a Custom List to Fill a Range

In order to use a custom list to fill a series, follow these steps:

1. ~~Enter the first items from the list in a cell.~~

2. Select the cell containing the first item from the list. Notice that the lower right corner of the cell contains a square dot. This is the fill handle. When you hover the mouse over the fill handle, the mouse cursor changes to a plus sign, as shown in Figure 29.3.

Figure 29.3
Watch for the mouse pointer to change to a plus sign. You can now click and drag the fill handle.

3. Click and drag the fill handle to the right or down. A tool tip appears showing the entry that will appear in the final cell of the selection. (Figure 29.4)

Figure 29.4
As you drag the fill handle, a tool tip indicates the value that will be placed in the final cell of the selection.

	A	B	C	D	E
1	MLB SCHEDULE FOR THIS WEEK				
2					
3		Blue Jays			
4	Sunday			Orioles	
5	Monday				
6	Tuesday				
7	Wednesday				
8	Thursday				
9	Friday				
10	Saturday				
11					

4. When you have reached the last entry in your list, release the mouse button. Excel will fill in the entries from the list.

Using a Custom List When Sorting

You may wish to sort a list into the same order specified in the custom list. This can be done, but you need to use the Sort dialog instead of the AZ or ZA buttons on the ribbon. Follow these steps:

1. Select a single cell in the column to be sorted.

2. On the Data ribbon, choose the Sort icon. The Sort dialog displays.

3. Initially, the dialog box will offer to sort by your column, sorting on values, with the Order of A to Z. Choose the dropdown for Order and choose Custom List…. The Custom List dialog appears.

4. Choose your custom list and click OK. You are returned to the Sort dialog box. The Order field now shows that the field will be sorted by your custom list, as shown in Figure 29.5.

Figure 29.5
After choosing a custom list, the Order field will indicate the first few entries of your custom list.

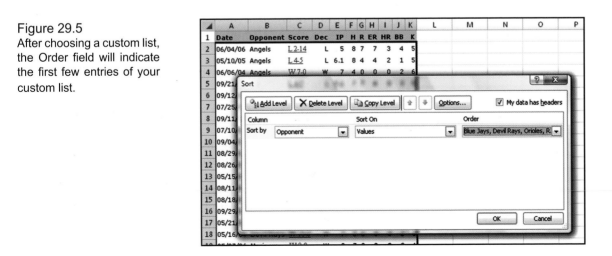

5. If you need to add additional sort fields, specify them in the Sort dialog.

6. Choose OK to sort the data. The data is sorted into the same sequence as your custom list.

Editing Your Custom List

Inevitably, items in your custom list will change. If you are a teacher, new students will move in and other students will move away. If you are a marketer, new products will be introduced. It is possible to edit your custom list. Follow these steps.

1. From the Office Icon menu, choose Excel Options.

2. Click the Custom Lists button in the Popular category.

3. On the left side of the Custom Lists dialog, click on your list. This causes the list to appear on the right side of the dialog (see Figure 29.6)

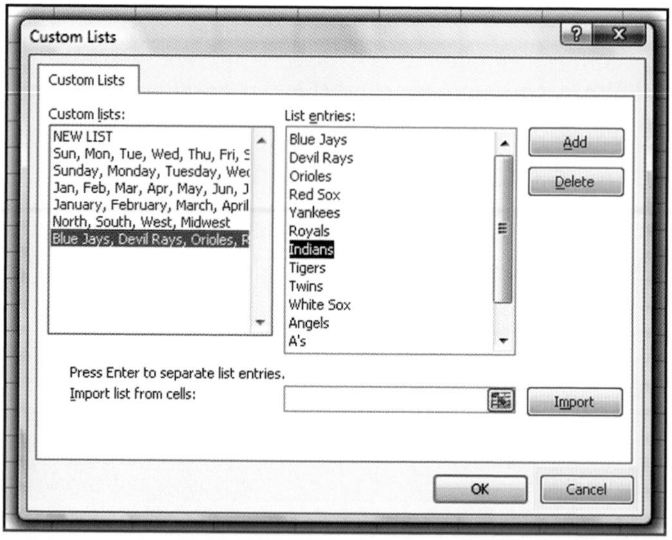

Figure 29.6
After choosing a list in the left list box, you can edit the items in the right list box. Click Add to commit the changes.

4. You can now treat the right side of the dialog as a rudimentary text editor (think NotePad). You can add items by typing the Enter key to create a new line. You can delete items by using the Backspace key. You can use Ctrl+X to cut a selected item and Ctrl+V to paste a cut item into a new location.

5. When the edits are complete, click the Add button to apply the changes to your list.

> Tip: Here is a cool tip from one of the audience at my Power Excel seminar. Sometimes, the first name in your list is nearly impossible to spell, making the custom list less beneficial. This person suggested using a simple heading as the first item in the list – something like Class1 for the students in the first period list. Type Class1, drag the fill handle, and then delete the first entry. You have to admit that it is easier to spell "Class1" instead of "Jailynn Kevitney".

✳ ✳ ✳

Chapter 30

Joining Text

You know that Excel is great at calculating numbers, but did you know that Excel can also perform calculations on text as well?

In Figure 30.1, you have a data set with first names in column A and last names in column B. You would like to join these together into a single cell in column C. Ideally, you would like the names in proper case instead of upper case.

Figure 30.1
You don't need to re-type the names in order to join them in column C.

	A	B	C
1	FIRST NAME	LAST NAME	Name
2	DENNIS	RAYMOND	
3	NATHAN	DUFFY	
4	JIMMY	SPENCER	
5	LOLA	BAIRD	
6	BRANDI	HAYNES	
7	DONALD	REEVES	
8	SHELLY	CROSBY	

The solution is a big word called concatenation. While you use a plus sign to add numbers, you use an ampersand to join text entries.

A formula of =A2&B2 would provide the result of DENNISRAYMOND. Since you probably want a space between the names, you will use one ampersand to join A2 with a space and then another ampersand to join B2 (=A2&" "&B2).

In Figure 30.2, the names are joined together, but they are still in upper case.

Figure 30.2
The formula joins A2, a space, and B2.

C2		f_x	=A2&" "&B2

	A	B	C
1	FIRST NAME	LAST NAME	Name
2	DENNIS	RAYMOND	DENNIS RAYMOND
3	NATHAN	DUFFY	NATHAN DUFFY
4	JIMMY	SPENCER	JIMMY SPENCER
5	LOLA	BAIRD	LOLA BAIRD

In order to convert the text to proper case, wrap the formula in the PROPER function. This function will capitalize the first character and every character that does not follow a letter. This rule works almost perfectly – the "C" in Campbell in C22 is capitalized and the "N" in O'Neal in C23 is capitalized. You will have to go through manually looking for improper capitalization – for example, the "K" in McKenzie in C24 is not properly capitalized.

Figure 30.3
The PROPER function works well, except when an interior letter should be capitalized, as in McKenzie.

	A	B	C
			C22 ▼ f_x =PROPER(A22&" "&B22)
22	JUDITH	CAMPBELL	Judith Campbell
23	CHRIS	O'NEAL	Chris O'Neal
24	ROBERT	MCKENZIE	Robert Mckenzie

> Tip: You might be tempted to delete columns A and B after joining the text in column C. Before you can do this, you must convert the formulas in column C to values. Select the range of data in column C. Use Ctrl+C to copy. Then choose Home – Paste – Paste Values to convert the formulas to their current value.

There is a particular problem when you attempt to join text with a cell that is formatted as a date or as currency. Although cell F11 in Figure 30.4 is nicely formatted, you lose the formatting when you join text with cell F11, as shown in cell A13.

Figure 30.4
When you join text with dates or currency, the result is an unformatted number.

A13 ▼		f_x ="Please remit "&F11&" on or before "&C3+C4					
	A	B	C	D	E	F	G	H
1	Invoice							
2								
3			Date:	3/14/2008				
4			Terms:	30				
5								
6			Quantity	Item		Each	Total	
7			133	R419		$11.32	$1,505.56	
8			186	L991		$11.00	$2,046.00	
9			187	Y103		$7.12	$1,331.44	
10			136	Y628		$13.17	$1,791.12	
11			Total				$6,674.12	
12								
13	Please remit 6674.12 on or before 39551							

The problem is worse when you join text and a date. The formatted date is converted back to a serial number. Most of your customers will not understand that a date 39,551 days after January 1, 1900 is in April 2008.

To solve the problem, you need to use the TEXT function. The first argument of the TEXT function is a date or a number. The second function is a custom number formatting code.

Figure 30.5
The red italic text in A14 is the formula used to generate A13.

◢	A	B	C	D	E	F	G	H	I
3		Date:	3/14/2008						
4		Terms:	30						
5									
6			Quantity	Item	Each	Total			
7			133	R419	$11.32	$1,505.56			
8			186	L991	$11.00	$2,046.00			
9			187	Y103	$7.12	$1,331.44			
10			136	Y628	$13.17	$1,791.12			
11			Total			$6,674.12			
12									
13	Please remit $6,674.12 on or before Sunday April 13, 2008								
14	="Please remit "&TEXT(F11, "$#,##0.00")&" on or before "&TEXT(C3+C4,"dddd mmmm d, yyyy")								

The corrected formula in A13 is ="Please remit "&TEXT(F11,"$#,##0.00")&" on or before "&TEXT(C3+C4,"dddd mmmm d, yyyy"). The difficult part of this formula is figuring out the proper custom numeric formatting code. Use the tip below.

Tip: If you have a cell that is already properly formatted, you can discover the code for that cell. For example, select cell F11 in Figure 30.5. Type Ctrl+1 to display the Format Cells dialog. Choose the Number tab, and then click on Custom in the Category list. The Type: box changes to display the custom number format. You can select those characters, type Ctrl+C to copy, and then later paste them inside of quotes as the second argument of the TEXT function.

Figure 30.6
After choosing the Custom category, the actual numeric formatting code for the selected cell appears in the Type: box.

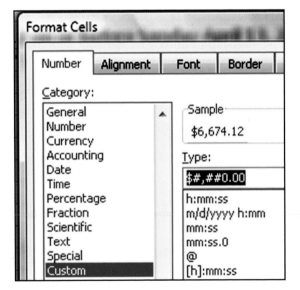

* * *

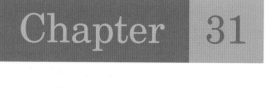
Splitting Apart Text

If you receive data from another system, you will be amazed at how often the data will have multiple fields in a single cell.

The process of splitting data in one cell to become data in multiple cells in called parsing data. In Excel, the feature is called Text to Columns.

Excel can handle two types of situations:

- In Fixed Width data, each column is defined by a certain width. This means that you might always find the Revenue field in the 54th through 66th characters of each cell. This format is popular from old COBOL computer systems.

- In Delimited data, each column is separated by a certain character. You will often find data separated by commas or tabs. However, Excel can handle any character that might be used as a separator.

> Tip: If you specify that a space character is the delimiter, you can use Text to Columns to break each word into a separate column. This can be useful for breaking a full name into two columns.

Splitting Apart Fixed Width Data

The dataset in Figure 31.1 may not look like a fixed width dataset.

Figure 31.1
This data does not appear to be fixed width due to the proportional fonts used in Excel.

	A	B	C	D	E	F	G
1	XYZ COMPANY						
2	ACCOUNTS RECEIVABLE AGING						
3	AS OF 6/30/2007						
4							
5	Customer		Current 1 - 30 31 - 60 61 - 90 > 90 TOTAL				
6	Agile Xylophone Corporation 0.00 250.00 0.00 0.00 0.00 250.00						
7	Alluring Opener Company 0.00 3,085.16 0.00 0.00 0.00 3,085.16						
8	Alluring Patio Traders 0.00 0.00 0.00 0.00 315.00 315.00						
9	Attractive Eggbeater Partne 0.00 0.00 0.00 0.00 215.82 215.82						

However, if you change the font to Courier New, you will see that the columns do line up nicely.

Figure 31.2
In a courier font, the columns basically line up.

```
Customer                       Current  1 - 30 31 - 60 61 - 90    > 90    TOTAL
Agile Xylophone Corporation      0.00   250.00   0.00    0.00      0.00   250.00
Alluring Opener Company          0.00 3,085.16   0.00    0.00      0.00 3,085.16
Alluring Patio Traders           0.00     0.00   0.00    0.00    315.00   315.00
```

1. To split the columns, select your data, including the headings, but not including the titles. In this case, you would select from A5:A39.

2. From the Data ribbon, select Text to Columns.

3. In the Convert Text to Columns Wizard – Step 1 of 3, choose that the data is Fixed Width and click Next.

4. As shown in Figure 31.3, Excel adds lines to the Data Preview to show where each field should be broken. Excel often guesses wrong, so spend some time examining the lines.

Figure 31.3
Make sure the column lines
are in the right position.

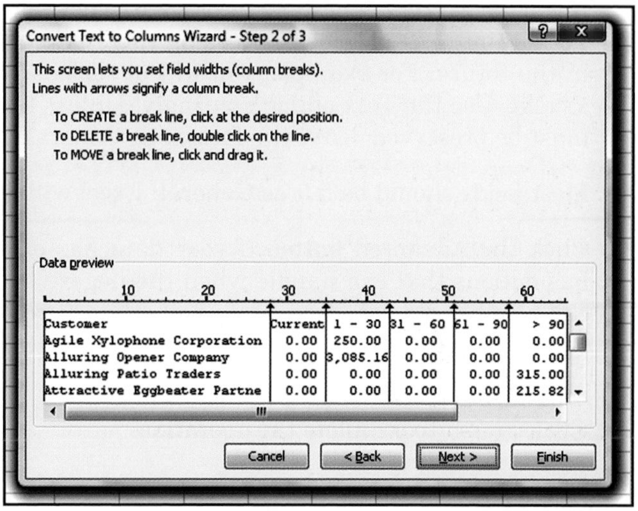

If a line is in the wrong position, click and drag to move the line. If you need to delete a line, double click the line. To add a new line, click in the Data Preview to show where the new line should be. It is OK to use the scroll button on the right side of the dialog to scroll down and see more than the first few records.

5. When you have the lines in the correct places, click Next.

6. In Step 3 of the wizard, you can assign field types to each column. First click a column in the Data Preview and then choose one of four options for the field at the top left of the dialog. You should definitely do this for date fields.

Figure 31.4
If you have a date field,
choose the column and
select the proper date style.

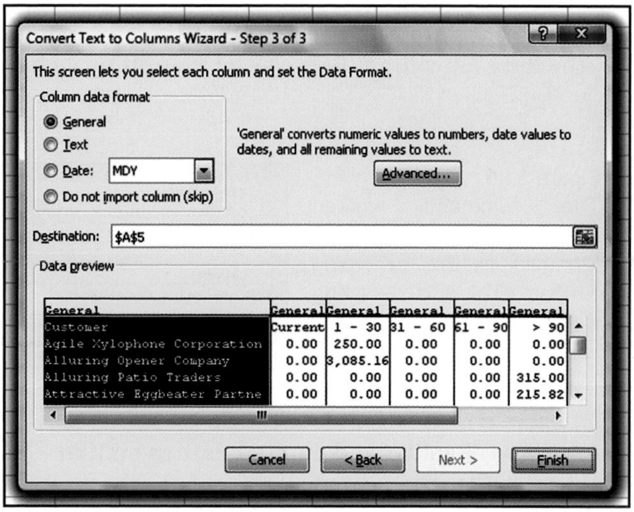

- If you have date fields, assign them as dates and choose the appropriate choice from the date format dropdown to show how the incoming data is arranged. For U.S. dates, you will usually select MDY for Month/Day/Year. If your data is from Europe, it might be in DMY for Day/Month/Year. Some clever COBOL programmers used to use YMD for Year/Month/Day.

- If you want to skip importing a field, choose Do Not Import Column (Skip). This is useful if every row contains the word "Customer" or a dash or something that you don't really need in the data.

- If you have a customer number or a zip code where you need to preserve leading zeroes, change the format to Text. However, using the Text choice will cause many headaches in your data in the future. For example, you will never be able to enter a formula in a column formatted as text. Use the Text option sparingly! Unless there are leading zeroes or trailing spaces that must be preserved, leave the format as General.

- Most fields should be left as General. Excel will decide if they are numeric or text.

- Click the Advanced button if your data has either of two anomalies. The Advanced button has options that can handle when the negative sign appears immediately after a number. It can also handle data from Italy and other European countries where a comma is used as the decimal separator and a period is used as the thousands separator.

7. Click Finish to complete the operation.

Figure 31.5
Some data is too wide for the default column width, resulting in ##### errors.

4							
5	Custome	Current	30-Jan	31 - 6C	61 - 9C	> 90	TOTAL
6	Agile	0	250	0	0	0	250
7	Alluri	0	######	0	0	0	######
8	Alluri	0	0	0	0	315	315
9	Attract	0	0	0	0	215.82	215.82

8. The Text To Columns command does not resize the columns and they almost always need to be resized. Select your new output range and choose Home – Format – AutoFit Column Width.

9. Scan your data to make sure that the parse command worked correctly. For whatever reason, the data for column B in row 21 was off by a character. Manually fix this data.

Figure 31.6
The command worked perfectly except for row 21. Manually fix this by typing 1100 in B21 and removing the 1 from the end of A21.

	A	B	C	D	E	F	G
1	XYZ COMPANY						
2	ACCOUNTS RECEIVABLE AGING						
3	AS OF 6/30/2007						
4							
5	Customer	Current	30-Jan	31 - 60	61 - 90	> 90	TOTAL
19	Fresh Paint Corporation	0	0	73	881.03	0	954.03
20	Guaranteed Doorbell Company	0	0	0	0	400	400
21	Improved Shovel Company 1	,100.00	0	0	0	0	1,100.00
22	Inventive Clipboard Corpora	0	0	0	0	55	55

The process of splitting delimited data is similar. The next example introduces a new twist – not having room for the parsed text.

Splitting Apart Delimited Data

In Figure 31.7, column A contains both a vendor code and a part number, separated by a dash.

Figure 31.7
You want to break the item # into two columns.

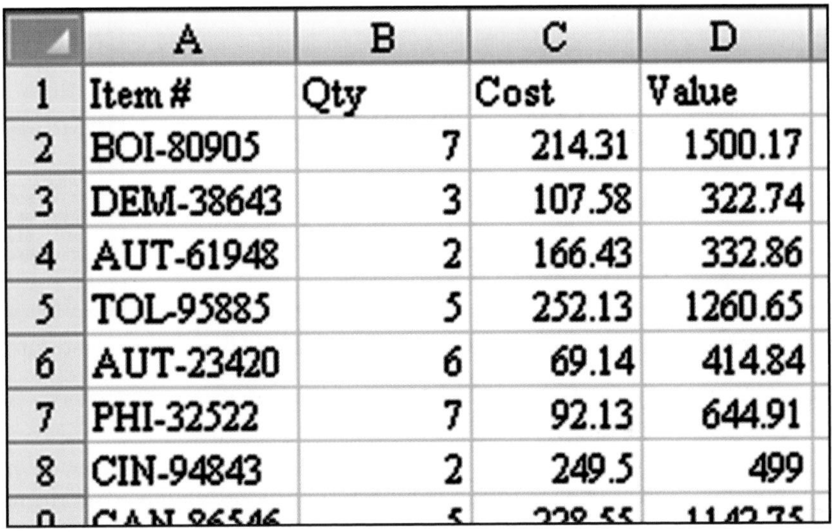

	A	B	C	D
1	Item #	Qty	Cost	Value
2	BOI-80905	7	214.31	1500.17
3	DEM-38643	3	107.58	322.74
4	AUT-61948	2	166.43	332.86
5	TOL-95885	5	252.13	1260.65
6	AUT-23420	6	69.14	414.84
7	PHI-32522	7	92.13	644.91
8	CIN-94843	2	249.5	499
0	CAN 96546	5	228 55	1142 75

If you specify that the dash is the delimiter, you can use Text To Columns to split column A into two columns.

The problem, though, is that the Text To Columns output would overwrite the quantities in column B. Before you use Text To Columns to break apart column A, you should insert at least one blank column to the left of column B.

To be safe, you might want to insert a couple of blank columns. Say that someone who keyed the inventory accidentally typed TOL-377-4 instead of TOL-37704. The Text to Columns command will assume that this field should be split to three columns. If you don't insert several blank columns between A and B, you will have the stray "4" character overwriting the quantity in column C.

Follow these steps to parse the data in Figure 31.7.

1. Select cells in columns B and C . Perhaps B1:C1 or B2:C2.

2. From the Home ribbon, select Insert – Insert Sheet Columns. This will insert two blank columns to the right of column A.

3. Select the data to be parsed. One shortcut is to select cell A2 and then press Ctrl+Shift+DownArrow.

4. On the Data ribbon, select Text to Columns.

5. In Step 1 of the Wizard, choose Delimited.

6. In Step 2 of the Wizard, you can choose the delimiter. Excel suggests using a Tab character, which is wrong. None of the other choices (Semicolon, Comma, or Space) will work. Check the box for Other and then type a dash in the Other field. The Data Preview window shows the data being broken apart into two fields.

Figure 31.8
Specify that fields are
delimited by a dash.

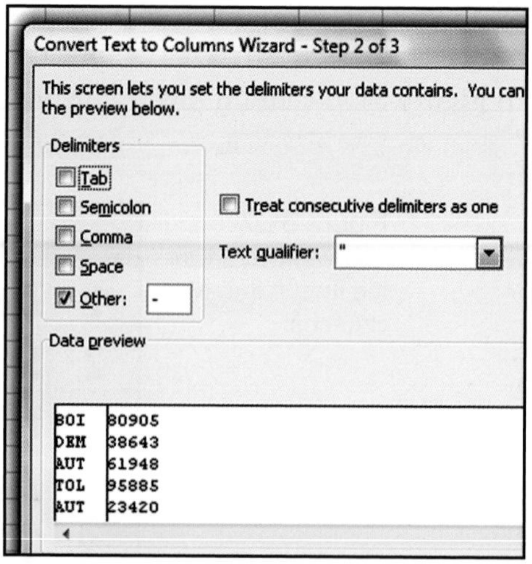

7. Click Next to go to the same Wizard Step 3 as discussed previously. Leave all fields as General.

8. Click Finish to separate the data.

9. You expect your data to fill two columns. See if any data accidentally spilled over to a third column. Select cell C1. Type the End key (usually above the numeric keypad). Type the Down Arrow key. If the cell pointer moves to A1048576, then you know that there is no data in column C. However, if the End+Down keystroke combination finds any data in column C, then you know that there was an extra dash in the original entry. In Figure 31.9, the data in row 14 was probably caused by an original value of TOL-337-4. Manually fix this. Repeat Step 9 until there are no further values in column C. You can then delete the extra column C.

Figure 31.9
An extra dash caused part of the item number to spill to a third column in row 14. If column C hadn't been blank, this value would have overwritten another cell.

	A	B	C	D	E	F
9	CAN	86546		5	228.55	1142.75
10	AUT	65244		1	174.76	174.76
11	DEM	14510		4	46.64	186.56
12	CLE	75366		12	200.32	2403.84
13	COL	80316		8	212.82	1702.56
14	TOL	337	4	11	95.29	1048.19
15	CIN	46679		2	127.88	255.76
16	PHI	73818		11	196.41	2160.51
17	PHI	29665		1	84.91	84.91

Separating SMITH, JOHN L.

Figure 31.10 presents an interesting dataset. The last name and first name represent data delimited by a comma. The first name and middle initial represent data delimited by a space.

Figure 31.10
This dataset has both comma and space delimiters.

	A	B	C
1	NAME		
2	FLORES, STEVE U		
3	WEAVER, KELLI F		
4	COLLINS, MARLENE E		
5	CAMPOS, CHAD M		
6	PERKINS, BILLY Y		
7	INGRAM, TIMOTHY B		

In this situation, you will use Text To Columns twice. Follow these steps.

1. Select the names in column A.

2. Use Text To Columns. Specify Delimited in Step 1 and Comma in Step 2. You will now have last names in column A, with First Name and Middle Initial in column B.

Figure 31.11
First, break the field at
the comma.

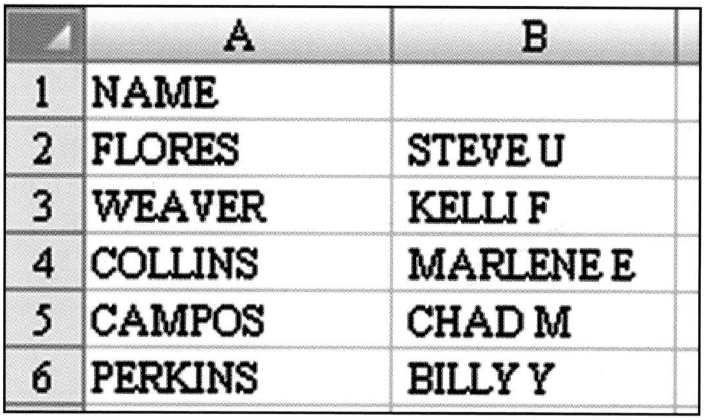

	A	B
1	NAME	
2	FLORES	STEVE U
3	WEAVER	KELLI F
4	COLLINS	MARLENE E
5	CAMPOS	CHAD M
6	PERKINS	BILLY Y

3. Select the names in column B.

4. Use Text To Columns. Specify Delimited in Step 1 and Space in Step 2.

5. In Step 3, you will notice that each name in column B starts with a space left over from the first Text To Columns. Choose the first column and specify that Excel should not make a new column out of this space by using the Do Not Import option.

Figure 31.12
Skip the initial space.

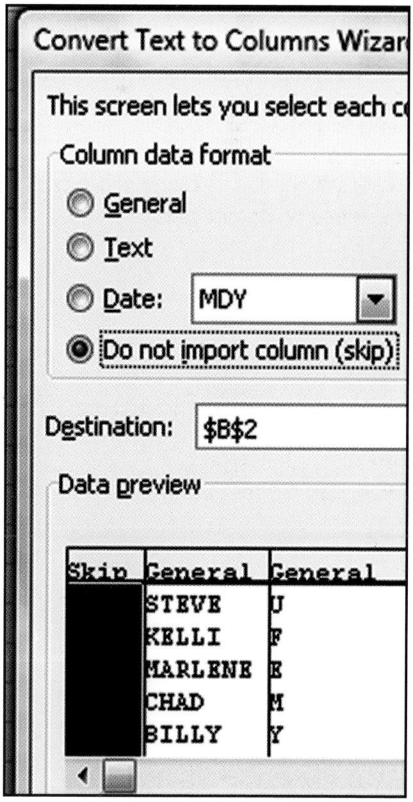

6. Click Finish to split apart first name and initial.

7. Select cell D1. This column should be blank. Type the End key. Type the Down Arrow key. If there are any values in column D, it might be a person with a two-word first name. Manually fix this entry. Repeat Step 7 until there are no values left in column D.

Figure 31.13
Watch out for people with two-word first names.

10	MCKEE	ROY	K	
11	KELLER	TERRI	P	
12	LANE	DIANA	T	
13	PATTON	MARY	ELLEN	J
14	MIDDLETON	DELORES	T	
15	BAXTER	THOMAS	V	
16	DANIELS	KELLI	D	

Using Text To Columns to Convert Text to Numbers

One annoying problem in Excel is when you have cells that look like numbers, but they actually contain text representation of numbers.

Many people try using Format Cells and changing the format from Text to Numeric. This fails because it will not fix incorrect entries already in the column!

1. Instead, select the column and use Data – Text To Columns.

2. Choose Fixed Width in Step 1. In Step 2, double click any field lines that appear.

3. In Step 3, specify a General format. Click Finish. Excel will convert the text numbers to real numbers.

✳ ✳ ✳

Chapter 32

Adding Subtotals Automatically

Automatic subtotals are not a new feature – they were added in Excel 97. However – if you have never used them, they will seem miraculous to you. Even if you have used the Subtotal command, read through this chapter, because there are some tricks available once you have subtotaled the worksheet.

In Figure 32.1, you have a large dataset. You would like to add a total for each customer that will total Quantity, Revenue, COGS, and Profit.

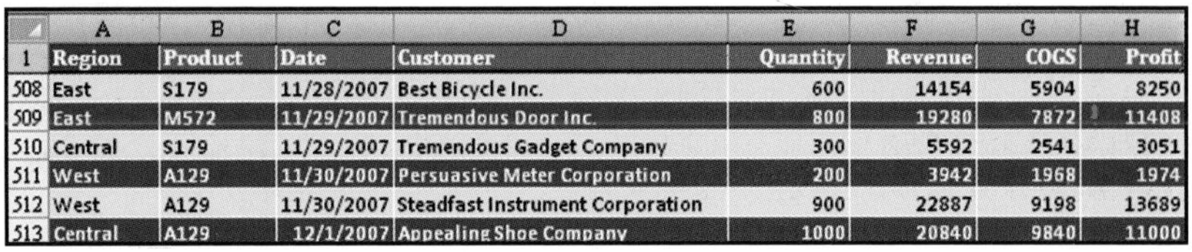

Figure 32.1
Your manager wants this data summarized by Customer.

	A	B	C	D	E	F	G	H
1	Region	Product	Date	Customer	Quantity	Revenue	COGS	Profit
508	East	S179	11/28/2007	Best Bicycle Inc.	600	14154	5904	8250
509	East	M572	11/29/2007	Tremendous Door Inc.	800	19280	7872	11408
510	Central	S179	11/29/2007	Tremendous Gadget Company	300	5592	2541	3051
511	West	A129	11/30/2007	Persuasive Meter Corporation	200	3942	1968	1974
512	West	A129	11/30/2007	Steadfast Instrument Corporation	900	22887	9198	13689
513	Central	A129	12/1/2007	Appealing Shoe Company	1000	20840	9840	11000

Follow these steps to add subtotals.

1. The data should be sorted by Customer. Select a single cell in the Customer column. On the Data ribbon, select the AZ sort button. Excel sorts the data by Customer.

2. On the Data ribbon, click the Subtotal icon.

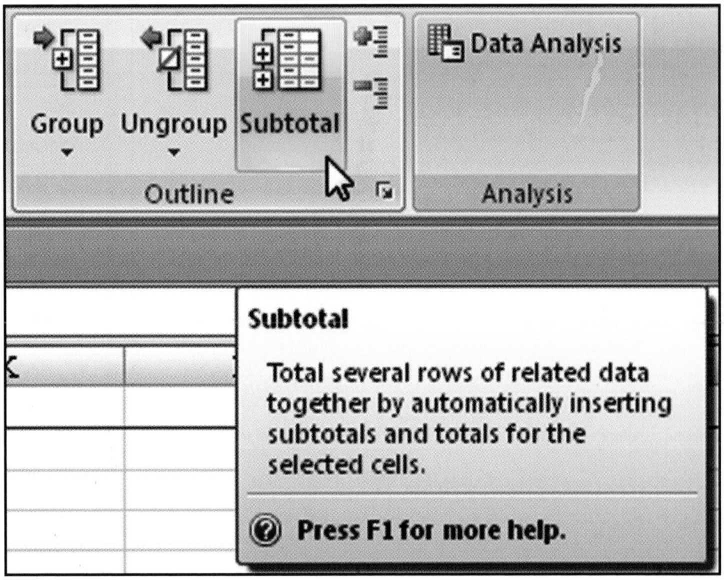

Figure 32.2
Find the Subtotal command on the Data ribbon.

Group Ungroup Subtotal

Outline

Data Analysis

Analysis

Subtotal

Total several rows of related data together by automatically inserting subtotals and totals for the selected cells.

② **Press F1 for more help.**

3. The Subtotal dialog always assumes that you want to subtotal by the left-most field and that the subtotal will be applied to the right-most field, as shown in Figure 32.3. Change Region to Customer, ensure the function is the Sum function, and add checkmarks to Quantity, Revenue, and COGS, as shown in Figure 32.4. If you want each customer on a new page, click Page Break between Groups.

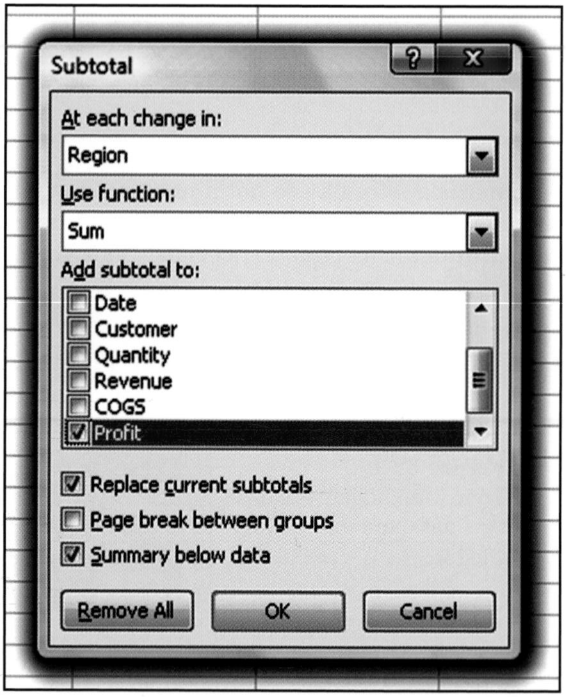

Figure 32.3
Initially, the dialog box proposed to subtotal by the left-most field.

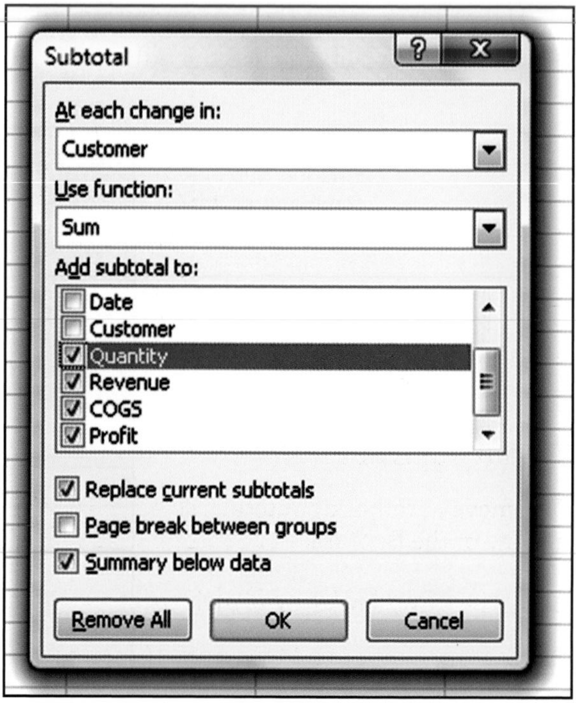

Figure 32.4
If your right-most field contains text, be sure to change the Function dropdown from Count to Sum.

4. Click the OK button. Excel quickly inserts new rows at every change in customer and adds new Subtotal functions as shown in row 6 and row 11 of Figure 32.5.

Figure 32.5
Excel quickly adds
the subtotals.

	Region	Product	Date	Customer	Quantity	Revenue	COGS	Profit
H6			fx =SUBTOTAL(9,H2:H5)					
1	Region	Product	Date	Customer	Quantity	Revenue	COGS	Profit
2	East	C780	4/13/2007	Agile Notebook Corporation	600	14004	5904	8100
3	Central	A129	6/24/2007	Agile Notebook Corporation	200	4060	1968	2092
4	West	J776	8/31/2007	Agile Notebook Corporation	800	18072	8176	9896
5	West	M572	11/4/2007	Agile Notebook Corporation	800	15104	6776	8328
6				Agile Notebook Corporation Total	2400	51240	22824	28416
7	East	M572	1/20/2007	Appealing Oven Corporation	800	14440	6776	7664
8	Central	S179	6/18/2007	Appealing Oven Corporation	1000	22140	9840	12300
9	East	S179	11/19/2007	Appealing Oven Corporation	1000	24420	10220	14200
10	West	N617	12/26/2007	Appealing Oven Corporation	500	11680	5110	6570
11				Appealing Oven Corporation Total	3300	72680	31946	40734

5. Notice that, to the left of column A, you have new buttons labeled 1, 2, and 3. These are the Group and Outline buttons, which are added automatically by the Subtotal command. Click the 2 button to see a summary of the Customer totals as shown in Figure 32.6. If you press the 1 button, you will see just the grand total. If you press the 3 button, you will see all of the rows again, as shown in Figure 32.5.

Figure 32.6
Pressing the "2" Group and
Outline button provides an
excellent view of just the
Customer totals.

	D	E	F	G	H
1	Customer	Quantity	Revenue	COGS	Profit
6	Agile Notebook Corporation Total	2400	51240	22824	28416
11	Appealing Oven Corporation Total	3300	72680	31946	40734
78	Appealing Shoe Company Total	33400	704359	311381	392978
119	Best Bicycle Inc. Total	23100	498937	219978	278959
168	Best Edger Company Total	29100	613514	275105	338409
173	Different Oven Company Total	1700	34710	16423	18287
226	Fascinating Camera Company Total	26600	568851	252522	316329
231	Fine Faucet Inc. Total	1900	42316	18764	23552
236	First-Rate Hairpin Company Total	2700	57516	26765	30751
293	Forceful Doghouse Traders Total	28900	622794	274978	347816
298	Functional Shingle Supply Total	2800	60299	27049	33250
303	Hip Bobsled Company Total	3000	62744	28644	34100
308	Inventive Opener Corporation Total	2000	46717	19961	26756
313	Inventive Wax Company Total	2600	55251	24632	30619
318	Magnificent Vegetable Inc. Total	2600	54048	23780	30268
323	Modular Chopstick Company Total	2300	50030	21612	28418
328	Modular Eggbeater Supply Total	3300	71651	32471	39180
333	New Lawn Inc. Total	2700	59881	25913	33968
338	Paramount Saddle Corporation Total	1600	34364	15576	18788
383	Persuasive Meter Corporation Total	19700	427349	189331	238018
388	Persuasive Meter Inc. Total	1400	31369	13730	17639
393	Secure Jewelry Inc. Total	1400	31021	13745	17276
454	Steadfast Instrument Corporation To	35700	750163	334614	415549
483	Supreme Yardstick Inc. Total	18700	406326	178585	227741
549	Tremendous Door Inc. Total	40400	869454	382170	487284
586	Tremendous Gadget Company Total	18600	390978	177281	213697
591	Vibrant Juicer Company Total	2000	39250	18614	20636
592	Grand Total	313900	6707812	2978394	3729418

Removing Subtotals

To remove automatic subtotals, select one cell in the dataset. Click the Subtotal button in the Data ribbon. In the Subtotal dialog, click the Remove All button.

Adding Two Sets of Subtotals

Say that you want to add two sets of subtotals – perhaps subtotals by Region and Product. The key step is Step 5 below. Follow these steps.

1. Sort by the inner field. Click a cell in the Product column and click the AZ sort button on the Data ribbon.

2. Sort by the major field. Click a cell in the Region column and click the AZ sort button on the Data ribbon.

3. Click the Subtotal button. Add subtotals to the major field first – in this case, the Region field. Click OK to add the Region subtotals.

4. Click the Subtotal button again. Change the first dropdown from Region to Product.

5. The key step is to uncheck the box for Replace Current Subtotals.

6. Click OK to add subtotals by Product.

You now have four Group & Outline buttons. Click the 3 button to see subtotals by Product within Region.

Figure 32.7
Two levels of
subtotals

		Region	Product	Date	Customer	Quantity	Revenue	COGS	Profit
	31		A129 Total			16,700	353,989	155,885	198,104
	65		C780 Total			17,300	366,651	164,400	202,251
	96		J776 Total			16,200	352,421	155,051	197,370
	126		M572 Total			16,700	356,757	159,346	197,411
	167		N617 Total			22,200	476,779	210,840	265,939
	208		S179 Total			22,200	469,282	208,352	260,930
	209	Central Total				111,300	2,375,879	1,053,874	1,322,005
	247		A129 Total			18,000	380,452	167,969	212,483
	279		C780 Total			17,400	371,967	165,915	206,052
	312		J776 Total			19,500	431,022	187,111	243,911
	342		M572 Total			17,300	363,746	163,257	200,489
	386		N617 Total			24,400	516,925	232,641	284,284
	424		S179 Total			19,800	428,891	193,526	235,365
	425	East Total				116,400	2,493,003	1,110,419	1,382,584
	453		A129 Total			17,100	372,336	163,442	208,894
	473		C780 Total			10,700	220,000	98,064	121,936
	508		J776 Total			19,900	414,841	186,496	228,345
	538		M572 Total			15,200	325,157	142,974	182,183
	565		N617 Total			12,800	287,370	124,396	162,974
	584		S179 Total			10,500	219,226	98,729	120,497
	585	West Total				86,200	1,838,930	814,101	1,024,829
	586	Grand Total				313,900	6,707,812	2,978,394	3,729,418

Copying Only the Subtotal Rows

Once you have data in the "2" summarized view, like you see in Figure 32.6, a natural reaction is to copy the subtotal rows and paste them to a new worksheet. Unfortunately, this also brings along the detail rows.

It is easy to copy only the subtotal rows, yet it is an incredibly obscure trick.

1. Add subtotals to a dataset and collapse the dataset using the 2 Group and Outline button.

2. Select from the final grand total row up to the first heading.

3. Type Alt+; (that is, hold down the Alt key while pressing the Semicolon key).

4. Click Ctrl+C to copy. You will see that Excel is selecting just the visible rows as shown in Figure 32.8. You can now paste to another worksheet.

Figure 32.8
Use Alt+; to select only
the subtotal rows.

1 2 3		D	E	F	G	H
	1	Customer	Quantity	Revenue	COGS	Profit
+	6	Agile Notebook Corporation Total	2,400	51,240	22,824	28,416
+	11	Appealing Oven Corporation Total	3,300	72,680	31,946	40,734
+	78	Appealing Shoe Company Total	33,400	704,359	311,381	392,978
+	119	Best Bicycle Inc. Total	23,100	498,937	219,978	278,959
+	168	Best Edger Company Total	29,100	613,514	275,105	338,409
+	173	Different Oven Company Total	1,700	34,710	16,423	18,287
+	226	Fascinating Camera Company Total	26,600	568,851	252,522	316,329

The key step is using Alt+; to select only the visible rows. Alt+; is the shortcut key combination that replaces Home – Find & Select – Go To Special – Visible Cells Only – OK. The Go To Special dialog is a powerful dialog. Figure 32.9 shows the ribbon location of the Go To Special command. Figure 32.10 shows the Go To Special dialog. This dialog is useful for selecting only the blanks, or only the errors, or only the formulas in a selection.

Figure 32.9
The Go To Special command is fairly well hidden.

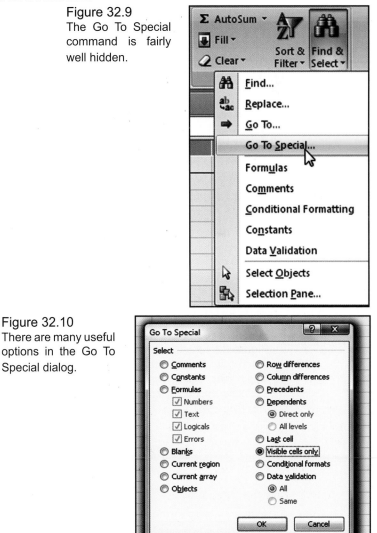

Figure 32.10
There are many useful options in the Go To Special dialog.

The Alt+; trick also works when you want to format the subtotal rows, as described in the next section.

Formatting the Subtotal Rows

The ability to select only the visible cells within a selection allows you to format the subtotal rows. Say that in Figure 32.7, you want the Product totals to be in teal and the Region totals to be in orange. Follow these steps.

1. Add subtotals by Region and Product.
2. Click the 3 Group and Outline button to see the Region and Product totals.
3. Select from the last Product total in H584 up to the first Product subtotal row in A31.

Figure 32.11
Select the range of Product subtotals.

	A	B	C	D	E	F	G	H
1	Region	Product	Date	Customer	Quantity	Revenue	COGS	Profit
31		A129 Total			16700	353989	155885	198104
65		C780 Total			17,300	366,651	164,400	202,251
96		J776 Total			16,200	352,421	155,051	197,370
126		M572 Total			16,700	356,757	159,346	197,411
167		N617 Total			22,200	476,779	210,840	265,939
208		S179 Total			22,200	469,282	208,352	260,930
209	Central Total				111,300	2,375,879	1,053,874	1,322,005
247		A129 Total			18,000	380,452	167,969	212,483
279		C780 Total			17,400	371,967	165,915	206,052
312		J776 Total			19,500	431,022	187,111	243,911
342		M572 Total			17,300	363,746	163,257	200,489
386		N617 Total			24,400	516,925	232,641	284,284
424		S179 Total			19,800	428,891	193,526	235,365
425	East Total				116,400	2,493,003	1,110,419	1,382,584
453		A129 Total			17,100	372,336	163,442	208,894
473		C780 Total			10,700	220,000	98,064	121,936
508		J776 Total			19,900	414,841	186,496	228,345
538		M572 Total			15,200	325,157	142,974	182,183
565		N617 Total			12,800	287,370	124,396	162,974
584		S179 Total			10,500	219,226	98,729	120,497
585	West Total				86,200	1,838,930	814,101	1,024,829
586	Grand Total				313,900	6,707,812	2,978,394	3,729,418

4. Type Alt+; to select the visible cells within the selection.
5. From the Home ribbon, choose Cell Styles – Accent 5.
6. Click the 2 Group and Outline button.
7. Select from the last Region subtotal in H585 up to the first Region subtotal in A209.

Figure 32.12
Select the range of Region subtotals.

	A	B	C	D	E	F	G	H
1	Region	Product	Date	Customer	Quantity	Revenue	COGS	Profit
209	Central Total				111,300	2,375,879	1,053,874	1,322,005
425	East Total				116,400	2,493,003	1,110,419	1,382,584
585	West Total				86,200	1,838,930	814,101	1,024,829
586	Grand Total				313,900	6,707,812	2,978,394	3,729,418

8. Type Alt+;.
9. From the Home ribbon, choose Cell Styles – Accent 6.
10. Click the 4 Group and Outline button. You will see that each level of subtotal has been assigned the selected color. Again, the trick here was using Alt+; in Steps 4 and 8 to select only the visible cells.

Figure 32.13
When you display the detail lines again, the subtotals appear in an offsetting color.

	A	B	C	D	E	F	G	H
1	Region	Product	Date	Customer	Quantity	Revenue	COGS	Profit
560	West	N617	1/13/2007	Tremendous Door Inc.	1,000	19,110	8,470	10,640
561	West	N617	1/23/2007	Tremendous Door Inc.	300	6,207	2,541	3,666
562	West	N617	12/26/2007	Tremendous Door Inc.	700	14,560	6,888	7,672
563	West	N617	3/21/2007	Tremendous Gadget Company	400	8,732	4,088	4,644
564	West	N617	4/4/2007	Tremendous Gadget Company	100	2,466	1,022	1,444
565		N617 Total			12,800	287,370	124,396	162,974
566	West	S179	3/6/2007	Appealing Shoe Company	500	10,155	4,235	5,920
567	West	S179	6/12/2007	Appealing Shoe Company	600	10,404	5,082	5,322
568	West	S179	10/11/2007	Appealing Shoe Company	200	5,002	2,044	2,958
569	West	S179	8/13/2007	Best Bicycle Inc.	300	6,522	2,952	3,570
570	West	S179	12/21/2007	Best Bicycle Inc.	800	18,304	8,176	10,128
571	West	S179	1/30/2007	Best Edger Company	1,000	19,250	8,470	10,780
572	West	S179	3/22/2007	Best Edger Company	800	15,856	7,872	7,984
573	West	S179	6/25/2007	Fascinating Camera Company	800	15,400	6,776	8,624
574	West	S179	7/20/2007	Inventive Opener Corporation	1,000	22,840	10,220	12,620
575	West	S179	2/18/2007	Persuasive Meter Corporation	400	9,088	3,936	5,152
576	West	S179	10/11/2007	Persuasive Meter Corporation	1,000	20,190	9,840	10,350
577	West	S179	5/4/2007	Supreme Yardstick Inc.	300	6,867	3,066	3,801
578	West	S179	5/6/2007	Supreme Yardstick Inc.	400	8,052	3,936	4,116
579	West	S179	8/15/2007	Supreme Yardstick Inc.	400	9,384	4,088	5,296
580	West	S179	2/17/2007	Tremendous Door Inc.	1,000	20,250	8,470	11,780
581	West	S179	8/4/2007	Tremendous Door Inc.	200	3,418	1,694	1,724
582	West	S179	5/2/2007	Tremendous Gadget Company	200	4,378	1,968	2,410
583	West	S179	7/27/2007	Tremendous Gadget Company	600	13,866	5,904	7,962
584		S179 Total			10,500	219,226	98,729	120,497
585	West Total				86,200	1,838,930	814,101	1,024,829
586	Grand Total				313,900	6,707,812	2,978,394	3,729,418

✳ ✳ ✳

Chapter 33

Using Speak Cells

It is possible for Excel to talk to you. I am not suggesting that you have so few friends that you need to talk to a computer. Instead, this is a great trick for proofing a spreadsheet.

Say that you have keyed in a lot of data and want to compare it to a printed piece of paper. Select the cells and choose Speak Cells. Excel will read the numbers on the screen and you can keep your eyes on the paper.

You can also use the Speak Cells on Enter feature to have Excel speak all new values entered in the workbook.

While the Speech Toolbar used to be featured on the Tools menu, the icons have been removed from the ribbon. You will have to customize the QAT in order to have access to this feature.

1. Right-click on the QAT and choose Customize Quick Access Toolbar.
2. In the left dropdown, choose Commands Not In the Ribbon.
3. Scroll down to the five icons that begin with "Speak". Add these icons to the Quick Access Toolbar by clicking the Add>> button.

Figure 33.1
You have to add the icons to the QAT to use them.

You can now select a range of cells and click the Speak Cells icon. Excel will read the cells to you.

Figure 33.2
Excel will read the selected cell to you.

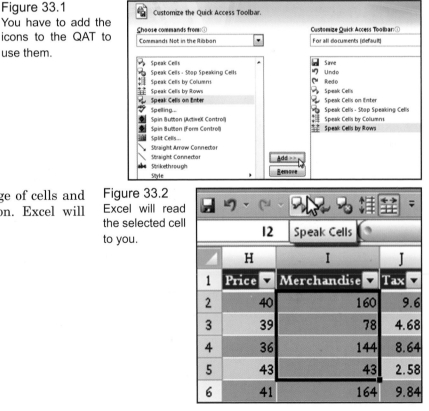

The complete suite of speech icons are as follows:

- Speak Cells – reads the current selection to you.
- Speak on Enter – reads cells as they are entered.
- Stop Speaking Cells – prevents Excel from continuing (useful if you inadvertently ask Excel to read a million cells).
- Speak Cells by Columns – reads the left-most column and then proceeds to the next column if you have Excel speak a rectangular range.
- Speak Cells by Rows – reads the first row and then proceeds to the next row if you have Excel speak a rectangular range.

> Tip: I just finished reading Good Days and Mad, a memoir by Dick DeBartolo of life in the offices of MAD magazine. Dick talked about the usual pranks that were common in the heyday of the magazine. It would seem that a great prank would be to customize the QAT, turn on Speak Cells on Enter, then remove the button from the QAT. The victim would return from lunch to find that Excel starts repeating everything that they type.

✳ ✳ ✳

Chapter 34

Recording a Macro

Every copy of Excel shipped since 1995 has an incredibly powerful macro recorder hiding behind the cells. This macro recorder allows you to automate repetitive tasks.

> Tip: Instead of using the macro recorder, you can learn Visual Basic for Applications and write amazing utilities that will automatically generate hundreds of weekly or monthly reports. For a 300+ page guide to Excel VBA, check out VBA & Macros for Microsoft Excel from QUE.

In this chapter, you will learn how to record two simple macros.

- Say that your job requires you to format certain cells with a particular format. Perhaps red bold font on a pink background with thick red overlines and underlines. You are constantly auditing worksheets and need to apply this format thousands of times a day. The first macro will add a FormatRedBold command to your personal macro workbook and add an icon to the QAT so that you can run the macro with a single mouse click.

- Say that you have a one-time repetitive task. You need to do a mail merge and someone has sent you data going down column A instead of across columns A, B, and C. You are facing the prospect of doing a few hundred Paste Transpose commands unless you can automate the process. The second macro will be a temporary macro stored in the data workbook that you will use to solve the current problem and then throw away. This macro requires you to understand an important concept called Relative References.

Preparing to Work with Macros

Most of the macro commands are hidden on a Developer ribbon. From the Office icon, choose Excel Options. In the Popular category, choose Show Developer Tab in the ribbon.

Figure 34.1
Enable the Developer tab.

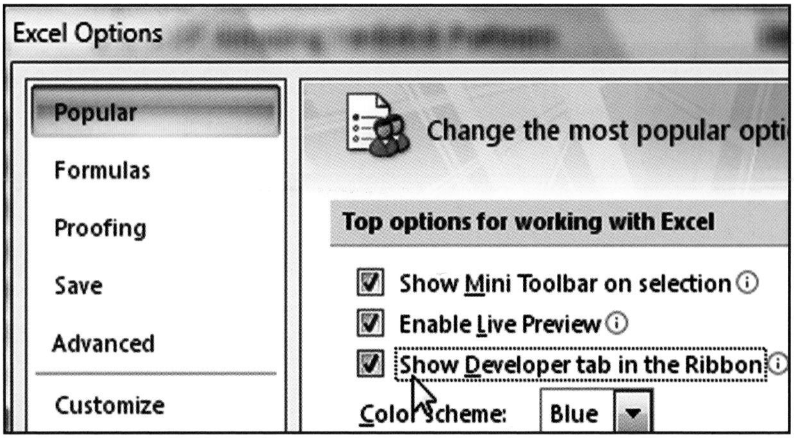

Choose the Macro Security icon from the Code group of the Developer ribbon.

Figure 34.2
Once the Developer tab is available, you have easy access to the security setting.

Choose Disable all macros with notification. This option lets you choose to enable macros that you have written but prevents macros in other workbooks from running.

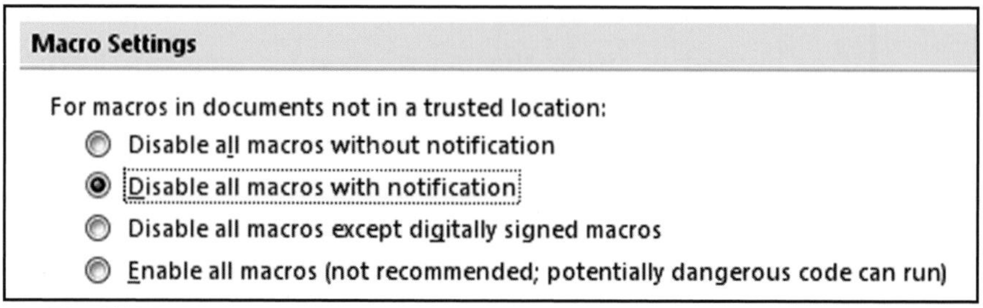

Figure 34.3
It is completely unintuitive, but this setting is the same as the Medium security setting in previous versions of Excel.

Macro Settings

For macros in documents not in a trusted location:
- Disable all macros without notification
- Disable all macros with notification
- Disable all macros except digitally signed macros
- Enable all macros (not recommended; potentially dangerous code can run)

Recording the FormatRed Macro

The first macro is a macro that you want to be available in all workbooks that you open. This macro will format the selected cell(s) with a bold red font, pink background, and thick red top and bottom borders.

1. In the Developer ribbon, click the Record Macro button.
2. In the Record Macro dialog, give the macro a useful name. Macro names can be up to 24 characters, but cannot have spaces in the name. In this case, FormatRed would work as a name.
3. You want this macro available in any workbook that you open. Choose to store the macro in the Personal Macro Workbook.
4. Add a description about the macro.

Figure 34.4
Fill out the Record Macro dialog before recording.

Record Macro

Macro name:
FormatRed

Shortcut key:
Ctrl+

Store macro in:
Personal Macro Workbook

Description:
Formats the selection with a bold red font, pink background, and thick red top & bottom borders.

OK   Cancel

5. Click OK to begin recording the macro.

6. On the Home ribbon, choose a red font. Click the Bold icon. In the Fill dropdown, choose More Colors and choose a pink color for the fill.

7. In the Borders dropdown, choose More Borders.

8. In the Border tab of the Format Cells dialog, choose a red color from the dropdown in the lower left.

9. Choose a thick line in the Style box.

10. In the Border area, click the top and bottom to apply a thick red border to the top and border of the cell. Click OK to dismiss the Format Cells dialog.

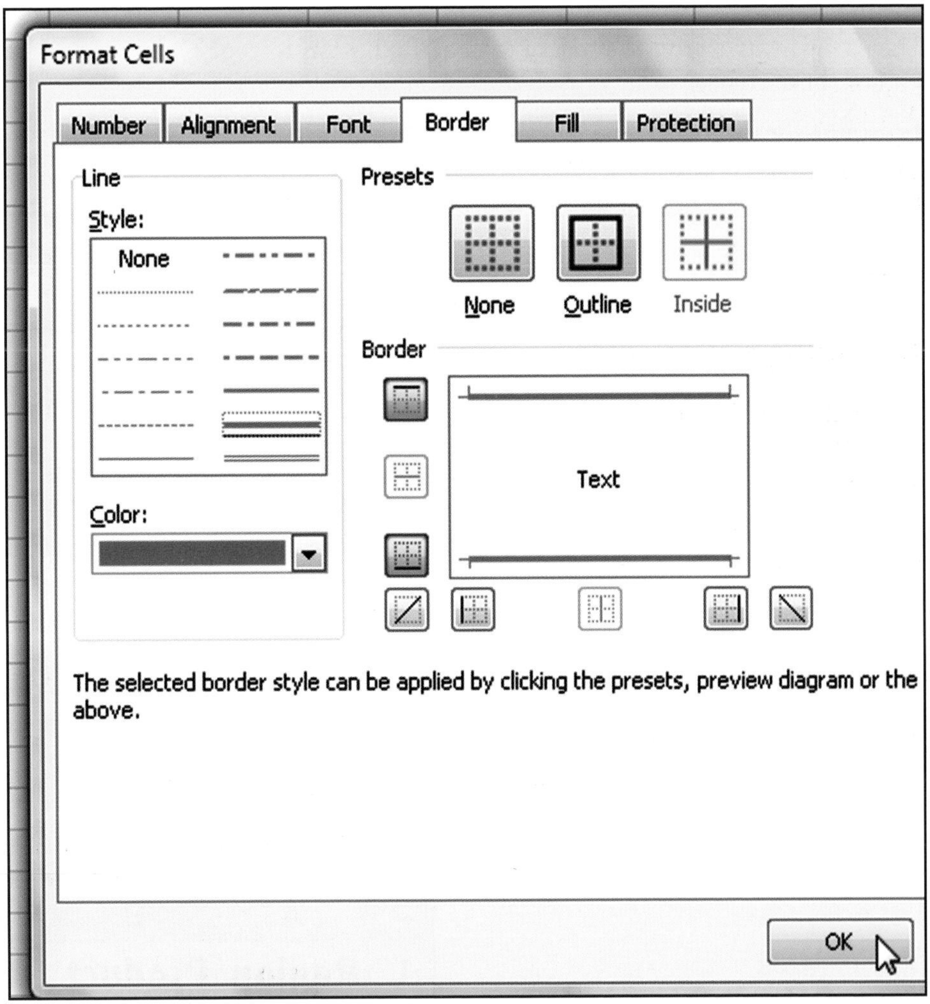

Figure 34.5
When using the Border dialog, you have to choose color and line style before drawing the borders on the right.

Format Cells

| Number | Alignment | Font | **Border** | Fill | Protection |

Line
Style:
None

Presets
None   Outline   Inside

Color:

Border

Text

The selected border style can be applied by clicking the presets, preview diagram or the above.

OK

In the lower left corner of the Excel 2007 window, there is a Stop Recording button. Click this to stop recording the macro.

Figure 34.6
The Stop Recording button is in the lower left of the Excel window.

Ready

A macro is currently recording. Click to stop recording.

Testing the FormatRed Macro

In the next section, you will add an icon to the QAT for the macro. But first, you should test the macro. Select another cell. From the View ribbon, click the Macros icon. Select the option for PERSONAL.XLSB!FormatRed and click Run. The new cell should receive the proper formatting.

Note that during the recording of your macro, you should not have moved the active cell. This allows Excel to format whatever cell is selected. If you accidentally chose another cell during recording, your macro may not work as desired. Try recording another macro; perhaps calling it FormatRed2.

Adding an Icon to the QAT for the FormatRed Macro

The easiest way to run the macro is to add a button to your Quick Access Toolbar for the macro. Follow these steps.

1. Right-click the QAT and choose Customize Quick Access Toolbar....

2. The Choose Commands From dropdown is on the top left of the customize dialog. Open the dropdown and choose the Macros category.

3. In the left listbox, choose PERSONAL.XLSB!FormatRed. Click the Add>> button to add the macro to the QAT.

4. On the right side of the dialog, click the newly added FormatRed entry. Click the Modify button at the bottom of the right listbox. Excel displays the Modify Button dialog.

5. Scroll through the Modify Button dialog to choose an icon that might indicate a red format to you. This is one area where Excel 2007 is lacking – in Excel 2003, there were 4000+ icons available. Excel 2007 offers only 200 icons. Of course, none of the icons look anything like bold red text on a pink background, so choose anything that is remotely similar.

6. At the bottom of the Modify Button dialog, type a new Display Name. This is the text that will appear as a tooltip when you hover over the icon in the QAT.

7. Click OK to close the Modify Button dialog. Click OK to close the Excel Options dialog.

The QAT now has a new icon. Select a new cell and click the icon in order to run the recorded macro on the selected cell.

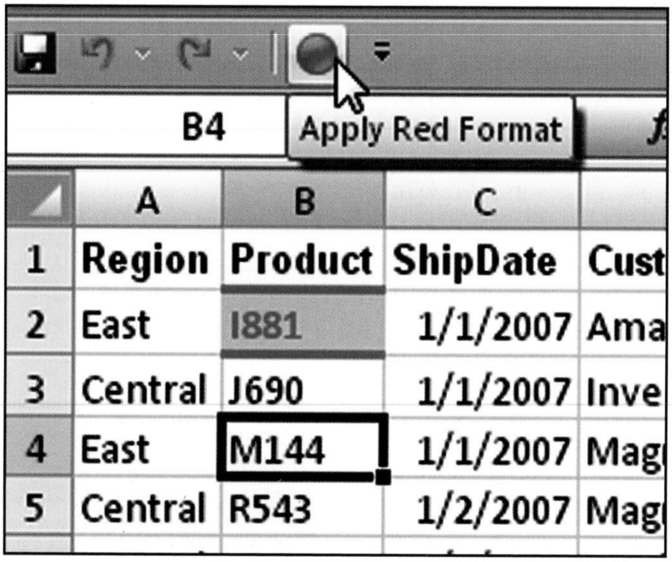

Figure 34.7
A custom icon in the QAT makes the macro easy to run.

Recording a Macro When the ActiveCell Will Move

There is an important concept for when you are going to record a macro that will change which cell is selected.

Consider the dataset in Figure 34.8. You want to do a mail merge in Word. The fields need to go across the columns instead of down the rows.

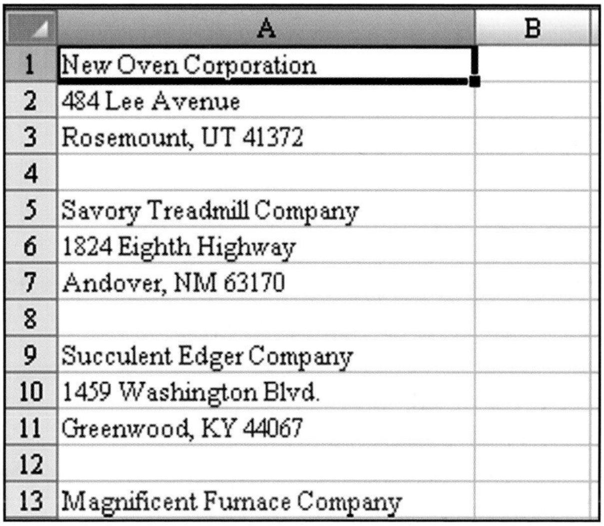

Figure 34.8
This data has the wrong layout for doing a mail merge.

	A	B
1	New Oven Corporation	
2	484 Lee Avenue	
3	Rosemount, UT 41372	
4		
5	Savory Treadmill Company	
6	1824 Eighth Highway	
7	Andover, NM 63170	
8		
9	Succulent Edger Company	
10	1459 Washington Blvd.	
11	Greenwood, KY 44067	
12		
13	Magnificent Furnace Company	

Say that you recorded a macro to fix one name. Excel would literally record these commands:

Cut cell A2 and paste to B1
Cut cell A3 and paste to C1
Delete rows 2, 3, and 4
Select cell A2

This is not a very useful macro. It is hard-coded to only fix data in cells A2:A4. There is only one record that will ever be in A2:A4.

You instead want to have Excel record your relative actions. If you start in cell A1 when you record the macro, you want Excel to record these actions:

Go down one cell. Cut.
Go up 1 and over 1. Paste.
Go down two cells and left one cell. Cut.
Go up 2 and over 2. Paste.
Go left 2 cells and down 1 cell.
Delete the current row and the next 2 rows.
Select the current row.

If you want Excel to record your relative actions, you need to click the Use Relative Reference button in the Developer ribbon.

Follow these steps to record a macro to fix one record in the current dataset.

1. Start on the name in cell A1.

2. Click the Record Macro button in the Developer ribbon. Excel displays the Record Macro dialog.

3. This will be a macro you use to solve the current problem and then you will never use it again. It is fine to leave the name as the generic name of Macro1.

4. Assign a shortcut key of Ctrl+a. Yes, Ctrl+a already means something. However, you will be running the macro for a minute and then you will throw it away, so it is fine to use a keyboard shortcut that is easy to hit.

5. For Store Macro In, choose This Workbook.

6. There is no need to fill in a description.

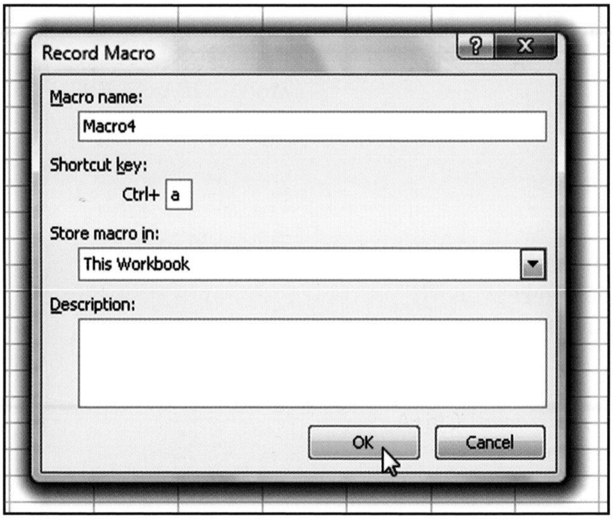

Figure 34.9
For a single-use macro, you don't need to fill in the description or even use a descriptive name.

Record Macro

Macro name:
Macro4

Shortcut key:
Ctrl+ a

Store macro in:
This Workbook

Description:

OK   Cancel

7. Click OK to begin recording the macro.

8. Click the Use Relative Reference icon in the Developer ribbon.

9. Use the keyboard instead of the mouse while recording the macro. Type the Down Arrow to move to A2.

10. Type Ctrl+X to cut.

11. Type the Up Arrow, Right Arrow, and then Ctrl+V to paste.

12. Type the Left Arrow, Down Arrow, Down Arrow.

13. Type Ctrl+X to cut.

14. Type the Up Arrow twice, Right Arrow twice, and then Ctrl+V to paste.

15. Type the Left Arrow twice and the Down Arrow once to move to the now-blank cell A2.

16. On the Home ribbon, choose Delete – Delete Sheet Rows. Repeat this command two more times.

17. At this point, you should have fixed the first record and deleted the blank rows. The cell pointer should be on Savory Treadmill Company in cell A2. Click the Stop Recording button in the Developer ribbon.

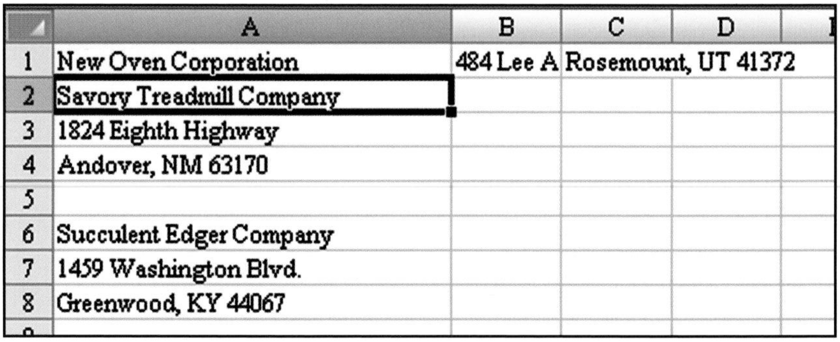

Figure 34.10
After fixing one record during the recording process, you worksheet looks like this.

	A	B	C	D	
1	New Oven Corporation	484 Lee A	Rosemount, UT 41372		
2	Savory Treadmill Company				
3	1824 Eighth Highway				
4	Andover, NM 63170				
5					
6	Succulent Edger Company				
7	1459 Washington Blvd.				
8	Greenwood, KY 44067				

To run the macro to fix the next record, type Ctrl+A.

Figure 34.11
Test the macro by running it to fix the next record.

	A	B	C	D	E
1	New Oven Corporation	484 Lee A	Rosemount, UT 41372		
2	Savory Treadmill Company	1824 Eight	Andover, NM 63170		
3	Succulent Edger Company				
4	1459 Washington Blvd.				
5	Greenwood, KY 44067				
6					
7	Magnificent Furnace Company				
8	993 Madison Blvd.				
9	Louisville, SD 76555				

If it appears that the macro is working, you can hold down Ctrl+A and watch as Excel runs the macro repeatedly. In less than a minute, Excel will have run the macro 100 times and fixed all of the records in your dataset.

Figure 34.12
Hold down Ctrl+A until all of the records are rearranged.

	A	B	C	D	E
90	Alluring Utensil Inc.	1422 Miller Street	Greenwood, OR 17893		
91	Real Necktie Inc.	666 Green Lane	Greenwood, CT 39687		
92	Guarded Raft Corporation	963 Eighth Blvd.	Bloomingdale, WY 86514		
93	Fine Gadget Corporation	1376 Highland Street	Middleton, UT 33287		
94	Fresh Adhesive Corporation	1763 Lee Lane	Louisville, SC 63650		
95	Fascinating Barometer Partners	1368 Spring Avenue	Akron, GA 73448		
96	Unique Shovel Inc.	1813 Cherry Circle	Middleton, KY 74753		
97	Brilliant Aquarium Inc.	646 Lake Street	Rochester, NY 44407		
98	Attractive Bobsled Inc.	858 Seventh Lane	City, FL 47192		
99	Wonderful Umbrella Company	1744 Lakeview Street	Bloomingdale, TX 26430		
100	Real Tackle Supply	295 Mill Blvd.	Fairview, IA 49657		
101	Top-Notch Thermostat Company	1361 Williams Blvd.	Franklin, NM 98939		
102	Mouthwatering Quilt Corporation	1948 Highland Lane	Peach City, ME 17304		

Macro Wrap-up

The macro recorder has some frustrating limitations. If you understand when to use the Use Relative References button, you can record fairly useful macros that will save you lots of time.

In most cases, any limitations of the macro recorder can be overcome by someone who knows Excel VBA. There are many fantastic resources on the web of people who will help you with simple VBA. The MrExcel Message board is staffed with volunteers who will help you tweak your VBA code (see Chapter 39 on page 160). Or, hire a consultant from MrExcel Consulting to put the code together for you for an inexpensive fee. Visit http://www.mrexcel.com/consult.shtml for details.

✳ ✳ ✳

Chapter 35

Solving Simultaneous Equations

Most of the math in this book is fairly simple. Excel is extremely powerful and can quickly solve complex problems.

I like the example in this chapter because I remember having to spend a lot of time in high school algebra solving these types of questions. If you are a fan of the Ask Marilyn column in the Parade Magazine, she often poses questions that require this type of logic.

It is fascinating to me that by mastering a few simple functions, you can now solve these problems with ease.

The Problem to Solve

While my books are sold in major bookstores like Borders, Chapters, Amazon, and Barnes & Noble, I do sell a lot of books directly to the buyer. I try not to compete on the price of a single book, but if you buy a bundle of books from MrExcel.com, you will save money compared to shopping at Amazon. Consequently, most of the orders that I ship are for a bundle of books.

Now, you might have learned from reading the acknowledgements in my books that my sister Barb processes, packs, and ships all of the MrExcel.com orders. Barb is in Arizona. However, when Barb is on vacation, I end up packing and shipping the books from Ohio. I don't have a scale in my office, and so I am always trying to guess the weight of a package as I fill out the FedEx air bill.

When I actually show up at the FedEx counter, I can find the weight of the final package to see if I was correct.

Today, I arrive at the FedEx counter with four boxes. The boxes contain various combinations of four books.

- Box 1 weighs 26.05 pounds. It contains two (2) Learn Excel, three (3) The Spreadsheet at 25, one (1) Pivot Table Data Crunching, and four (4) Special Edition Using Excel 2007.
- Box 2 weighs 9.75 pounds. It contains one (1) Learn Excel, one (1) The Spreadsheet at 25, one (1) Pivot Table Data Crunching, and one (1) Special Edition Using Excel 2007.
- Box 3 weighs 30.4 pounds. It contains five (5) Learn Excel, four (4) The Spreadsheet at 25, three (3) Pivot Table Data Crunching, and two (2) Special Edition Using Excel 2007.
- Box 4 weighs 25.3 pounds. It contains four (4) Learn Excel, two (2) The Spreadsheet at 25, four (4) Pivot Table Data Crunching, and two (2) Special Edition Using Excel 2007.

Assume that the box and packing material weighs exactly one pound in each case. Solve to figure out the weight of each individual book. This type of problem is known as solving a system of simultaneous equations.

Solving the Problem

Rows 2 through 5 of Figure 35.1 restate the information from above. Note that the weights are 1 pound lighter than described above to account for the box. Also, I've used A for Learn Excel, B for The Spreadsheet at 25, C for Pivot Table Data Crunching, and D for Special Edition Using Excel 2007.

In A7:F11, I've built a table describing how many of each book was in each box and the weight of the box. For example, A8:D8 shows the number of each type of book in Box 1 and F8 shows the weight of the books in that box.

Figure 35.1
The range in A8:D11 represents the coefficients of the equation.

	A	B	C	D	E	F	G	H	I
1									
2	Box 1 weighs 25.05 pounds. It contains 2 A, 3 B, 1 C, and 4 D.								
3	Box 2 weights 8.75 pounds. It contains 1 each of A, B, C, D.								
4	Box 3 weighs 29.4 pounds. It contains 5 A, 4 B, 3 C, and 2 D.								
5	Box 4 weighs 26.3 pounds. It contains 4 A, 2 B, 4 C, and 2 D.								
6									
7	A	B	C	D		Ans			
8	2	3	1	4		25.05			
9	1	1	1	1		8.75			
10	5	4	3	2		29.4			
11	4	2	4	2		26.3			
12									

The range A8:D11 contains the coefficients of the original problem. This range is four rows by four columns.

Select a new 4x4 range. Type the formula =MINVERSE(A8:D11). Do not type the Enter key. Instead, hold down Ctrl+Shift while pressing Enter. This keystroke tells Excel that you want a single formula that will return the answer in the 16 selected cells. You will notice in the formula bar of Figure 35.2 that Excel added curly braces around the formula. You don't type these braces.

Figure 35.2
Set up a MINVERSE array.

A14						●	*fx* {=MINVERSE(A8:D11)}		
	A	B	C	D	E	F	G	H	I
7	A	B	C	D		Ans			
8	2	3	1	4		25.05			
9	1	1	1	1		8.75			
10	5	4	3	2		29.4			
11	4	2	4	2		26.3			
12									
13	MINVERSE								
14	0.5	-4	0.3	0.6					
15	-1	3.3	0.3	-1					
16	-1	2.8	-0	-0					
17	0.5	-1	-0	0.4					
18									

Select a new range that is four cells tall by one column wide. Use the =MMULT function to matrix multiply the MINVERSE range by the weights in F8:F11. The function is =MMULT(A14:D17,F8:F11). Again, do not type Enter. Instead use Ctrl+Shift+Enter.

Excel will produce the answers shown in Figure 35.3. Those answers are the weights of the four individual books. Learn Excel is 3.5 pounds. Special Edition Using Excel is 4.1 pounds, etc.

Figure 35.3
MMULT the MINVERSE by the answers to find the solution.

	A	B	C	D	E	F	G	H	I	J
	H8						fx	{=MMULT(A14:D17,F8:F11)}		
7	A	B	C	D		Ans		Solution		
8	2	3	1	4		25.05	A=	3.5		
9	1	1	1	1		8.75	B=	0.25		
10	5	4	3	2		29.4	C=	0.9		
11	4	2	4	2		26.3	D=	4.1		
12										
13	MINVERSE									
14	0.5	-4	0.3	0.6						
15	-1	3.3	0.3	-1						
16	-1	2.8	-0	-0						
17	0.5	-1	-0	0.4						

The Math Behind the Solution

The MINVERSE function is the magic function in the solution. It creates a matrix inverse. The MINVERSE array has a special property. When you multiply the original array by the MINVERSE array, you will have an array with mostly zeroes and a one along the diagonal of the array.

Figure 35.4
The special property of the MINVERSE array is that, when multiplied by the original array, the answer contains only ones along the diagonal.

	A	B	C	D	E	F	G	H	I	J
	D23						fx	{=MMULT(A8:D11,A14:D17)}		
7	A	B	C	D		Ans				
8	2	3	1	4		25.05				
9	1	1	1	1		8.75				
10	5	4	3	2		29.4				
11	4	2	4	2		26.3				
12										
13	MINVERSE									
14	0.5	-4	0.3	0.6						
15	-1	3.3	0.3	-1						
16	-1	2.8	-0	-0						
17	0.5	-1	-0	0.4						
18										
19	MMULT									
20	1	0	-0	-0						
21	-0	1	0	-0						
22	0	0	1	-0						
23	-0	0	-0	1						
24										

It is interesting that the worksheet in Figure 35.3 is a general purpose worksheet that can solve any system of four equations. You can type in new values in A8:F11 and the result in H8:H11 will be the solution behind the problem.

Tip: If you are a fan of math and formulas, check out Chapters 23-27 of Special Edition Using Excel 2007. In those chapters, I've attempted to produce real-world applications for all of Excel's 350+ functions.

* * *

Chapter 36

Cool Uses for Excel – Solving Sudoku

Sudoku is an addicting puzzle craze that is sweeping newspapers. There are at least four different tools in Excel for helping you solve Sudoku, but I really like the free Sudoku Assistant tool by Jobey Jones.

Figure 36.1
Enter the puzzle from the newspaper in the upper left green grid.

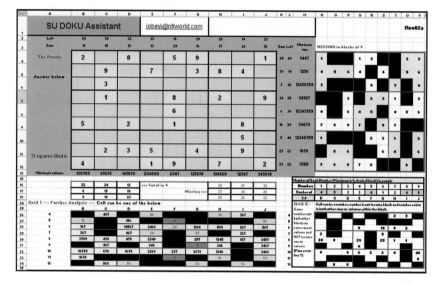

The program provides five different analysis tools. Any square in Grid 1 that lights up in green has only one possible answer. As you fill those in the original grid, new cells will often have only one answer. I like this tool because it teaches you the logic of solving Sudoku on your own.

Figure 36.2
The possible numbers for each open box in the puzzle. The cells in bright green are the ones to solve first.

Grid 1 --- Further Analysis --- Cell can be one of the below								
	B	C	D	E	F	G	H	I	J
4		467		46			38	367	
5	18		156		2				56
6	167		14567	2468	24	1268	569	267	567
7	367		467	34		57		367	
8	3789	478	479	2349		257	1345	137	3457
9		467		349		7	346		3467
10	16789	678	1679	2368	237	2678	1346		3468
11	1678				7		16		68
12		568	56			68		36	

This tool, as well as several others is available for download from http://www.mrexcel.com/tip109.shtml.

✳ ✳ ✳

Chapter 37

Calculating Texas Hold-Em Probabilities

We have a gang of friends who occasionally get together for a night of Texas Hold-Em. In this card game, each person is dealt two cards face down. Everyone then shares five cards dealt face up in the center of the table. The person with the best hand wins.

Texas Hold-Em has become very popular. There are a couple of cable TV programs that televise Texas Hold-Em tournaments, which possibly means that there are too many cable channels available!

Usually, I show an example in my books that talks about using the COMBIN function to decide when the jackpot is large enough that you should play the lottery. In this book, I will switch up to show how to use COMBIN, FACT, and FACTDOUBLE to calculate some odds in Texas Hold-Em.

> Note: While writing Special Edition Using Excel 2007, I needed to find a real-life example for every Excel function. I initially hit a wall when trying to find a use for =SQRTPI and =FACTDOUBLE. Reader Dwayne Kuemper of Canada pointed out that FACTDOUBLE is not completely useless – it can be used to calculate Texas Hold-Em Probabilities. So, now we are only left with SQRTPI as the only seemingly useless Excel function.

Using the COMBIN Function

At the start of a hand of Texas Hold-Em, you are dealt two hole cards. These are initially the only two cards that you see. How many possible combinations might you be dealt?

This question is how many ways are there to choose two cards from a fifty-two card deck. The COMBIN function will solve this problem. Use =COMBIN(52,2) to show how many combinations are possible when dealing two cards from a fifty-two card deck.

Figure 37.1
The COMBIN function is great for figuring out the number of possibilities.

◢	A	B	C	D	E	F	G
4	Number of different starting hands. How many ways to choose 2 cards from a 52 card deck?						
5	1326	=COMBIN(52,2)					

Out of the 1326 possible combinations, many are of equivalent value. One suit is not worth more than another suit. The only questions are (a) do you have a pair of matching values, and (b) if you don't have a pair, are your cards of the same suit or not.

There are 13 possible pairs that you can be dealt (A,A through 2,2).

Of the suited cards, you have 13 possible first cards x 12 possible second cards. Since A,3 is worth the same as 3,A, divide by 2 to get 78 different suited hands.

Of the unsuited cards, you also have 13x12/2 or 78 hands.

Thus, there are 13+78+78, or 169 different possible values of starting hands.

Figure 37.2
There are 169 different shapes of hands you can have in the initial deal.

	A	B	C	D	E
7	Analysis of the first two hole cards in your hand				
8	Pocket Pairs		13		
9	Suited Hands		78	=13*12/2	
10	Unsuited Hands		78	=13*12/2	
11	Total Poss. Hands		169	=SUM(C8:C10)	
12					
13	How many hands can a single opponent have?				
14	1225	=50*49/2			
15					

Analyzing a Single Opponent

You know the two cards in your hand. If you have a single opponent, how many combinations of cards might the opponent have? There are fifty possibilities for the first card, and forty-nine for the second card. That makes 1,225 possible hands for a single opponent.

After an initial round of betting, the dealer flops the first three community cards. You now know the two cards in your hand, plus the three cards in the flop. This reduces the number of possible combinations for your single opponent to 47x46/2 or 1081, cards.

Figure 37. 3
Once you see the cards in the flop, it reduces the possibilities that can exist in your opponent's unseen hand.

	A	B	C	D	E
13	How many hands can a single opponent have?				
14	1225	=50*49/2			
15					
16	After the 3 card flop, how many hands can a single opponent have?				
17	1081	=47*46/2			

Possible Boards in a Two-Person Showdown

Say that in a two-person game, after the initial deal, both players go all in and show their cards. How many possible combinations of the five-card board might be dealt? You know four cards. This leaves forty-eight cards. To find how many ways there are of dealing five cards from a forty-eight card deck, use =COMBIN(48,5) to see that there are 1.7 million combinations.

Figure 37.4
Four cards of the 52-card deck are known. There are 1.7 million possible five-card boards that can now be dealt.

	A	B	C	D	E	F	G
19	In a 2-person game, say that you both go All-In after the initial deal and show your cards.						
20	You now know 4 of the cards. How many possible combinations of the 5-card board can be dealt?						
21	This is 5 cards chosen from the remaining 48 cards that you haven't seen:						
22	1,712,304	=COMBIN(48,5)					
23							

Multi-Player Games

In a Texas Hold-Em Tournament, you are usually playing against several players.

If you are playing against two opponents, how many combinations of cards might there be after the initial deal? You know your two cards. The first opponent would have =COMBIN(50,2) possibilities. The second opponent would have =COMBIN(48,2) possibilities. You are not concerned with which opponent will beat you, so you have to divide by FACT(2). There are 690,900 possible combinations in a game with two opponents.

If you are playing against three opponents, how many combinations of cards might there be after the initial deal? You know your two cards. The first opponent would have =COMBIN(50,2) possibilities. The second opponent would have =COMBIN(48,2) possibilities. The third opponent would have =COMBIN(46,2) possibilities. You have to divide by FACT(3). There are 238 million possible combinations.

Figure 37.5
The number of combinations increases geometrically as the number of opponents increases.

	A	B	C	D	E	F	G
24	Given your 2 hole cards, how many combinations of hole cards when you are playing 2 opponents?						
25	690900	=COMBIN(50,2)*COMBIN(48,2)/FACT(2)					
26	Given your 2 hole cards, how many combinations of hole cards when you are playing 3 opponents?						
27	238,360,500	=COMBIN(50,2)*COMBIN(48,2)*COMBIN(46,2)/FACT(3)					

To generalize this formula, if you are playing N opponents, the formula is =COMBIN(50,2*N) times the Double Factorial of 2*N -1. The Excel function for Double Factorial is =FACTDOUBLE.

Figure 37.6
As far as I know, this is the only real-life example where you can use the FACTDOUBLE function.

	A	B	C	D	E	F	G
28	Given your 2 hole cards, how many combinations of hole cards when you are playing n opponents?						
29	N						
30	2	690900	=COMBIN(50,2*A30)*FACTDOUBLE(2*A30-1)				
31	3	238,360,500					
32	4	56,372,258,250					
33	5	9,707,302,870,650					
34	6	1,261,949,373,184,500					
35	7	126,735,772,764,100,000					
36	8	9,980,442,105,172,910,000					
37	9	622,114,224,555,779,000,000					

In a ten-player game, you have your 169 possible initial hands, times the 622 quintillion combinations of opponent hands, times the number of combinations of dealing five cards from the remaining 32 cards =COMBIN(32,5). This works out to 2.1 x 10^28, or 2.1 Octillion, combinations. If Excel could analyze 10,000 hands per second and you networked 20,000 computers, it would require 3.4 quadrillion years of computing power to analyze all of the possible combinations.

To read more about further analysis of Texas Hold-Em, check out the great Wikipedia article at http://en.wikipedia.org/wiki/Poker_probability_(Texas_hold_'em).

* * *

Chapter 38

Download Cool Spreadsheets from Office Online

Rather than create your own spreadsheets, there are hundreds of free spreadsheets that you can download from Office Online.

1. From the Office Icon, choose New.
2. In the New Workbook dialog, look along the left side for a list of categories. Choose a category such as Budgets.
3. The center of the dialog will offer thumbnails of a personal budget, family budget, expense budget, event budget, marketing budget and more. To try out a file, click the thumbnail and choose Download.

Figure 38.1
There are hundreds of free sample workbooks available in the New Workbook dialog.

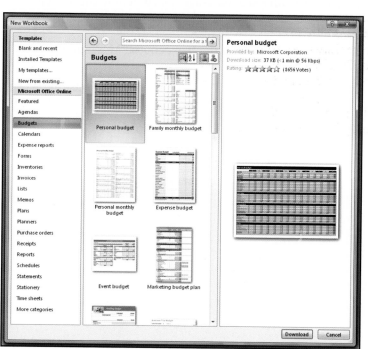

Be sure to check out the More Categories option on the left. There are spreadsheets for Address Books, Games, ID Cards, Itineraries, Quizzes, Scorecards, Tournament Brackets, and more.

Caution! You must be using a legal version of Microsoft Excel 2007 in order to download the templates from Office Online.

✳ ✳ ✳

Chapter 39

Get Excel Answers from the MrExcel.com Board

If you are an Excel fan, join our community of Excellers at the MrExcel Message Board.

The board was launched in 1999 as a way to provide answers for questions people have about Excel and Excel VBA.

Since the launch, the community of Excellers at the message board has answered over 200,000 questions. Every question and answer is archived at the site and is searchable.

If you ever have an Excel question, post your question with sufficient detail. Usually within minutes, others will either ask clarifying questions or provide assistance.
To get to the MrExcel message board, follow these steps:

1. Visit www.MrExcel.com.

2. From the left navigation box, choose Message Board.

Figure 39.1
Use the left navigation to find the message board.

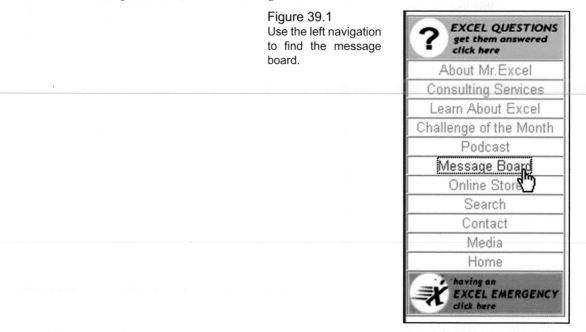

3. Using the top right links, choose to Register. We ask for your e-mail address and for you to verify that you are age 13 or over.

Figure 39.2
The Register link is towards the upper right corner of the site.

4. After registering, click on the Excel Questions forum.

Figure 39.3
Other forums exist for
Access, the Lounge, and
questions in languages
other than English.

> Question Forums
>
> **Excel Questions**
> **All Excel/VB questions** - formulas, macros, pivot tables,
> general help, etc. Please post to this forum in English only.
> Moderator <u>Moderators</u>

5. Click on New Topic.

Figure 39.4
The New Topic button
appears just above the
list of topics.

6. Build your question and click Submit.

> Tip: If you need to show an Excel spreadsheet in your post, download Colo's
> HTML maker from the link at the bottom of the forum. This tool will convert a
> range of your spreadsheet into HTML that can be posted at the board.

✳ ✳ ✳

Chapter 40

Document Themes & Cell Styles Across Microsoft Office

Three components of Microsoft Office 2007 allow you to easily create documents that look like they belong together. If you are preparing a presentation in PowerPoint 2007, an introduction in Word 2007 and some tables in Excel 2007, all of these documents can look similar using Document Themes.

Cell Styles Borrowed from Word

Gurus of Microsoft Word have known about using styles for a decade. In Excel 2007, Microsoft promotes styles in Excel, adding a dropdown right on the Home ribbon offering 42 built-in styles as shown in Figure 40.1.

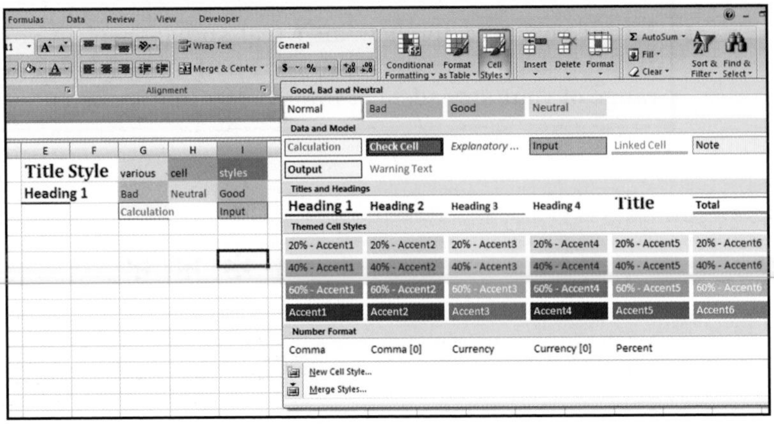

Figure 40.1
Excel offers 42 built-in cell styles on the Home ribbon.

Yes, you could customize Excel 97 to add a style dropdown to the toolbar. Yes, this seems like a gimmicky way to avoid using regular formatting. However, before you reject the idea, wait until you see how Excel styles interact with document themes.

Document Themes, Borrowed from PowerPoint

If you dabble in PowerPoint, you know that you can change the slide background. You may or may not have noticed that when the slide background changes, the fonts, colors, font sizes and effects also change. As I create a PowerPoint document, I try to choose a background that matches my message.

In PowerPoint 2007, Microsoft offers 20 themes. With each theme, you get new colors, fonts, effects, and a choice of backgrounds. Microsoft added these same 20 themes to Word 2007 and Excel 2007. If you choose a certain theme in PowerPoint, choose an identical theme in Word and Excel to make your entire report look like it came from the same application. You can staple together pages that came from Excel, Word, and PowerPoint. Provided you used the same theme in all of the applications, the documents should look similar.

Choosing a New Theme

So far, most of the images in this book have been created using the Office theme. This is the default theme in Excel 2007. Figure 40.2 shows a worksheet with several elements; shapes, SmartArt graphics, a photograph, a chart, WordArt, and cells formatted with various cell styles.

Figure 40.2
This document is in the Office theme.

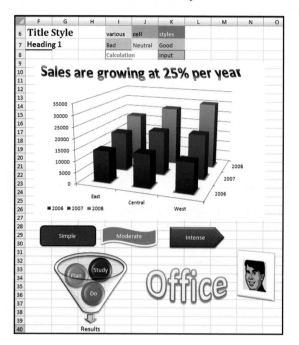

To change the look and feel of your document, choose a new theme from the Themes dropdown on the Page Layout ribbon. Figure 40.3 shows the document in the Verve theme.

Figure 40.3
Change to Verve theme for new colors, fonts, and effects.

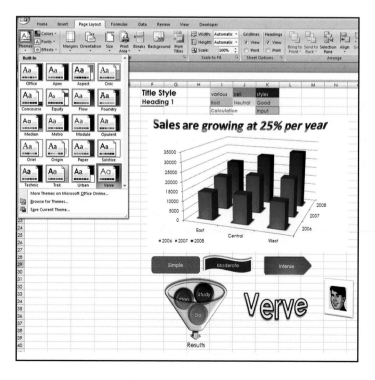

Themes range from subdued, such as Paper (Figure 40.4) to gaudy (take your pick from Metro, Opulent, or Verve).

Figure 40.4
The Paper theme is a bit more subdued.

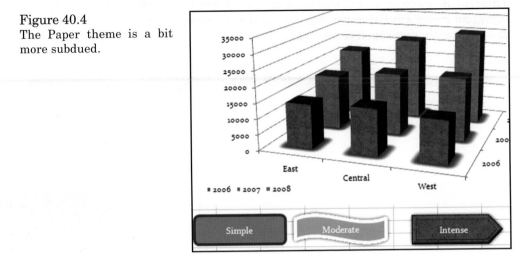

When you change a theme, you inherit new fonts, colors, and effects. The Colors dropdown shows the palette for each of the 20 built-in themes (Figure 40.5).

Figure 40.5
Colors available in the built-in themes.

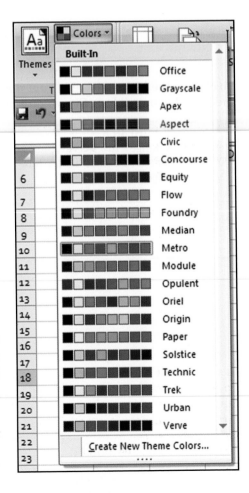

While colors are fairly easy to understand, the Effects dropdown seems confusing.

Throughout Excel 2007, galleries typically offer styles from plain to moderate to intense. For example, the Shape Styles gallery ranges from plain styles at the top, to moderate styles in row 3 & 4 to intense styles in row 6. (Figure 40.6)

Figure 40.6
Many galleries in Excel 2007 range from simple to moderate to intense.

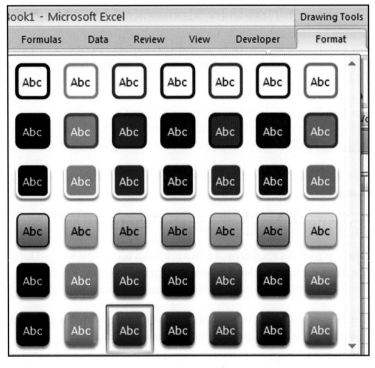

The effects dropdown shows three shapes for each theme. The circle is meant to indicate the effects when you choose simple styles. The arrow is meant to indicate effects when you choose moderate styles. The rectangle is meant to indicate effects when you choose Intense styles. (Figure 40.7)

Figure 40.7
The effects dropdown gives a clue to the effects in each theme, if you understand the code.

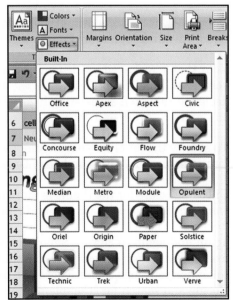

If you study Figure 40.7, you can guess that Metro is going to apply a jeweled effect to intense styles and Paper will apply a texture to moderate styles. Technic offers a glow around the moderate styles. Module uses a double-line for simple styles. You are certainly wondering why you should care. This becomes important when you want to design your own theme.

Designing a Theme to Match Your Company Colors

Microsoft allows you to create new themes. You can share these themes with others in your company. Thus, you could create a company theme with your company colors. Or, you could simply mix and match fonts from one theme, colors from another theme, and styles from a third theme.

Creating a Theme by Mixing and Matching

On the Page Layout ribbon, use the Colors, Fonts, and Effects dropdown to define a new theme. Choose Colors from the Verve theme, Fonts from the Apex theme, Effects from the Opulent theme.

On the Themes dropdown, choose Save Current Theme. Save the theme as MyTheme. A theme gets saved as a file with a .thmx extension. Excel will automatically save the file in the appropriate folder, usually %appdata%\Microsoft\Templates\Document Themes.

The next time you start Excel 2007, your theme will be in a built-in section of the Themes dropdown.

Sharing Your Theme with Others

Open Windows Explorer. In the address bar, type %AppData% and press Enter. Excel will find the application data folder for your operating system. From there, browse to Microsoft, then Templates. You will see the theme that you saved, stored as a .thmx file.

You can copy this .thmx file and save it in the similar folder of every computer in your department, and everyone will have access to the same theme.

Creating a Theme to Match Your Company Colors

While you are allowed to customize colors and fonts in your theme, you must start with one of the 20 built-in effects.

Open the Effects dropdown in the Page Layout ribbon. Choose one of the 20 built-in effects themes. Read the paragraph after Figure 40.7 to understand how the thumbnails work.

Your theme will need a title font and a body font. If your company has a font that is used to render your logo, this is appropriate for the title font. (Visit www.Chank.com if you need a custom font designed to match an existing logo). For the body font, you should choose something simple such as Cambria, Arial, or Times.

To specify the fonts for your theme, use Page Layout-Fonts-Create New Theme Fonts. Specify the font to be used for titles and body copy.

Choosing colors for the theme is more difficult. You need to specify a color for text and titles (black works great...), a color for text and titles on a dark background (white?), a color for hyperlinks and followed hyperlinks, and then 6 accent colors. The accent colors are the colors that will come up again and again in charts, SmartArt, shapes, WordArt, etc. Use your company logo colors for the first accent colors. Unless your company has six accent colors, you will need to find complementary colors for your logo colors. There are free tools on the web for finding complementary colors. Go to Google and search for "Complementary Color Tool".

On the Page Layout ribbon, choose Colors, Create New Theme Colors to display the dialog in Figure 40.8. For each color, choose the dropdown and then More Colors. You can specify the Red, Green, Blue components for the selected Color (see page 91 for assistance with color codes).

Figure 40.8
Specify company colors in the Theme Color dialog.

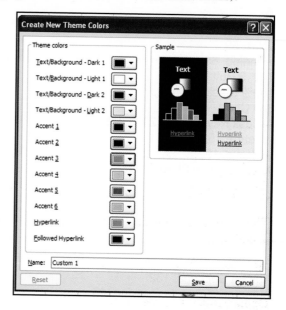

Finally, use Page Layout, Themes, Save Current Theme. Specify a name for the theme (perhaps your company name?).

When you restart Excel, you will be able to choose your custom theme from the dropdown. The document, charts, graphics will all use colors from your company logo. (Figure 40.9)

Figure 40.9
A custom theme using the MrExcel colors.

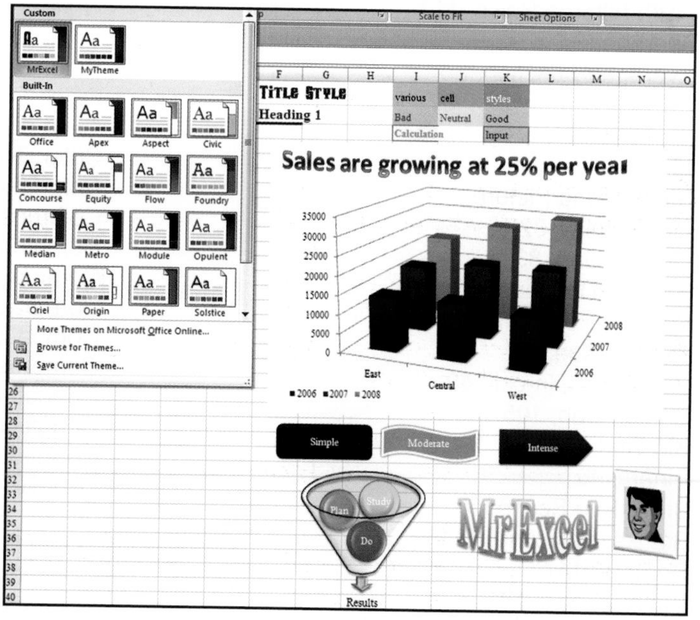

Themes are a great tool for branding documents from Word, PowerPoint and Excel into a single cohesive document.

✳ ✳ ✳

Index